California Gardening

Los Angeles Times
CALIFORNIA GARDENING

A Practical Guide to Growing Flowers, Trees, Vegetables, and Fruits

by Robert Smaus

HARRY N. ABRAMS, INC., PUBLISHERS, NEW YORK

Project Director: Darlene Geis
Editor: Joan E. Fisher
Designer: Darilyn Lowe

Library of Congress Cataloging in Publication Data
Smaus, Robert.
    Los Angeles times California gardening.

    1. Gardening — California. I. Los Angeles times.
II. Title. III. Title: California gardening.
SB453.2.C3S6 1983   635'.09794   83-2671
ISBN 0-8109-1258-9

Published in 1983 by Harry N. Abrams, Incorporated, New York

Printed and bound in Japan

JACKET FRONT: California poppies and red flax (photograph
by Robert Smaus)
JACKET BACK. Top: Marigolds and other warm weather annuals in
a garden by Roger Boddaert (photograph by Bill Ross)
Bottom left: Cabbage and pak choy (drawing by Cathy Pavia)
Bottom right: Radishes, from left to right, are White Icicle,
Crimson Giant, Burpee White, Champion (photograph by Douglas
Kennedy)

PAGE 1: Fuchsias and begonias in the shady garden
PAGE 2: Fall-planted, spring-blooming annuals include white
alyssum, a snapdragon called Sprite, and violas

Contents

61 The Rock Garden

67 The Rose Garden

83 The Wild Garden

95 The Working Garden

127 The Shady Garden

141 The Kitchen Garden

192 Credits

The Basic Garden

The California garden is different — different enough to devote a book to, and special enough to intrigue gardeners who do not live here. This book is an introduction to the plants and the practices that make the California garden so distinct. Though it speaks to the California gardener, it is for anyone interested in how gardens are grown in California, or in what we grow in them.

More than anything else, this book is about plants, and it is these plants that make the California garden unique. Californians themselves are often not aware of the differences and often miss the opportunities provided by the special nature of their gardens.

Not only can we grow the traditional plants from our English garden heritage — the hollies and hollyhocks or their close cousins that adapt so well to California's kind climate — but we can also grow many more wonderful things from warmer parts of the world.

Climate, of course, is the reason we can grow this amazing array of plants, and California's is legendary: it is mild, seldom too hot or too cold, and it is dry, with rainfall only in winter. It is a "summer-dry subtropical" climate, part of a select community of similar climates that are more commonly called "Mediterranean" that cover less than 3 percent of the earth's surface.

Well over half of what we grow comes from one or another of these summer-dry subtropical areas — the Mediterranean itself, South Africa, and especially Australia. This remarkable lot of plants is reason enough to get interested in gardening. Rather than the deep green foliage of plants from rainier climates, theirs ranges from subtle shades of steel blue to gray and olive. Their flowers come in brilliant colors — some actually shimmer because they are so bright; others combine shades most unfamiliar to us. They have their own dry aesthetic, and using them to form a garden is a challenge. Because they are so difficult to grow elsewhere, there is little precedent to follow, and growing them can be an adventure. But while they are the backbone

of the California garden, they are certainly not the only plants we grow.

Because California is a subtropical climate, we can grow an equally splendid group of plants from the subtropical parts of Central and South America, Africa, China, Japan, and New Zealand. Mostly what we have to remember to do is water, because these plants come from rainier places. These plants are better known than the group previously discussed but still not widely grown since cold is not to their liking.

There are, in fact, very few plants at all that can't be grown in California. We are privileged indeed. The word "hardy," of utmost importance throughout much of the garden world, has almost no meaning in California. This book singles out plants that are rarely, if ever, mentioned in other garden literature because they are not "hardy" — such plants as fuchsias, eucalyptus, and iceplants that are special to California.

Only the most tropical or cold-requiring plants are difficult to grow outdoors here — plants as opposite as orchids and lilacs — though clever gardeners have even coaxed varieties of these to grow in our even-tempered climate. Few places are fortunate enough to have such a palette of possibilities. There is much uncharted territory, and we are still learning what will grow here and how to grow it.

If your garden is not full of these fascinating plants, if you have not succumbed to their special beauties or haven't been challenged by their unfamiliar textures and colors, you are missing out on an adventure. If you must suddenly move to a less kind climate, you will have missed an opportunity to become acquainted with an international array of plants as interesting as the countries they come from. We hope this book will make this abundant variety more familiar to Californians, and perhaps introduce some of these plants to intrepid gardeners everywhere.

It is hoped that this book will entice you all enough so that you can't wait to get out into the garden. You will find

Two silvery plants from sunny climates, *Centaurea gymnocarpa* and yellow-flowered *Helichrysum petiolatum*, grace this path in a Santa Monica garden

The end of the California climate is the Sierra Nevada Mountains.

The Pacific Ocean controls this territory with its cooling fogs, stabilizing influence.

Santa Ana winds sneak through here.

The Tehachapi Mountains divide north from south.

pertinent information presented in a quick and uncomplicated fashion so no time is wasted and you can get right outside come Saturday morning. Good gardens are made when more time is spent weeding than reading, and good gardeners wear out the knees of their jeans a good deal faster than the seat. For fast reference there are suggestions for plants that will thrive in the California climate, followed by instructions for the planting and care of each.

This information is important, as are the basics described on the following few pages. Underlying the complexities that are a garden are some surprisingly simple practices. These techniques — preparing the soil, the proper way to plant, water, and fertilize — are not difficult, but they are different in California. Every garden practice, from what we add to the soil to how we prune a rose, has been challenged and often changed to better suit our climate. There are definitely right ways and wrong ways to go about it, so it's a wise idea to spend an evening studying this basic

information before venturing out the next morning. These basics should become second nature, the beginning of a green thumb. You'll be amazed how your garden will grow given a good start.

Climate

Not all of California basks in an identical climate, and, to a great extent, where you live determines what you can grow. Mountain ranges are the great dividers. The state is neatly split in half by a transverse mountain range, the Tehachapi. Beginning at the base of the southern Sierra, it swings west to hit the sea near Point Conception, just north of Santa Barbara. Above the Tehachapis is Northern California; below, Southern California. Winter storms from the Gulf of Alaska often poop out at the Tehachapis, so Southern California is generally drier. It is also definitely warmer, in winter and summer, just enough so that frost-tender or

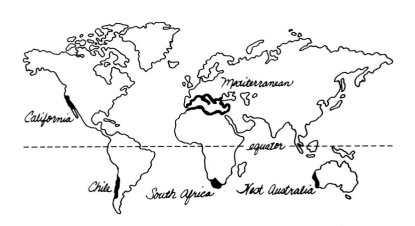

heat-loving plants can be grown here, including Southern California's famous palm trees, but also exotic things like bromeliads and cycads.

Northern California, on the other hand, is just cool enough to grow plants that need cold winters and cool summers, such as flowering fruit trees and rhododendrons, that are difficult in the southern half of the state. Plants that do better in one half of the state than the other are so noted throughout this book.

How far you live from the ocean also determines what you can grow. Here the great dividers are the Coast Ranges, or, more specifically, the inner coastal ranges, which block the ocean breezes that tend to moderate temperatures. On the eastern side of the Diablo Range, the Santa Susanas, the San Gabriels, and similar mountain ranges, the climate is a lot hotter in summer (in the southern half of the state it is desert), and usually a lot colder in winter (the low desert around Palm Springs is the exception). But most people live on the western side of these mountains in what we call "coastal California." In this book when we say something does best near the coast we mean it in its broadest sense. This coastal area includes all of the San Francisco Bay Area (including the Santa Clara Valley) and all of the Los Angeles Basin (including Orange County), and most of San Diego. Many plants need the mild temperatures or the extra humidity found along the coast. A very few (fuchsias, for instance) require it to an extent that they can only be grown in a narrow band along the coast. In this book these will be singled out as doing "best near the beach."

Inland, as used, refers to the inner valleys, such as the San Ramon and Livermore in Northern California, or the San Fernando and Perris-Hemet in Southern California. In these valleys, the ocean breezes only influence the weather some of the time, so they get hotter, colder, and drier. The great Central Valley is barely, if ever, influenced by the ocean but it is still mild enough to grow most of the plants in this book.

The Central Valley is a good example of another clima-

MORE ABOUT MEDITERRANEAN CLIMATES

Shown in the drawing above are five remarkably similar climates, called "summer-dry subtropical" or, more commonly, "Mediterranean," of which California is one. The others are important to California because from them come so many of the plants we grow. Note that they are all on the western side of continents, and that they are equidistant from the equator. They are dry but not desert, since they receive reliable rainfall. Adjoining each of these coastal climates are the great deserts of the world.

These Mediterranean regions stay dry in summer because of a worldwide weather phenomenon called "subtropical anti-cyclones," which are huge, stable masses of warm air that form over the oceans on the western edge of continents. Rain falls in winter because these pools of air move farther out to sea and toward the equator, clearing the way for storms originating in the polar regions. In California this stable mass of air is called the "Pacific High."

Though subtropical, these climates are dry rather than humid, and since they are so close to the ocean, they are moderated by the ocean's relatively constant temperature. It is seldom terribly hot or cold.

This unique set of climatic circumstances has produced an unusually interesting group of plants that combine a certain delicacy made possible by mild temperatures with a toughness necessary to withstand prolonged summer drought. Two countries in particular have a tremendous inventory of interesting plants — South Africa and Australia. But all of these summer-dry climates have contributed to California gardens some of the most fascinating plants we grow.

THE AUSTRALIAN BUSH

If the Australian countryside looks familiar to a Californian, it is because so many of our plants are actually theirs. Eucalyptus, acacias, bottlebrush, pittosporums, melaleucas, leptospermums, grevilleas — even if the names aren't recognizable, a native Californian would certainly know the plants.

Without a doubt, Australia has contributed more to our landscape, especially trees and shrubs, than any other country. A rough tally shows that more than a thousand have been grown here at some time. It isn't surprising that Australian plants do so well in our gardens; the climates are remarkably similar. In fact, many do better here because our strict quarantine laws allow only pest-free plants to enter the country. Very few eucalyptus in California are bothered by insects, but every tree in Australia is nibbled.

While much of Austra-lia's land is desert and barren, two strips of vegetation several hundred miles wide by several thousand miles long run along each coast. In these two belts lies a tremendous variety of habitats, from subtropical rain forest to alpine meadows. Long isolated from the rest of the world, Australian plants (and animals) have had plenty of time to go their own way. Many of the major Australian plant groups exist nowhere else. The eucalypts, for

instance, are found only in Australia.

Plants from all parts of Australia are grown in California, but Western Australia has the most similar climate and the most exciting plants. Much drier than the rest of Australia, it bursts into bloom like California's own hills after the winter rains, with fields of wildflowers (mostly everlastings or strawflowers) and an incredible array of flowering trees and shrubs. The rocky outcrop shown here, just outside Perth and just past the rainy season, is covered with drought-toughened eucalyptus, black-trunked grass trees (Xanthorrhoea) *and survival-bent shrubs. With a little imagination it could just as easily be a California hillside covered with oaks or digger pines, yuccas, and shrubs from our own chaparral.*

While it may seem that most Australian plants have found their way to California gardens, there is still a wealth of plant material yet to be tried. And nurseries and botanic gardens are showing new interest, especially in Western Australian plants, because they are so appropriate for our gardens and because drought tolerance in landscape plants is becoming increasingly important in California. It's a good bet that in the years ahead, even more California plants will be from Australia, so keep your eyes open for them.

Grass trees and gnarly eucalypts in the West Australian bush

tic factor — elevation. In general, the higher you live, the colder, but low-lying hills often experience warmer nights in winter because cold air tends to roll downhill and settle in the valley bottoms. Around the edges of the Central Valley, citrus can be grown safely because the ground is a little higher. This is also true of many hillside areas, just above valley floors — they are as warm, but nights don't get as cold — they are choice gardening areas anywhere in the state. In the southern half of the state, these are the most subtropical zones, where avocados, for instance, do best.

Southern California has a few additional phenomena. In fall and winter, dry Santa Ana winds sweep in from the east. Contrary to popular belief, they do not originate in the desert but in the Great Basin area between the Sierra and the Rockies. This wind follows the passing of storm fronts first coming from the north, then from the east. It may be a hot or cold wind, but it is always dry. It is strongest around the mouth of canyons, and gardens in its path take quite a beating now and then, but generally it is not as great a threat as it seems.

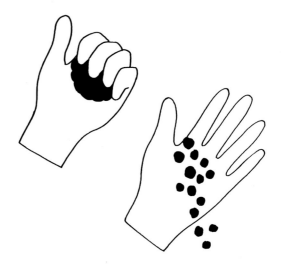

Soil Preparation

Gardening is too often made out to be more difficult than it is. The practices and principles are really quite simple and vary only subtly from plant to plant. The fundamentals discussed here — soil preparation, planting, watering, and fertilizing — are easy to learn but relatively inflexible. In the garden, plants need a specific set of conditions for healthy abundant growth.

Good gardens begin with good soil. Once a plant is in the ground, little can be done about the soil; most problems later on, from pests to poor growth, can be traced to hurried soil preparation. Take your time in preparing the soil and there will be few problems later on. It's not easy work, but in the garden nothing is more important or more rewarding. Soil that has been turned and amended is a delight to work in and makes every future step from weeding to watering a lot easier.

Most soils, whether they are sand or sticky clay, can be prepared the same way. The object is to make a pleasant home for the plant's roots. Roots need a careful balance of air and moisture (not too much of either), as well as nutrients and an unobstructed path as they grow. To provide these conditions, you can add amendments that fluff up the soil, allowing air and moisture to penetrate easily. These amendments are usually found in some kind of organic matter. In California, redwood sawdust or ground fir bark are the most common. Because the soil organisms responsible for decomposition consume nitrogen in the process, both products are sold with nitrogen added. Otherwise the organisms would rob the soil of any available nitrogen, depriving plants of this most important nutrient.

What do soil amendments such as these do in the ground? First, they physically separate the individual soil particles. If you squeeze a handful of moist clay soil (the most typical garden soil), it sticks together. Mix amendments into it and it won't, because the amendments keep the particles of soil from sticking together. Separating the particles of soil with amendments makes it easier for water and air to penetrate. At the same time, any excess water quickly drains deeper into the soil, away from the critical root area.

"Good Drainage" and Root Rots

At least half the plants mentioned in this book require "good drainage." A soil with good drainage lets water move down through the soil, away from the root area. If the soil gets too soggy or too saturated, air — which is just as important as water to roots — is excluded. In California drainage is critical because of various organisms called "root rots" or "water molds," which thrive in soggy, airless soil, especially during warm weather. These are responsible for the death of more plants than any other cause.

sandy soil   amended sandy soil   clay soil   Amended clay soil

For air and moisture to be in balance, a certain amount of water must remain in the soil. This is the secondary job of a soil amendment in clay soils, and the primary job in sandy soils that have naturally good drainage. Organic amendments act like little sponges, absorbing and holding water for the plant, while still allowing air in the spaces between the particles of amendment.

Gypsum, Compost, Planting Mixes, Manure

There are other more expensive products, such as peat moss and leaf mold, sold as soil amendments that work like ground bark or sawdust. Gypsum is still another kind of amendment, especially valuable in California's clay soils. It chemically separates soil particles but doesn't improve

PREPARING A GARDEN BED

Begin by watering the ground several days in advance. Make sure it is thoroughly soaked. A day or two later turn over a sample shovelful. If the soil crumbles, it is ready to work. There is a magic time somewhere between too wet and too dry when most soils, even adobes, crumble easily, which makes the mixing of amendments possible.

The labels on most packaged amendments and fertilizers tell how much to use. If you use the most commonly available kinds you will need the amounts shown in the drawing for each hundred square feet: four three-cubic-foot sacks of organic soil amendment, ten pounds of gypsum, and two pounds of a complete, all-purpose fertilizer (a one-pound coffee can holds about two pounds of a granular fertilizer). These amounts are not critical—a little more or less makes little difference, just as long as they are thoroughly mixed into the soil.

With the materials on hand, first turn the soil over with a spade or spading fork. These two tools are not shovels. They are flat, not curved, and

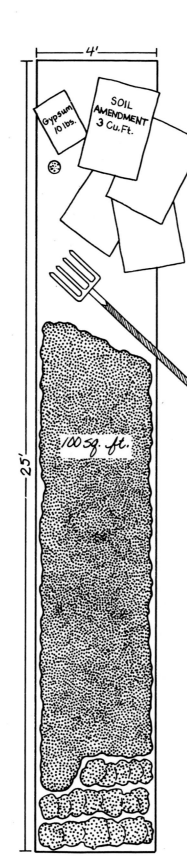

water retention so it is best used with an organic amendment, as described here.

Lime, often added to acid soils in the East, should never be used in California's already alkaline soils. Some amendments are called "planting mixes" and contain fertilizers as well as organic matter, but they cannot be used in the large quantities required to perceptibly improve a soil. They can be used in conjunction with soil amendments that do not contain fertilizers or to refresh a soil that has previously been improved with other amendments. Planting mixes are particularly valuable in flower and vegetable beds that are replanted frequently, and should be used each time.

Homemade compost is of course a valuable soil amendment, but it must be thoroughly rotted or it will steal nitrogen from the soil. To make compost, simply pile garden debris and wait. Make sure to separate grass clippings with bulkier material or the clippings will pack together to become the perfect fly-breeding medium. To speed up the composting process, keep the pile moist and occasionally stir it up to allow air inside. Adding a little fertilizer also helps. If you also chop the material up with a commercial grinder or even a pair of shears, it will decay still faster. Using all of these tricks, you can produce compost in two months or less. A simple pile will take at least a year.

Steer manure is in a category by itself. The best that can be said for manure is that it must somehow be disposed of and gardens are a likely place. Most packaged manure contains a lot of mineral salts, which is detrimental to plants. In California, where salts are already a problem in the soils, manure must be used sparingly. It is more a fertilizer than an amendment and should be used as such.

Fertilizer for Planting

It is a good idea to mix fertilizer into the soil when preparing the soil for planting. It is especially important to mix in

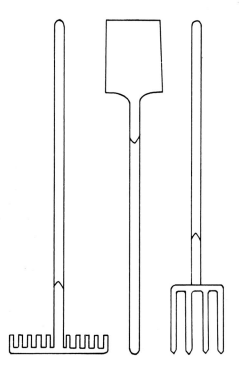

The basic tools: flat steel rake, spade, spading fork

phosphorus, since this important fertilizing element cannot be carried into the soil by watering, as other plant foods can. It must be placed where the roots are, not on top of the soil. When preparing the soil, choose a fertilizer that is high in phosphorus, or add superphosphate or bone meal, which are essentially pure phosphorus.

Professional gardeners often use special slow-release fertilizers in pellet or tablet form, which provide fertilizer for a year or more. They work best placed in the bottom of the planting hole, a few inches beneath the plant.

How Much?

What quantities of these amendments and fertilizers do you work into the soil? In the diagram at left is a typical garden bed and the proper amounts that will make the soil fertile and easily manageable. Such heavy soils as adobe may require more organic matter, and sandy soils less, but you won't go wrong using the amounts shown. When preparing garden beds, it's easiest to divide them into one-hundred-square-foot sections since that is what most label recommendations are based on.

Soil amendments and fertilizers must be thoroughly mixed into the soil. If they are not, they cannot do their jobs, and the next time you dig in the garden you'll find clumps of one or another. Remember, the amendments must physically separate the soil particles. If you are preparing a large area, it's easiest to rent a rototiller, though you can do it all by hand if you do a little each day. Turning soil is hard work.

their edges are pointed or sharpened. To turn soil, dig the spade in as deep as you can, pull back on the handle, and without lifting turn the soil on its side, not upside down. Break up clods with the back of the spade. This first digging loosens and pulverizes the soil. Work in a line, first turning one row, then another just behind it, as shown in the drawing.

Now spread amendments over the ground and sprinkle the fertilizer and gypsum on top. Repeat the entire digging and turning process, taking the time to mix soil and amendments completely.

A rented rototiller is a good investment once the soil has been loosened with a spade. It is an excellent soil mixer, but only the largest size will dig deep enough for the initial loosening process. Soil must be prepared at least six inches deep and preferably a foot if it is to benefit the roots. Roots of course go much deeper, and the deeper you dig the better, but the top six inches is critical since this is where good drainage is required.

When everything is thoroughly mixed, give it the squeeze test: scoop up a handful of moist, amended soil and squeeze it. It should

crumble when you loosen your grip. If not, add more organic amendments. Even though this requires yet another round of soil turning, it is your last chance to make any real improvement in the soil, and every spading helps mix the ingredients.

After everything is mixed, the soil will be noticeably higher than it was, but wait a day or two and then pack the soil down by walking all over it (for large areas you may wish to rent a water-fillable lawn roller). Now rake it flat and level and remove all clods and rocks near the surface. Water thoroughly, and the soil should settle to within an inch of its original height. You can plant before this final watering or wait a couple of days and then plant, watering once more after planting.

You now have good garden soil, the best investment you can make and the best guarantee for a healthy garden. Weeds will pull out with the slightest tug, and carrots too. Watering will be easier, and you will need to use less water. Should you happen to water too long or too often, it will quickly drain away. Dig your hands in. What a delight, and what a joy for plants.

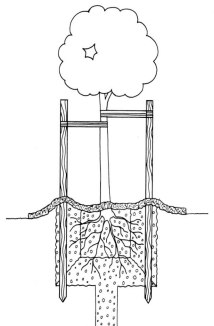

CULTIVATE OR MULCH?

To cultivate the soil, one simply loosens the very surface, usually with a tool called a cultivator that has four short prongs. Mulching means to cover the soil with something. In the vegetable garden plastic is used; elsewhere some kind of organic matter is preferred. The best mulch is homemade compost, or freshly shredded leaves and twigs from a compost grinder or shredder such as the tree services use.

The reasons to cultivate or mulch are similar. When soil is cultivated or loosened, it's easier for water and air to penetrate. Cultivated soil also creates what is called a "dust mulch," which enables soil to retain water better. And, if done often enough, it keeps weeds from growing.

Mulches do almost the same thing. They too keep water in the soil from evaporating and the surface from baking hard, so it is easier for water and air to penetrate. Mulches also keep

the soil from eroding, even on level ground where soil tends to become silt as the organic particles are washed from it. If the mulch is thick enough (four to six inches), it will prevent weeds from growing, but it may harbor earwigs, sowbugs, and other minor pests. Mulches should never touch the trunk or base of the plants or they may encourage fungous disease. If the mulch is organic it will eventually decay and become part of the soil.

It is important to do one or the other — mulch or cultivate — or maybe both. For certain plants that are shallow rooted, such as azaleas and camellias, mulches are best because cultivation would disturb the roots. Around other plants you might try this: first cultivate the soil, then add a mulch several inches thick. As the mulch decays, cultivate it into the soil and add more mulch material. This can be done on a seasonal basis in flower beds or once every few years around more permanent plantings.

Time to Plant

Next to soil preparation, planting is the most important part of gardening. Most garden failures are not caused by the nursery, the soil, or even the weather, but the way a plant is put into the ground (seeds are a separate matter, see page 26). Trees, shrubs, and ground covers will have few problems in life if planted correctly — growth will be faster, winds won't topple them, even insects are less likely to cause trouble. An old gardener's adage sums it up: it is better to plant a dollar tree in a ten-dollar hole than a ten-dollar tree in a dollar hole.

Learning proper planting techniques is not difficult, but each step is as important as the next. There are no shortcuts. If you're planting a tree (the most complicated and time-consuming procedure), it should end up like the drawing (upper left) when you're finished. Shrubs require less work than trees, and smaller plants still less, but the basic rules apply to all. The directions that follow apply to larger plants such as trees, shrubs, vines, and perennials from gallon cans.

Smaller plants require a similar procedure, only with fewer steps. Once the soil is thoroughly prepared you can plant. It's just as important to make sure these are not root bound, that the soil is packed firmly around them, and watering is critical the first few weeks. While it is possible to overwater larger plants right after planting, small plants should never be allowed to dry out because their roots, only inches below the surface, are subject to rapid evaporation.

Digging the Hole

Holes should be twice the width of the container the plant comes in, and several inches deeper. Make the sides of the hole jagged; if it's a perfect circle the roots have a tendency to go around in circles instead of pushing into new ground.

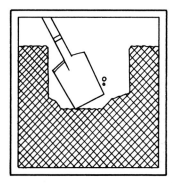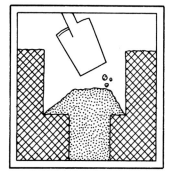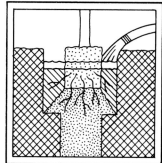

For trees in clay soils it is a good idea to dig a narrower hole at the bottom with a clamshell-style post-hole digger (as shown). Dig this hole as deep as you can; it helps drain excess water.

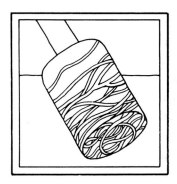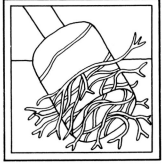

Untangling the Roots

When you take the plant out of its container, check the roots. If any are circling around the root ball, they must be straightened out or they will continue to grow that way. The idea is to aim the roots in the right direction so they expand out into the new soil. If the plant is extremely root bound, you may have to make shallow cuts on four sides with a knife. Otherwise just grab hold and pull the roots loose.

This is a critical point in the planting process. It is better to lose a lot of roots and soil than plant something that is root bound. It is not uncommon to dig up plants that have not grown as they should, only to find that their roots are still growing as they were in the nursery container. Be rough if you must, but untangle those roots!

Putting the Dirt Back

The soil that goes back into the hole should be mixed with organic matter: 50 percent dirt, 50 percent amendment, and a touch of fertilizer. Form a flat-topped cone of soil in the bottom, as shown, pack it down, then set the plant on top, carefully spreading out the roots. Fill the hole with amended soil until it is two-thirds full. Thoroughly water to help settle the soil, then finish filling. Extra soil can be mounded around the perimeter of the hole to form a watering basin.

Be sure to stomp it down. The soil put back in the hole must be compressed to be nearly as dense as the surrounding soil. Otherwise, it will drain too quickly and dry out too fast. When packed correctly, it will slow the water just enough to allow penetration to the root ball of the new plant. Wait a few days if the soil is wet, but don't be gentle — pack it down. Use your hands as you fill the hole, then use your boot near the top.

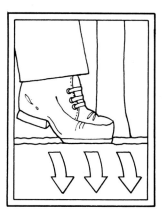

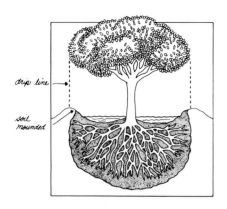

WATERING WISDOM

Though roots spread farther, the bulk are just below the foliage inside what is called the "drip line," as shown in the drawing above. This is where it is most important to water. Watering the spaces between plants only encourages weeds and is a waste of water. It is far more important to make sure that the area inside the drip line is thoroughly watered to encourage roots to grow deep where they are safe from the irregularities of watering and are less likely to compete with the roots from other plants.

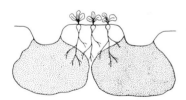

Watering basins as seen in the drawing above are one way to ensure that only the important ground is wetted, and that the water sinks deep into the ground. Make watering basins by mounding up soil with a hoe to form a six-inch ridge. Fill the basin several times with water to make sure it soaks deep into the soil.

Furrows, or irrigation ditches, are a practical way of watering things planted in rows, like vegetables, or strawberries, or even roses. Furrows on either side of a slightly raised bed work best because they supply the plant with water on both sides.

Note that the water has a tendency to spread out as it goes deeper so it actually reaches under the bed. One benefit of watering this way is that the soil on top of the bed stays dry, which discourages the growth of weeds and eliminates the need to cultivate.

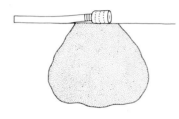

Special soaker nozzles are the best way to apply water inside a furrow or basin. They go on the end of the hose and diffuse the force of the water so it is less erosive.

Drip irrigation systems work like dozens of small soakers. Each little "emitter" only waters a very small area. The water slowly trickles out and soaks right into the ground. True drip systems run all the time, but most kinds used in gardens are run for several hours, then are turned off, like sprinklers. They must run long enough for the water to soak deep into the ground. Drip systems are probably the best way to water plants in California, but they are difficult to install and not terribly flexible, or attractive.

Finishing Up

Trees should be thinned to compensate for roots lost during planting. Don't just nip back ends—take out entire small branches. Support a droopy tree with two sturdy stakes (not the temporary one the tree came with) about a foot on either side, and tie it with plastic tape. This method of staking supports a tree but also helps it build the strength to stand on its own. Research has shown that tying a tree directly to a stake weakens the trunk. Like muscles in an arm, the trunk will not be strong unless it can move and flex in every breeze. A properly staked tree will be able to stand on its own within a year. A tree tied flat against the stake may never gain the strength necessary to remain upright itself.

Build a watering basin around the plant to help funnel water to the roots. Finally, put a several-inch-thick mulch around all plants to keep down weeds.

Watering

One thing that sets California apart from other places is the need to water year round. Even drought-tolerant plants need water the first year or so, and most plants need a regular supply. In other parts of the country there is adequate water just below the surface, so a little water is all that's needed.

Watering would seem an easy task, but many gardeners go about it the wrong way. There is one simple rule that applies to almost all plants, but it is seldom heeded: *water as seldom as possible but when you do, water thoroughly.* "Thoroughly" means letting the water run a long time so it soaks deep into the soil, and if you are standing there holding the hose, this is impossible. Use one of the techniques shown in the drawings. When the water penetrates far into the soil, it stays there for a long time, safe from evaporation. It also encourages roots to go downward since they grow where there is moisture. Deep underground, roots find a more constant environment. Near the surface they must deal with fluctuating temperatures and soil that is wet one day, dry the next.

Watering too frequently or for too short a time encourages roots to grow near the surface — moisture seldom sinks deep enough in the soil. It also tends to encourage root rots because the soil surface stays wet too often.

Thorough watering is especially important in Southern California because of the high salt content of its water (particularly that from the Colorado River), which can damage plants. Thorough watering "leaches" the soil of salts — the water carries the salt down past the roots. With container plants, it's a good idea to fill them with water several times every now and then to wash the salts out or let the hose trickle slowly for twenty minutes or so.

How long you should water varies tremendously with the type of soil in your area. Water has a difficult time penetrating clay soils but once it's there it tends to stay for weeks. On clay soils, let the water run a long time, but then don't water for at least a week. Adding soil amendments makes it easier for water to soak in. On sandy soils, water sinks in quickly but doesn't last long, so water for shorter periods and more often, or add soil amendments that help hold water in place.

The best way to determine how long and how often to water is to do a little test once in a while. Let the water run for half an hour, then dig a hole and see how far it has soaked in. If it isn't several feet deep, let the water run longer and try the test again, in another spot. If you do this at several times of the year, you will soon get a real "feel" for watering.

On the plus side, they waste very little water since they wet only a specific area. They also encourage deep root growth and discourage weeds.

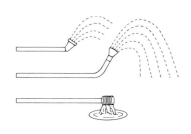

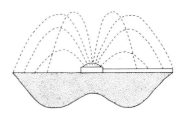

Canvas soaker hoses are a good way to water long narrow beds. Or they can be doubled back to water wider areas. They apply water the right way, so it soaks deep and does not flood.

Sprinklers are the easiest but least effective way to water. First, they do not apply water as evenly, as seen in the drawing above. They water areas that do not need it and they erode the soil surface so it compacts and crusts. For sprinklers to be effective they must be run a relatively long time but they often apply water faster than the ground can soak it up. Sometimes it is necessary to water until puddles form, then stop until the ground has soaked it up and water again. Lawns are the best use of sprinklers since they are difficult to water any other way.

Plants in pots should be watered with one of the hose-end attachments seen here. The first is a special

device used for bonsai but it works well on other container plants, especially young seedlings being grown in pots. It puts out a gentle, fine spray that falls like rain, if the nozzle is pointed up as shown. The device below it is similar but more coarse. Or use a watering wand (the last device shown). This has a series of disks that brake the force of the water so it is not erosive.

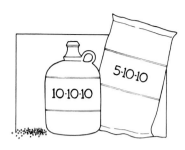

FERTILIZERS . . . SOME CHOICES

Discussed below are some ways fertilizers are packaged. Most are available as granules or liquids. Granules are generally the easiest to use in the garden, and liquid forms go to work faster because they are carried into the soil with the water they are mixed with. However, watering right after using a granular fertilizer has a similar effect.

Some of these fertilizers are much more potent than others and they can "burn" plants if applied too liberally. These are noted. Remember that fertilizer must immediately be washed from the plant leaves to prevent "burning."

all-purpose fertilizers.
These are the best bet for general use in the garden. Most contain a good balance of the major nutrients and all of the minor nutrients. They should also contain a balance of fast-acting nitrogen and slow-release nitrogen. Look for such numbers as 6-6-6 or 6-8-6.

fertilizers to mix into the soil before planting. *Few are sold this way, but any fertilizer higher in phosphorus than the other nutrients is intended to be used this way. Look for such numbers as 6-12-6.*

slow-release fertilizers.

While both of the fertilizers above are formulated to release some nitrogen slowly, there are products, used mostly on plants in containers, that provide nitrogen for several months to a year. Mag-Amp is one that can last a year but must be mixed into the potting soil. Osmocote works lying on the surface of the potting soil, and slowly releases nutrients for three to four months.

fertilizers for more flowers.
To encourage flowering, gardeners often use fertilizers that contain phosphorus and potassium but no nitrogen. There is little scientific evidence that this works, but withholding nitrogen does keep the plant from putting its energy into growth so that it may turn its attention to blooming. Fertilizers sold for this purpose are called Hi-Bloom, Superbloom, and so on, and have such numbers as 0-10-10 or 2-10-10 on their labels.

acid-type fertilizers. *Some of the formulations of nitrogen tend to make the soil more acidic, favored by certain plants. These are often sold as azalea and camellia fertilizers.*

citrus, rose, and vegetable fertilizers. *These are essentially all-purpose fertilizers but those intended for citrus should have the important trace elements —iron, zinc, and manga-*

Fertilizing

In most garden soils, plants do survive with little or no fertilizer, but what a difference it can make! Most plants thrive on the stuff. Anything grown primarily for flowers or fruit and any grass (including bamboo) will do dramatically better if fertilized often, and fertilizer can coax dramatic growth from basic landscape plants.

Nitrogen is responsible for growth in plants, and how fast if affects the plant can be determined by carefully reading the label on the package. Most packages list numbers like 4-6-4 or 10-10-10 right on the front. The first of these numbers is the percentage of nitrogen in that particular fertilizer, but this is not as important as how that nitrogen is formulated, which is on the back of the package. There you will find the total nitrogen divided into two or more kinds. Nitric or nitrate nitrogen goes right to work as soon as water touches it, in warm or cold weather. It also disappears quickly since it is easily washed out of the soil with practically the next watering. Ammonic or ammoniacal nitrogen goes to work a little slower but lasts a lot longer. This form only works in warm weather. Water insoluble nitrogen (W.I.N.) is released slowly to plants over a long period. Organic nitrogen, a less precise term, is nitrogen that slowly becomes available to a plant over a long period. Most fertilizers are a blend of two or more of these forms so there is a combination of immediate as well as longer-lasting effects.

The phosphorus content is the second number on a fertilizer label. Not much is known about what this element does for a plant, but it is known that if there is not enough, plants will grow slowly. What you need to remember about phosphorus is that it doesn't move in the soil. While other fertilizer elements can be washed down into the soil with watering, phosphorus is quickly attached to soil particles and stays put. It is best mixed into the soil before planting.

The third percentage listed on a fertilizer label is potassium. It's almost as important as nitrogen, and plants use a lot of it . . . for what is not clear.

Calcium, magnesium, and sulfur are minor fertilizer elements usually included in what is called a "complete" fertilizer. They too are usually present in most California soils but adding more certainly doesn't hurt.

Although iron, manganese, and zinc are also minor, or "trace," elements, they are vital ones because often they are unavailable to plants in California soils. Their absence may be dramatically displayed by a plant's leaves, which turn yellow except around the veins. They are best used in a chelated form, which ensures that they will not be grabbed up by the soil before the plant can put them to use.

Fertilizers containing all or some of these elements are available in a bewildering array. All are composed of the same basic elements, and most plants do just fine with a fertilizer that contains all of them in relatively equal proportions. There are times when a specifically formulated fertilizer does the job a little better, but there is no magic formulation.

nese. An all-purpose fertilizer with these elements will suffice.

lawn fertilizers. *Typically, these are formulated for slow release because lawns are especially susceptible to "burn." Many are also combined with insecticides, fungicides, and herbicides to control various lawn problems.*

natural fertilizers. *Most work very slowly, but last. Bone meal (5-15-10) is a source of phosphorus, blood meal (13-0-0) of nitrogen, and they are often combined to make a more balanced product. Cottonseed meal has a little of all three nutrients (6-2-1). Sewage sludge and poultry manure are usually formulated to be good all-purpose fertilizers. All of these are best used at planting time mixed into the soil.*

fish-based fertilizers. *Made from fish remains, they are slow acting and usually have other fertilizers added to make them more potent.*

wood ashes. *Saved from the fireplace they can be used as a source of potassium and trace elements. Sprinkle lightly throughout the garden and work into the soil.*

highly soluble fertilizers. *These are usually sold in small quantities with names like Hyponex, RapidGro, Spoonit, and Miracid. They are strong, concentrated fertilizers that dissolve easily in water and are*

used mostly on container plants. They must be used with caution or they will "burn" the plant, so many people use them half-strength, twice as often. Most are high in nitrate nitrogen so they work fast even in cold weather.

fertilizer tabs and sticks. *These are simply pushed into the ground near the plant, and as they dissolve they release nutrients. Some tabs are dissolved in special dispensers that inject the nutrients into the ground — a good way to fertilize trees and shrubs.*

fertilizers with soil penetrants. *Penetrants or "surfactants" make water "wetter" so it easily soaks into the ground. This helps fertilizers soak in.*

The Flower Garden

This collection of plants has been described simply as "an old-fashioned flower garden" by Los Angeles landscape architect Joseph P. Copp, Jr.

The Flower Garden

Flowers alone are a good enough reason for having a garden. If you roll up the lawn, take away the trees and shrubs, break up paths and patios, and grow nothing but flowers, you will still have a glorious garden.

What we call flowers fall roughly into two groups: annuals, or bedding plants, and perennials. They are all plants grown primarily for their flowers. Trees and shrubs may also have flowers, but they have other, more important work to do in the garden. Flowers need only be pretty.

Annuals live just one season and make the splashiest show. From this magnificent display of blossoms comes the seed for their regeneration and survival. Some "annuals" are actually longer lived in nature, but in the garden we treat them as one-season plants because they get raggedy beyond that and look better replanted. True annuals last only one season because that is their lot in life, usually an adaptation to a short growing season in their native lands. Perennials are the garden stalwarts, lasting at least several years, with some kinds assuming the status of permanent plants in the landscape. In the not-too-distant past, the two were seldom combined. Annuals were planted in beds (hence the term "bedding" plant) and perennials were planted in separate borders. But in California, where one season just drifts into another, this distinction has become fuzzy, and mixing annuals and perennials works out remarkably well. Each helps hide the other's shortcomings — one is blooming while the other fades — guaranteeing that something always has center stage. Gardens planted with both never look bare.

Try it — it's almost impossible to go wrong. Mix all kinds of flowers and even toss in some bulbs and small shrubs. Besides benefiting from your garden's beauty, you'll find that it's also a good way to discover and learn about plants because you'll be planting a variety.

In the garden at the left, both annuals and perennials are used to good effect by landscape designer John Catlin. The annuals in this flowery mix include long-stemmed Ice-

In April, six months after fall planting, this happy mix of annuals and perennials is in full bloom

24

FLOWER TALK

Botanical terminology terrifies many gardeners. However, it's not as difficult as it seems, and if you know just a few key words it is much easier to understand descriptions in books or catalogues. So here's a start with some elementary terms.

Most flowers have just four basic parts: the **petals** are the most noticeable part of most flowers. They may be separate (like a rose) or joined together to form a tube or trumpet (like a petunia). Collectively, the petals are called a **corolla.**

The **sepals** go unnoticed on most flowers but if you look behind the petals you will see them—little green parts that seem to support the petals. On some flowers (like fuchsias) they are colorful parts of the overall flower. Collectively, sepals are called a **calyx.**

Stamens contain the male reproductive parts of the flowers and carry the pollen. Sometimes they are quite decorative, as they are on fuchsias.

Pistils are the female part of the flower. Seeds are formed at their base.

Daisies are a little different. They all belong to the same huge family, **Compositae**, and are worth learning about because half of the flowers we grow are daisies of one kind or another.

What appears to be just one daisy flower is actually a composite of many tiny flowers. Each "petal" is actually a flower—pull one off and see tiny reproductive parts at its base. These are called **ray**

flowers. The center contains dozens of much tinier flowers called **disk flowers**. Supporting all of this is a **bract**. Some composites have only one or the other of these flowers. Marigolds and zinnias, for instance, have only ray flowers and no central disk.

Flowers are further described as being single, semi, or double. Single means the flower has a normal set of petals, usually not more than six. Semi-double means it has more than normal but not so many petals that they hide the center of the flower containing the stigmas. Double flowers are the most deluxe, with so many petals that the center of the flower is completely hidden.

Sometimes flowers are described as rose flowered, or peony flowered. Rose forms look like roses, usually with semi-double flowers and slightly wavy petals. Native Californians may have more trouble with the latter description, since we don't grow peonies, but a peony form is usually fully double and very ruffled.

land poppies, low-growing pinkish alyssum, and yellow pansies way in back. Perennials include the pink-flowering bulblike *Tulbaghia violacea* in the foreground, purple-flowered *Convolvulus mauritanicus* spilling over the wall, a blue-flowered felicia, and a few clumps of gold and mahogany gaillardias. The plant at the base of the wall, *Nierembergia* Purple Robe is a good example of why the distinction between annual and perennial has blurred. Is it annual or perennial? California gardeners use it either way in the flower garden. It blooms most heavily in the spring, and if it is cut back soon after the flowers fade it returns to bloom in the summer. On the other hand, it is so quick and easy to grow that it is often simpler to replant it or replace it with something a little more summery.

There is yet another distinction slowly dissolving in California's kind climate: that of seasons for certain flowers. Nierembergias can be planted in fall or spring, blooming in spring or summer. Especially in the southern half of the state, more and more flowers are being discovered that do well at many times of the year. Nevertheless, there are two major planting times that result in two major flowering seasons. Spring's flowers are best planted in the fall, and summer's flowers in the spring. Perennials can be planted in either season, but fall is generally favored. On the following pages, annual flowers are grouped into one or the other flowering season, but the distinction actually isn't as neat as it appears here. Planting—and flowering—go on year round in the California garden.

THE BEST WAY TO PLANT

In the lists that follow, the best procedure for planting each annual is suggested. Most annuals can be planted from seed, sown directly in the ground, which is ultimately the best way because the roots are never disturbed. It is also the most "iffy" method because all sorts of things can go wrong in the open ground, from marauding snails to sudden downpours that wash seed away. To prepare ground for seeding, water for several hours several days in advance, providing a reservoir of water. Work in amendments if necessary, then rake and smooth soil. Sow seed and be sure to keep moist until germination.

Sowing seed in small pots or flats provides more control and is an easier way to sprout seeds. Watering is easier too, though more diligence is required. Plantlets are also safer from seedling nibblers. When plants are several inches tall with a few sets of leaves, transplant them into the garden. A few annuals, however, must be sown directly in the ground because they do not transplant well.

Buying plants in flats (large but shallow wooden or plastic trays) or small plastic packs is a surefire way to

Fall-planted, spring-blooming annuals in the garden of Mary Ellen Guffey include white alyssum, a snapdragon called Sprite, and violas

Spring's Flowers

Spring gardens are the best . . . at least that's the consensus of flower gardeners throughout California. It might be the rain, or the clean winter air, or it could be the mild weather. Whatever the reason, flowers that bloom in the spring seem to be the freshest and prettiest, and the time to plant them is in the fall.

In California, spring-blooming annuals grow during cool weather. Since they need some early warmth for roots to become established, it's preferable to plant them in late September or October. This guarantees a warm start and a long growing season. It also means they'll be finished blooming by the time the garden is ready for spring planting of summer flowers. Wait too late in the fall and they'll sulk through winter and bloom part way into summer.

This garden in Malibu (left and below), shown full bloom in April, was mostly planted in the fall. There is a backbone of perennial plants, but over half the plants are annuals — what we call "spring's flowers" in the lists that follow — and they are replanted every fall. These one-season plants put their all into flowering, the reason the garden is so colorful.

April's flowers include stock, snapdragon, and arching larkspur

plant. The process of separating plants, either by pulling them apart or cutting apart with a putty knife, ensures that the roots are not tangled, or "root bound." Root-bound plants will never grow as they should, and will dry out too fast and look stunted all their lives.

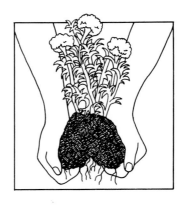

Another option is to plant from quart (four-inch) plastic pots. This method brings speedy results because plants are often blooming size but they are also more likely to be root bound. If roots are tangled, matted, or circling, drastic action is required. If roots have formed a white mat at the bottom of the container, pull this off completely — the plant will survive. If roots are simply tangled, "butterfly" the root ball as shown in the drawing. Dig your fingers into the bottom of the root ball and gently split it halfway up. **feed, feed, feed.** Because annuals grow so fast, they need more fertilizer than most other plants. Frequent feeding is often the only difference between a so-so garden and a grand one. In the garden shown here (left and below) the soil is thoroughly prepared each time something is planted. Compost and a complete granular fertilizer are worked into the soil with a spading fork to make it fluffy and fertile. In addition, all the plants are fed with a liquid fertilizer every three weeks until they bloom. Most flowers are cut or pinched off as they fade to promote new growth, and when they are finally finished blooming they are run through a compost grinder and added to the compost pile to become food for the next generation. One look at this garden and it's obvious that all this nourishment pays off.

Southern California extras. In addition to the spring-blooming flowers listed on the following pages, these can be planted in the fall in Southern California's mild climate:

ageratum	nicotiana
cosmos	petunia
lobelia	scarlet sage
marigold	verbena

Hollyhock

Larkspur

The Best of Spring's Annuals

annual African daisy. Delightful foot-tall daisies in pastel shades of yellow and orange that flourish in the desert where they will colonize the landscape but do well throughout California. Look best by the hundreds and must be planted from seed scattered freely.

sweet alyssum. Loose mounds of white to pinkish lavender flower clusters grow only six inches tall, perfect for filling in between other plants. Dwarf kinds are the most kempt looking. Will reseed but plants get progressively more rangy with each generation. Sow from seed scattered about, will bloom in only six weeks.

bachelor's buttons. Some people may know these as cornflowers. They make two-foot-tall bushy plants with blue, pink, or white flowers. Easy to grow from seed, packs, or pots.

calendula. Big, rich orange or yellow composite flowers on foot-tall plants. One of the most reliable plants for mid-winter bloom if planted early in the fall. Easy to grow from seed, packs, or pots.

calliopsis. An annual coreopsis with yellow daisy flowers marked with maroon, one and a half to two feet tall. Long stems give the look of a wildflower. Sow from seed.

Canterbury bells. An annual campanula with spikes as long as three feet and bell-shaped flowers in shades of blue, violet, pink, and white. Grow from seed or packs.

Chrysanthemum multicaule. This and the following daisy are so new they have yet to acquire common names. This one has butter yellow flowers and grows about six inches tall, with most of that stem. Best grown from packs or pots.

Chrysanthemum paludosum. These look like ten-inch daisy bushes covered with white flowers. Excellent filler between other plants, and they usually reseed. Best grown from packs or pots.

Sweet peas

Nierembergia Purple Robe

Sprite snapdragons

Bachelor's buttons

Chrysanthemum paludosum (left) and *C. multicaule*

Pansy Orange Prince

dianthus. The annual kinds grow as loose mounds of tiny carnation flowers and stay under a foot tall. They come in shades of pink, red, and white. Merry-Go-Round has white flowers with red centers. Easy to grow from seed, packs, or pots.

English daisy. Actually a perennial that works best as an annual because it doesn't survive summers well. Small tufted daisy grows to six inches with big white, pink, or rose flowers. Needs moisture. Grows best from packs or pots.

hollyhock. Giants of the spring flower garden, some grow to ten feet, others stay around four feet. Flowers are in shades of magenta, pink, yellow, crimson, and white. A disease called rust makes them nearly impossible to grow in some areas. Easy to grow from seed or pots.

Iceland poppy. Wonderful, crinkly poppy flowers in shades of orange, yellow, coral, pink, and white, the colors just a little too bright to be called pastel. The strain named Champagne Bubbles has the biggest flowers, shortest stems. Tall one- to two-foot spindly stems sometimes topple when watered from overhead or after rain. Spectacular when planted in masses, from packs.

larkspur. Annual delphiniums that form two- to four-foot slender spikes in unbeatable shades of blue, rose, and pink. Best from seed, transplants may topple.

linaria. Resembling tiny snapdragons, they grow only to a foot. A graceful, airy filler in many shades of red, purple, yellow, even orange. Best grown from seed scattered about.

nemesia. Foot-tall plants covered with yellow, orange, or red flowers, and just about every shade in between. Best grown from packs or pots.

nierembergia. Technically a perennial, it is more often planted as an annual. Spreading mounds of clear blue-violet or white flowers. Excellent filler between taller plants. It should be in every garden. Best grown from packs or pots.

pansy and **viola.** Pansies have dark contrasting markings, violas are solid colors, both bloom in shades of blue, purple, yellow, maroon, and apricot. Johnny-jump-ups have tiny

purple and yellow flowers. All are under a foot tall and most will last longer than other fall-planted annuals, well into mid-summer. Easily grown from seed started in flats, or from packs, pots.

phlox. The annual kinds grow about a foot and a half in shades of dark magenta, rose, lavender, and white. From seed or packs.

scabiosa. The annual kinds grow to three feet tall with flowers in blue violet, pink, and white atop long stems. Best grown from seed.

snapdragon. A bewildering array of heights, types, and colors, from six inches tall to three or four feet, in every color but blue and including some that don't "snap," much to the disappointment of children. If you can only plant one kind, try Sprite. Cut back after flowering, it often returns to put on one more show. Grow from seed or packs. Planted from four-inch pots, they may topple.

stock. Muted lavender, pink, and white flowers are sweetly scented on one- to two-foot-tall plants with grayish foliage. Grow from seed or packs.

Swan River daisy. Wonderful little lavender or rose daisies on foot-tall plants. Best grown from seed sown in masses.

sweet pea. There are two distinct kinds. Bush types stay low and full, below two feet. Vining types can climb to over twelve feet and are perfect on fences. Bright pastel shades of pink and lavender, as well as white, purple, and red. Best grown from seed soaked in water the night before planting. Working fertilizer into the soil before planting is especially important; never let plants go without water.

sweet William. These are foot-tall carnation relatives with a decidedly old-fashioned look. Big clusters of flowers in shades of red, rose, pink, and white. Grow from seed, packs, or pots.

Virginia stock. Tiny flowers bloom in shades of pink, lilac, white, on eight-inch plants. Grow from seed scattered about; flowers appear in just a few weeks.

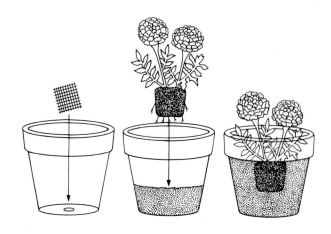

PLANTING IN POTS

For some reason, much mystery surrounds container gardening but, actually, nothing could be simpler. Annuals are especially easy to grow in containers because they flower and finish blooming before the potting soil wears out, the reason other container-bound plants fail to thrive after a few years.

There is little logic to making your own potting mix, and plain dirt won't do, so begin by buying a bag of potting soil. Though most commercial mixes contain some fertilizer, it helps to mix in a little more before planting. Do the mixing in a large plastic dishpan. An "all-purpose" fertilizer with around 5 percent nitrogen, 10 percent potassium, 10 percent phosphorus, and trace elements like iron and zinc works best. You won't need much. Two tablespoons will be enough to improve a dishpan of potting soil. Some gardeners also stretch commercial mixes by adding dirt from the garden. A handful or two is about right for a dishpan of mix. Or you can add a handful or two of sand, perlite, or vermiculite (two mineral

products sold at nurseries) to make a faster-draining mix for finicky plants. Of course, if you don't want to bother, potting soil right from the bag will suffice.

Put a little square of window screening over the drainage hole of the pot (to keep out slugs and sowbugs that might nibble on roots), then fill the container part way with potting soil. Don't put gravel, bits of broken pots, or any other substance in the bottom of the pot. These unnecessary materials, which are supposed to improve drainage, only occupy space that roots could be using. Firmly pack the potting soil into the bottom of the container, then plant, packing more soil around plants. Make sure soil is compacted or it will dry out too fast. Also make sure you haven't overfilled the container — leave an inch of space at the top or soil will spill out every time you water. Water immediately.

After the first three weeks, fertilize container plants monthly if they are annuals or other plants that grow fast and bloom often. Fertilizing once every three months is sufficient for plants that are not so vigorous. Water often the first few weeks because some potting mixes need time to settle down, and if they dry out early on, it may be difficult to get the soil properly moist.

Summer's Flowers

Summer's flowers are the brightest and the boldest in the garden, as radiant as the sun itself. Most need heat (the two most popular, marigolds and zinnias, come from sunny Mexico), and they shouldn't be planted until the weather swears to stay warm. In California this usually means planting in March or April, or even waiting until May or June.

Two of the brightest summer annuals — marigolds and gloriosa daisies — dominate this garden by Roger Boddaert. The marigolds are present in their many forms. There are small-flowered French marigolds, big American hybrids, and just about every size in between. The small white daisies interspersed are *Chrysanthemum paludosum*, an annual that seems to grow in any season. The big white flowers are shasta daisies, a perennial. Ageratum, a bluish flower that always photographs purple, grows in the clay pots. (The young vines beginning to climb the trellis are *Mandevilla Alice de Pont*, a subtropical vine that only grows in nearly frost-free locations.)

In California, summer's flowers aren't as easy to grow as those of spring. Warm weather brings out bugs and disease that may bother them, and regular watering becomes more critical, but they are a tough lot born to grow in the sun. On the following pages are some of the best grown as annuals.

right: Naughty Marietta, a French
marigold

below: Sunny summer flowers in a
Santa Monica garden

Nicotiana

Zinnia

The Best of
Summer's Annuals

ageratum. Flat, fuzzy clusters of violet-blue flowers cover this foot-tall plant throughout summer. Good as a filler, or in the front row. Best planted from packs or pots.

sweet alyssum. As good in the summer as it is in winter and spring, it grows in low mounds of white or purplish flowers. Midnight, a dark purple variety, and Wonderland, a pinkish purple one, are less likely to fade in summer's heat. Dwarf kinds are dense, stay under four inches. Best grown from seed.

balsam. This has camellialike flowers in shades of pink, rose, and red. An old-fashioned plant that looks a little lost in the modern garden. Grows from one to two feet tall, from seed, packs, or pots.

celosia. There are two kinds, crested cockscomb with bizarre, contorted flower heads, and plume celosia with feathery plumes. There are varieties of each that grow from one to three feet tall and both come in outrageous shades of yellow, orange, gold, and crimson. Best grown from packs or pots, and best planted by themselves since colors don't combine well.

cosmos. Bushy plants with vivid, daisylike flowers on long, thin stems. There are two distinct kinds, one with brilliant yellow or orange flowers and one with flowers in shades of pink, mulberry, and white. Both have the same airy effect in the garden, growing to three feet tall or more. Easy to grow from seed, packs, or pots.

bedding dahlia. These miniature dahlias are always grown as annuals in California. Most kinds stay under one and a half feet, and the colors are superb shades of yellow, orange, red, pink, and white. Best grown from packs or pots. Need more moisture than most flowers.

gloriosa daisy. Huge daisy flowers on tall but graceful plants growing to four feet. Flowers usually golden, often with dark mahogany markings, though some are completely mahogany in color. Irish Eyes has a bright green center. Easily grown from seed, packs, or pots.

golden fleece. *Thymophylla tenuiloba* is a very big name for a very dainty yellow daisy flower with fine, threadlike foliage that never grows taller than a foot. Best grown from packs.

lobelia. Six-inch-tall plants often with dark reddish foliage and bright blue to violet flowers. A good filler that contrasts nicely with summer's many golden flowers. Best grown from packs or pots.

marigold. Summer's favorite flower hardly needs describing. The tiniest are the Signet marigolds that have almost ferny foliage and delicate little flowers that are vivid yellow, orange, or crimson. These look best in masses, like wildflowers. Most are only eight to ten inches tall; easy to grow from seed or packs.

The mid-sized French marigolds come in single and double flowered forms, in yellow, orange, and crimson, often marked with maroon. All are neat and tidy and low growing, eight to fourteen inches tall.

The taller American or African marigolds grow one and a half to three feet tall with the biggest flowers on sturdy stems. Most are shades of yellow or orange.

Triploids are the newest wrinkle. These so-called mule marigolds are crosses between French and American varieties, ending up with big blooms on short plants. Since they don't produce seed, they seem to flower forever. Easy to grow, but not every seed will germinate so plant more than you need. All other marigolds are easy to grow from seed, packs, or pots.

nicotiana. Graceful stems from one to three feet tall are covered with tubular flowers in shades of pink, deep red, and white, including some pleasing greenish whites. Easy to grow from seed, packs, or pots.

petunia. Until quite recently, petunias were surefire summer flowers, but smog and fungous diseases have made them difficult to grow in many areas. On the horizon are more

Gloriosa daisies

Golden fleece

vinca. The best annual for really hot weather, it is also long lasting, well into winter. A foot tall with neatly growing white flowers with red eyes or rosy pink flowers. Until recently it was called *Vinca rosea*, now it is *Catharanthus roseus*, but most people just call it vinca. Best grown from packs or pots.

zinnia. The brightest of summer flowers, zinnias come in many sizes, forms, and colors. The newest are dwarfs, most notably the foot-tall Peter Pan series, though there are zinnias even smaller. Tall zinnias reach two to two and a half feet tall. There are Giant Double types (the best known), Giant Tetra types (dahlialike flowers), and Giant Cactus types (lots of narrow, pointed petals). All come in brilliant shades of yellow, orange, pink, rose, scarlet, cream, and a mediocre violet. Zinnias should only be planted after the weather becomes warm in late spring. Prettiest when planted as a mix of colors. Easy to grow from seed or packs. Become root bound in pots.

resistant varieties. In the meantime, petunias are best grown early in the season before summer's heat and smog descend. There are single- and double-flowered forms with the singles making the biggest impact in the garden. And there are Grandifloras and Multifloras, the former with large flowers, the latter with more, but smaller, flowers and a neater appearance. Both come in shades of pink, red, salmon, purple, white, and even a pale yellow. All are under a foot tall and are best grown from packs or pots.

portulaca. Low-spreading succulent plants with shimmering flowers almost too brilliant for the garden, in shades of yellow, orange, red, cerise, coral, and white. Loves hot weather. Easy to grow from seed or packs.

scarlet sage. Brilliant red flower spikes top foot-tall plants. Loves hot weather, easy to grow from seed, packs, or pots.

verbena. Usually planted as annuals, these low-spreading plants will last several seasons in Southern California. The kinds sold as bedding plants have rounded clusters of white, pink, red, or violet flowers, grow under a foot tall, and should be planted two feet apart. They are seldom out of bloom. Very useful in foreground of garden. Best grown from packs or pots.

Vinca rosea (actually *Catharanthus*)

Strawflowers and a few herbs drying upside down

Flowers That Last Forever

Everlastings or strawflowers can be grown like any other annual planted from seed. First they put on a show in your garden, then you pick them, let them dry, and use them in flower arrangements or dried bouquets. The dried blossoms hold their shape and lose only a little color, though most of the leaves wither.

You can plant an entire garden of everlastings, or you can plant just a few here and there among other flowers. They'll need a full day's sun and average soil, but little else, which isn't surprising since most come from climates similar to California's. Over half are native to western Australia. Everlastings don't even need much water. If planted in the fall, winter rains will help with irrigation.

Gardeners on the coast can plant everlastings in fall or early spring. Inland, plant them in the fall. If planted later, the flowers will open too fast in the hot weather and won't dry properly. Most of them prefer growing in cooler weather.

Strawflowers are always grown from seed. Most nurseries carry seed of the common strawflower (*Helichrysum*) and mixed packets containing several kinds of everlastings.

Pictured here are some of the best yet easiest to grow. If you want all the everlastings shown, you'll have to order seed from a mail order company. George W. Park Seed Co., Greenwood, South Carolina 29647, has the biggest selection of everlastings.

Most of the seeds are easy to handle and sow, although the seeds of *Anaphalis* are very tiny. Statice seeds must be separated from each other by breaking them apart.

There's a right time to pick each of these everlastings for drying. That information is included in each listing. The best time of day to cut is midafternoon, on a day that is sunny and warm (a few of these flowers only open on sunny days).

Cut a good length of stem with each flower so it can be used in arrangements. Bundle the cut flowers with some twine and hang them upside down (flowers toward the ground) in a cool, dark place. The garage is often a good

Ammobium alatum　　　　　Swan River everlasting　　　　Globe thistle

spot. However, if your garage is dusty you might want to wrap newspaper cones around the flower bundles. A large, vented clothes bag would be another good place in which to hang the flowers to dry.

winged everlasting (*Ammobium alatum* Grandiflora). Three-quarter-inch-wide flowers on four-foot-tall stems, anchored to a foot-wide clump of foliage. Pick while still in bud.

globe thistle (*Echinops ritro*). Prickly and two inches wide, the globes should be picked for drying before flowers open (sooner than shown). It's a perennial that looks like a two-foot by two-foot artichoke plant.

strawflowers (*Helichrysum bracteatum*). Easy to grow flowers, two and a half inches across, in many colors on three-foot-tall, foot-wide plants. Pick before flowers fully open.

Helipterum humboldtianum (sold as *H. sandfordii*). These grow twelve to twenty inches tall, four to six inches wide, with bunches of flowers to four inches across. Pick when fully open.

Helipterum roseum (also sold as *Acroclinium*). Pretty pink flowers atop grassy tufts two-and-a-half feet tall by six inches wide. Pick in bud or as flowers open.

Swan River everlasting (*Helipterum manglesii*). Dainty, papery, inch-wide flowers, usually sold as *Rhodanthe*. A spindly plant — fifteen inches tall, six inches wide. Pick anytime.

sea lavender or statice (*Limonium sinuatum*). A broad, flat head several inches wide formed by tiny flowers on a sturdy twenty-inch stem, twelve inches across. Pick anytime.

love-in-a-mist (*Nigella damascena*). Pretty in flower. Dry the balloonlike pods that follow blossoms. Thorny looking parts are actually soft leaves. Plants grow twenty inches tall, twelve inches wide.

Helipterum roseum

Limonium sinuatum

PERENNIAL CARE AND MAINTENANCE

All perennials require a little diligence. Short-lived perennials from mild climates need the least care. The common Marguerite daisy is a perfect example. It grows and blooms continuously for two or three years, then either collapses or gets so raggedy that it must be pulled out and replaced by a new plant. The only care required is the occasional removal of dead flowers. Severe pruning will seldom rejuvenate perennials of this sort and may in fact kill them outright.

Another group of perennials, also originating mostly in mild climates, of which agapanthus is a good example, is long lived, almost permanent. They grow and spread, forming larger and larger clumps that benefit if dug up, divided, and given a fresh start every few years. Leave them alone as long as you can, but if they don't flower as they used to, that means it's time to divide.

Herbaceous perennials, the kind that die down for the winter in colder climates, are the trickiest. In mild climates, where winter may not arrive with the chill they're accustomed to, they may flower and need cutting back several times a year, but in general they follow the pattern shown in the drawings below.

In spring and summer they grow and flower, usually from a closely knit clump of roots. Look carefully at the base of such plants and you'll see not just one stem but many growing out of the ground.

After flowering, they should be cut back, some almost to the ground, others by half or a third. From this base they will regrow and bloom.

Fall through February is the best time to dig and divide perennials. Some require dividing because the centers of the clumps slowly die out, leaving gaping holes. Others need dividing just because they have spread too far. A few require it because they just seem to need a fresh start in life, perhaps because they have depleted the soil. Always cultivate and improve the soil before replanting a perennial.

To divide any plant, first dig it up and try separating chunks with your hands. If this doesn't work, resort to an old kitchen knife or a sharp spade.

Summer

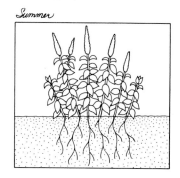

Fall & Winter

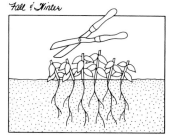

Perennials

Perennials are simply plants that live for more than one season. In colder climates, most perennials die down for the winter and return each spring. These are "herbaceous" perennials. But in California, many of our best perennials look good year round. Some are short-lived, lasting only a few years and blooming the entire time; others slowly grow into bigger and bigger clumps, persisting for years. In this sense, a perennial is any plant that lasts longer than an annual without ever quite becoming a shrub or equally woody and permanent part of the garden. Perennials are primarily grown for their flowers, but some are cultivated for exquisite foliage.

Traditionally, perennials are planted by themselves in grand, flowery borders. Perennial borders, as developed by the English, are legendary, surrounded by a great mystique that has caused more than a few good gardeners to shy away from anything called a perennial. They always sound so difficult to grow, so exacting in their requirements. But there is no mystery here. Perennials are as easy to grow and use as any other plant.

Combined with annuals and bulbs, they give backbone to the flower garden. In a new garden, they grow fast and bloom right away so they can take the place of such permanent plants as shrubs and trees the first few seasons. In mature landscapes they can be mixed in, under or around shrubs and ground covers, where they become highlights of color or form — the first thing you notice when you step out into the garden in the morning.

The traditional border can even be a possibility in California, but it must adapt to the milder climate. Pictured here is landscape designer Chris Rosmini's garden of perennials in Los Angeles. Unlike the traditional border it also

Sunset on a Southern California perennial garden

includes flowering shrubs, bulbs, and annuals — even though perennials are in the majority here — ensuring that something is always in bloom, even in the dead of winter. Fruit trees form the backdrop, a retaining wall of broken concrete elevates the flowers nearly to eye-level, and a path of used brick allows access while providing definition.

The California perennial garden has a more natural appearance than the rigid formality of the traditional border because the seasonal changes don't stop and start the growing process as they would in a colder climate. While some plants are at their best any time of year, others aren't there yet or are already past prime. There is no headlong rush to bloom before frost, so the garden doesn't come to regimented perfection. Things are more relaxed here.

While most perennials are quite easy to grow, all need to be fiddled with in some fashion, if only to be finally pulled out and replaced. Herbaceous perennials need the most attention. Remember, perennials do not live forever; while some are described as "permanent," they should not be planted and forgotten. In return for a little care and grooming they will reward you with flowers or foliage considered by many to be the prettiest in the plant kingdom.

The list of perennial plants on the following pages provides just a sampling and includes all the commonly available kinds, with just a few harder-to-find (but not harder-to-grow) teasers thrown in. Perhaps these will lead you on to further discoveries, for there are literally thousands of perennials to be tried.

Perennials are usually started from plants, but can be sown from seed in pots. It's best to sow seed in August and plant them in the garden in fall. Fall and the month of March are best times to plant perennials from divisions or containers.

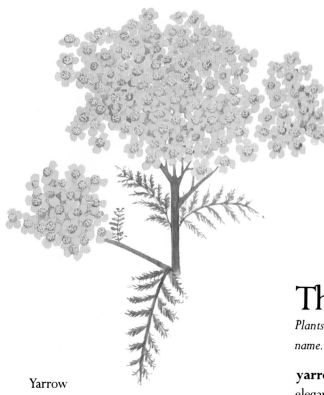

Yarrow

Agapanthus

The Best Perennials

Plants are listed in alphabetical order according to botanical name.

yarrow (*Achillea*). Flat-topped clusters of tiny flowers on elegant stems with low clumps of fernlike foliage, often silvery. Most flower in summer. After flowering, cut stems to ground. Should be divided every few years. Tall kinds include *Achillea filipendulina* Gold Plate and Coronation Gold (bright yellow, three feet tall) and *A. ptarmica* The Pearl (white, two feet tall). Smaller kinds include *A. taygetea* (bright yellow, eighteen inches tall), *A. tomentosa* varieties (yellow to cream, ten inches tall), and *A. clavennae* (white, ten inches tall).

agapanthus. Bold, bulblike clumps of foliage look good year round. All have clusters of blue or white flowers atop tall stems in late spring. Easily divided but it is seldom necessary. *Agapanthus orientalis* is tallest with flower spikes to five feet. *A. africanus* with spikes to two feet is more useful. Peter Pan is a tidy miniature with spikes eighteen inches tall.

kangaroo paw (*Anigozanthos*). Sword-shaped leaves make low, thin clumps. Fascinating fuzzy flowers in odd color combinations come atop tall stems. Seldom needs dividing. *Anigozanthos flavidus* is yellow-green with red tips on stalks five feet tall. *A. pulcherrimus* is similar but half the size.

columbine (*Aquilegia*). Wonderful, graceful plants. Most have flowers with contrasting colors from pink to yellow to bluish. McKana hybrids are most common. Cut to ground in late fall. Division possible, but easy to grow from seed. Replant every few years.

African daisy (*Arctosis*). Most perennial African daisies are hybrids, in unusual shades of pink, red, purple, yellow, orange, and white. They make gray-green, gazanialike clumps, but the recent Venidio-Arctotis hybrids spread to

McKana's
Giant columbine

Arctotis

38

Asteriscus sericeus

Coreopsis Sunray

several feet. Divide and restart every few years as centers die out.

artemisia. Valued for their silvery-white foliage, flowers are unimportant. *Artemisia frigida* grows to one and a half feet, *A. schmidtiana* grows to two feet (a variety of this, Silver Mound, grows only a foot tall). All can be sheared back if they become rangy with age. Can be divided, but considered permanent once planted.

aster. Of the many asters, two do especially well in California. The Michaelmas daisies (hybrids of two American asters, *A. novae-angliae* and *A. novi-belgii*) make graceful, spreading masses of daisy flowers in shades of pink, red, and purple with two- to three-foot stems. They bloom in fall and should be cut to ground in winter, when they are easily divided, a necessary task every few years. *Aster frikartii* is a loosely bushy daisy with bright lavender blooms that last all summer and fall. Shear off flowers to prolong bloom. Needs to be restarted every few years.

Asteriscus sericeus. A foot-tall mound of exquisite silver leaves with yellow daisies neatly on top. Lives several years, then slowly dies. Sometimes sold as *Odontospermum.*

bellflower (*Campanula*). Most campanulas have white, pink, or more often, lavender or blue bell-shaped flowers. *Campanula persicifolia*, the peach-leaved bluebell, has spikes to two or three feet and grows easily from seed. It should be divided every other year and may bloom several times a season if fading spikes are removed. *C. rapunculoides* makes spikes two feet tall that spread vigorously, verging on weedy. Frequent division keeps it in bounds and helps flowering. Cut to ground after flowering. Two short bellflowers are *C. isophylla*, which trails to two feet and looks splendid dangling over a wall or raised bed, and *C. poscharskyana*, which spreads to become a ground cover. Both need restarting every few years. All bloom in late spring.

valerian (*Centranthus ruber*). An old-fashioned plant that blooms all the time, with clusters of magenta or white flowers. Grows to three feet. Quite permanent, but may be divided.

Marguerite (*Chrysanthemum frutescens*). The daisy bush. Most grow quickly to four by four feet. Besides the common whites and yellows, there are new forms with silvery foliage, fancy flowers. One of the best is a double pink. Bloom most of the year. Prune lightly to encourage flowering; replace plants every few years as they get woody.

shasta daisy (*Chrysanthemum maximum*). Low-spreading clumps of dark green foliage with large, white daisy flowers, single or double, on sturdy two- to three-foot stems. Little Miss Muffet is a valuable foot-tall dwarf. All do best if divided every few years, in the fall. Cut flowers to ground after bloom.

bush morning glory (*Convolvulus*). *Convolvulus cneorum* makes a foot-tall, slightly spreading bush of silky, silvery leaves with white, morning-glory flowers. Alas, it is short-lived. *Convolvulus mauritanicus* grows only six inches tall, spreading several feet, with green foliage and lavender flowers. It should be cut back every few years, and eventually must be replaced.

coreopsis. The king of yellow flowers, tall kinds include *Coreopsis grandiflora* and *C. verticillata*, both to two and a half feet with bright golden flowers. *C. auriculata* Nana spreads to form a six-inch-high mat. The best is a new variety named Sunray that makes a dense clump one and a half feet tall, is seldom out of bloom, and is easy to grow from seed. Coreopsis plants bloom and bloom but at some point the dead flower heads should be sheared off, unfortunately along with the current crop of flowers. A good time for this is fall, when they may come right back into bloom. Divide every few years in fall or winter. Makes a good cut flower.

delphinium. White, pink, lavender, and blue flowers bloom on dense spikes. There are many kinds, but the very

A Pacific Hybrid delphinium

Pride of Madeira

tall (to six feet) Pacific Hybrids of *Delphinium elatum* are the most common. Spikes need staking early in the season. Dwarf varieties, such as Blue Fountains, are easier to grow. Easier still are bushy varieties of *D. belladonna*, growing to three or four feet. However, all delphiniums are somewhat difficult. They need rich, moist soil, a place out of the wind, and no overhead watering. Delphiniums are grown like annuals, though they may persist for more than one season. Short kinds are best grown in the fall from seed; buy taller kinds as small plants purchased fall through spring. After they bloom cut back just below bottom flower, wait for side spikes to form, then remove rest of old spike.

carnations and pinks (*Dianthus*). There are over three hundred kinds of perennial dianthus. The taller ones are known as carnations. Look for garden types that don't need staking. Pinks are shorter, more delicate, with smaller flowers. They usually last longer, forming dense mounds of grayish foliage. *Dianthus deltoides, D. gratianopolitanus, D. plumarius*, and their many varieties are among the best. Most bloom in spring and again in fall if lightly sheared. Somewhat difficult to divide, they are best replanted every few years.

African iris (*Dietes*). Called *Moraea* until recently, these three-foot-tall, irislike plants bloom off and on all year. The small, flat flowers are usually white with orange and brown blotches. There is also a smaller kind with a soft yellow flower. A permanent plant but can be divided.

pride of Madeira (*Echium fastuosum*). A big, elegant plant growing to six feet in bloom. From many long stems covered with blue-gray leaves come spikes of deep blue flowers. Occasionally prune lightly and cut off dead spikes. Reasonably permanent in coastal gardens.

erigeron. Two are right at home: *Erigeron glaucus*, a California native beach aster that grows about a foot tall, spreads slowly, and has neat lavender daisy flowers. Grows best near the coast. Needs replanting every few years. *E.*

FAR LEFT: *Geranium sanguineum* Prostratum

LEFT: *Gaillardia*

Felicia

karvinskianus, from Mexico, is a low, tumbling plant with tiny white daisies that turn to pink. Reseeds itself so it appears permanent.

euryops. Resembles the common daisy but lasts much longer in the garden. Golden daisies bloom on open bushes to four feet tall. Foliage is deep green. Prune lightly to keep in shape, otherwise reasonably permanent.

felicia. Lovely blue daisies on a tidy, mounding plant that seldom grows taller than two feet but may spread as wide as four feet. Blooms appear year round. It only looks good the first two or three years, and should be replaced with new plants. Light pruning helps blooming.

gaillardia. Most kinds grow about two feet tall and have big daisy flowers in warm shades of yellow and red with contrasting bands of orange or maroon. Goblin is an especially neat foot-tall variety with dancing yellow flowers. Blooms in summer and fall; seed heads are attractive. Eventually rots and must be replaced.

geranium. These are true geraniums, not to be confused with *Pelargonium*, the plant most people call geraniums. Many are good perennials, including *Geranium sanguineum* with deep purple flowers and spreading growth under a foot, and its variety Prostratum (often called *G. lancastriense*) lower still with bright pink flowers. *G. pratense* has electric blue flowers, grows to two feet tall, seeds about. All kinds bloom in summer, have leaves like snowflakes, and can be divided if necessary.

gerbera. These South African plants produce huge daisylike flowers in deep, warm shades of yellow, orange, red, and pink. Clumps of dark green foliage stay under a foot tall and should be cut in half with a spade every few years and be replanted. Plant gerberas a little high in the ground to prevent crown rot. Thin the inner leaves to let in sun if they don't bloom well.

Geum chiloense. Brilliant yellow-orange or scarlet-orange flowers bloom on graceful, branching, two-and-a-half-foot

Duplex gerberas in full glory, great for cutting

Pet Set, a dwarf iris

Candytuft

Coral bells

stems early in spring. Foliage makes a tidy, foot-tall clump of dark green. May not bloom the first year. Divide and replant every few years, or replace.

daylily (*Hemerocallis*). One of the toughest perennials, flowers look like lilies with foliage like that from a bulb. There are tall varieties to six feet, and dwarfs only a foot tall. Flowers in shades of pink, rusty red, orange, and yellow bloom year round. Evergreen kinds are best. Divide in fall, when clumps get too large.

coral bells (*Heuchera*). From foot-tall tufts of roundish leaves come dainty three-foot spikes of pink, red, or white flowers in spring and summer. Need several years to look their best. Divide clumps in fall when centers begin to die out. It's all right if divisions have only a few roots each.

candytuft (*Iberis sempervirens*). Low-growing mounds of narrow, deep green leaves completely obscured by short spikes of white flowers in spring and early summer. Snowflake is an especially dense variety. A good filler among taller perennials. Shear after flowering to keep growth dense. Most grow a foot tall or less. Division is difficult but plants are quite long-lived.

iris. Bearded and many other kinds of iris are perennial plants growing from rhizomes that resemble sweet potatoes. The bearded kind are best known, and with a little looking can be found in heights from such foot-tall dwarfs as Pet Set to the more common four-foot-tall varieties. All bloom in late spring but some have a bonus bloom again in the fall (this trait is called "remontant"). A dozen reblooming varieties that do especially well in California gardens are: Autumn Echo, Autumn Leaves, Bess Gergin, Cascade Pass, Cherished, Halloween Party, Homecoming, Pink Feathers, Red Polish, Touché, Wedding Vow, and Zulu Warrior.

Iris clumps should be divided every three to four years in the fall. Cut rhizomes apart with a knife and discard old shriveled rhizomes at center of the clump. Trim tips of leaves and tidy up roots, then replant.

poker plant (*Kniphofia*). A robust plant with tall, sword-shaped leaves that can become ratty looking, so it is best planted behind other perennials. Tall kinds grow to four feet with flowers shooting up to six feet, but there are also smaller varieties and species. Flowers form dense clusters, usually shading from yellow to orange or red. One variety blooms in winter, but most in summer. Common kinds are very permanent. Use a sharp spade to cut chunks from root mass if division is necessary.

lion's tail (*Leonotis leonurus*). A shrubby plant that grows five or six feet tall. Upright branches are covered with orange tubular flowers in summer, fall, and even the dead of winter. Cut stems halfway back after they bloom. Permanent.

statice (*Limonium perezii*). Low tufts of broad leaves produce foot-tall spikes of flat-topped flower clusters. Flowers are deep purple with white centers and last a long, long time. Plants may be divided but this is seldom necessary.

nierembergia. One kind, *Nierembergia hippomanica*, is planted as an annual but trimming after flowering may make it last a season or two more. Longer lived is *N. scoparia* (*N. frutescens*), a graceful, shrubby, white-flowered plant growing to two feet tall. Eventually needs to be replaced.

evening primrose (*Oenothera*). The Mexican evening primrose (*Oenothera speciosa childsii*) is the best. Spreads to form low masses of soft pink flowers. Cut to ground after flowering. Easy to divide. Must be kept in bounds.

geranium (*Pelargonium*). Geraniums grow best in coastal gardens, and require a bit more work elsewhere. Geraniums can be long-lived. Cut them back occasionally to keep their shape; replace when their time has come. There are basically four groups:

Garden or common geraniums (*Pelargonium hortorum*) are shrubby with fat, succulent stems. They produce big balls of blooms in soft or bright shades of pink, red, orange,

Salvia farinacea Victoria

Penstemon gloxinioides

lavender, and white. There are also fancy-leaved kinds. Most grow to about three feet, and need little care.

Martha Washington geraniums (*P. domesticum*) are more erect, with larger individual flowers than the common kinds though there are fewer to a cluster. Flowers are usually marked with contrasting colors, and leaves are toothed.

Ivy geraniums (*P. peltatum*) are trailing plants that can be used for ground covers. Flowers are like those of the common geranium and stand above the crinkly foliage on short stems.

Scented geraniums are grown for their interesting foliage and fragrances. Nutmeg (*P. fragrans*) and lime-scented geraniums (*P. nervosum*) make nice little shrublets, and the velvety-leaved, peppermint-scented *P. tomentosum* will make a three-foot-tall bush in part shade.

penstemon. There are many kinds, but two do best mixed with other perennials. *Penstemon gloxinioides*, the border penstemon, comes in shades of pink and deep red, with rangy growth to two or three feet tall. If cut back after flowering in spring, they bloom again in summer. *P. heterophyllus*, the blue bedder penstemon, is a much neater plant to about one-and-a-half feet tall, with flowers that sometimes approach true blue. Both kinds are short-lived and must be replaced after several years.

Physostegia virginiana. Bright lavender-pink or white flowers bloom on three-foot stems that spread slowly to form pretty thickets. After flowering in the early fall, cut to ground. Dividing is easy, but this is only necessary to keep it in bounds.

Rehmannia elata. From small clumps of foliage come two-to three-foot spires of pink or white flowers that bloom most of spring and into summer. A slowly spreading plant, it is easy to divide, when it becomes necessary with age.

yellow flax (*Reinwardtia indica*). With bright yellow flowers that bloom in the dead of winter, it spreads into a bushy

shape about three feet tall. Divide in spring. Viral disease may turn stems brown and make it short-lived.

salvia. Of the many varieties, the most popular are of *Salvia farinacea*. Two salvias found in the herb section at nurseries make attractive perennials — *Salvia officinalis* and *S. sclarea*, the clary sage. Some new introductions from South America, as yet unnamed, have shocking red or deep purple flowers, and grow to three or four feet. Most are long-lived and must be replanted when they become too woody.

dusty miller (*Senecio cineraria*). A coarse plant with distinctively cut gray leaves and pale yellow flowers. Growing to two feet tall, it spreads slowly and should be lightly sheared in fall. A close to permanent plant, it can be divided and restarted if the growth gets too ragged.

lamb's ears (*Stachys byzantina*). Low clumps of large, woolly, white leaves are the attraction. Flowers in summer with pinkish blooms on short stems. It spreads slowly and is easy to divide if necessary.

betony (*Stachys officinalis*). Low-spreading clumps of leaves produce two-and-a-half-foot-tall spires of very pretty purple flowers in early summer and again in fall if cut back. It is easily divided if necessary.

society garlic (*Tulbaghia violacea*). Forms large clumps of delicate bulblike foliage with clusters of pinkish flowers most of the year. Unpleasant odor when cut. Easy to divide if they get too large. *Tulbaghia fragrans* lives up to its name and smells better but isn't nearly as attractive.

speedwell (*Veronica*). There are many kinds, and most have graceful blue spikes. Hybrids, like Shirley Blue, are best. Most grow no more than two feet tall. Should occasionally be divided. Many rebloom if cut back after flowering.

The Bulb Garden

Spring finery: Lady Derby hyacinths, Darwin tulips
Gudoshnik and Orange Juice, and King Alfred daffodils

true bulb   corm   tubers   rhizome

The Bulb Garden

Bulbs are nature's surprise. From the round, papery packages we call bulbs and the equally undistinguished brownish lumps called "corms" and "tubers" come some of the prettiest of all flowers. They burst forth with a suddenness that can only mean that spring is here, even if there are no other signs about.

Few plants are so foolproof. Plant them in the fall and forget them until spring, when they will explode with color. Their season is short and they will soon retreat underground, but if properly chosen and cared for they return year after year.

Certain bulbs, such as tulips and hyacinths, were developed for climates colder than California's. Without the necessary winter chilling, and perhaps because of the summer's heat, those favorites may not return the following year. In colder parts of the country, and even in some parts of California, they can be garden stalwarts. In the milder parts of the state they are best treated as bedding plants, planted in masses or even in pots.

There are, however, many lesser-known bulbs and bulblike plants that thrive in California's endless summer. They come from similar climates, like those of South Africa or the Mediterranean. While tulips and daffodils may have developed bulbs as a defense against a cold winter, these others use their bulb stage to survive a long, dry summer, and then suddenly bloom with the first rain. There should be room for both kinds in the garden.

Tulip bulbs, freesia corms, and ranunculus tubers ready to plant

BULBS, CORMS, AND TUBERS

For the gardener there are a few important distinctions between true bulbs and "bulbs" that are actually corms or tubers. True bulbs include two of the most popular plants: daffodils and tulips. The onion is a true bulb whose concentric rings are typical. The layers, called "scales," are actually specialized leaves, and are storehouses of plant food. From the top of each bulb comes only one sprout, so a single bulb will produce just a single set of leaves, though many bulbs develop baby bulblets that will also produce leaves. From time to time, these should be dug up, pulled off, and replanted.

Corms are fat, specialized sections of stem, and include crocuses and most of the South African bulbs. There are no rings or scales in the cross section, but there is a papery covering. It is often difficult to determine which side is up on a corm, but look for a small, flattish base plate on the bottom and a little pointed eye on top. Corms only last one season, but as foliage withers a new corm forms atop the old for next year's bloom. On either side cormels will form, babies that won't bloom for several years. Removing cormels sometimes makes corms bloom better.

Tubers least resemble bulbs in appearance. They too are technically fattened stems but they don't have the papery covering of corms or true bulbs, and sprouts often occur all along the tuber. The potato is a good example. Some tubers disappear as the plants grow but new tubers will form at the end of the season. Other tubers get larger each year. Ranunculus, anemones, and cyclamen are actually tubers that are called "bulbs."

Plants with other underground storage devices such as rhizomes, tuberous rhizomes, and tuberous roots belonging to such plants as iris, agapanthus, calla, and dahlia are usually not considered "bulbs," but perennials.

For years, gardeners have put a little bone meal in the bottom of every bulb planting hole. Why? Because bone meal is mostly phosphorus, an important fertilizing element for bulbs, and because phosphorus doesn't move in the soil. If you sprinkle it on top, there it stays. It must be mixed into the soil so it is near to plant roots.

But bone meal is probably not enough. Although it certainly can't hurt, there is some doubt as to whether it becomes available fast enough to benefit most

47

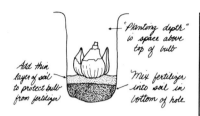

bulbs. Superphosphate, also high in phosphorus, may be the better choice to place under bulbs, or try a complete fertilizer, such as a 5-10-10, intended just for bulb planting.

Many bulb growers do this: at planting time mix bone meal or superphosphate into the soil beneath the bulb, then cover it with a little additional soil, preventing direct contact between fertilizer and bulb, which may harm the bulb, but ensuring that the phosphorus will be close to the roots. Then, when the emerging foliage is about three inches high, fertilize with an ordinary liquid or granular fertilizer so that nitrogen, the plant food most responsible for growth, is available at just the right time.

In the drawing above, showing where to put bulb fertilizers, note that the "planting depth" of a bulb is the distance from the top of the hole to the top of the bulb, not the depth of the entire hole. Planting depth of individual bulbs will be discussed in the following pages.

King Alfred daffodils in a field of baby blue eyes

Tazetta daffodils are good choices in California; this is Cragford

perianth, made up of segments or petals

corona, also called a "cup" or "trumpet"

Daffodils for Spring

If spring has a symbol, it is the daffodil. Color alone would make it resplendent — bright yellow blooms that chase away the gray of winter like tiny suns. But they are also as versatile as they are lovely. In most regions daffodils can be permanent plants (though avid growers usually dig up bulbs, divide, and replant every three years). They withstand heat and cold, sun or partial shade, heavy or light soils. They can be planted by the hundreds on hillsides, in little clumps by the front door, or in pots. In short, they are near-perfect plants, and it would be a shame to let the fall planting season pass without putting a few in the ground.

There are hundreds of varieties, from the huge trumpet types, such as Califlora, to the tiny species, such as *Narcissus bulbocodium*, only inches tall. Daffodils don't stay in bloom for long but different kinds bloom at different times. In California blooming can begin as early as December and continue into late April. So by careful reading of catalogues or by experimentation, it is possible to select daffodils that will flower one right after the other, for a long succession of bloom.

Daffodil blooms always face south, toward the sun, so make sure they won't turn their backs on you. Except in areas where fall feels more like summer, they are best planted as early as possible, preferably in September, so they have plenty of time to form roots. Although most bulbs look best when planted fairly close together, daffodils are the exception. Their nodding flowers should not touch, so space large bulbs at least eight inches apart and smaller bulbs four inches apart. The rule of thumb is to cover bulbs with soil two times as deep as the bulb is tall. (For example, a big three-inch bulb should have six inches of soil over it.) When planting bulbs in pots, the necks of the bulbs should stick out of the soil to allow more room for roots underneath. In the ground or in pots feed bulbs with 5-10-10 fertilizer when foliage is about three inches high.

DAFFODIL LINGO

Here are some of the commonly used terms for this popular flower:

daffodil. *The common name for all* Narcissus.

narcissus. *The botanical name for the entire genus, but also indiscriminately applied to any daffodil that appears delicate or has a small cup.*

jonquil. *Often used interchangeably with daffodil, the jonquil is actually one type of daffodil,* Narcissus jonquilla.

perianth. *The ring of segments that appear to be petals is called the perianth.*

corona. *The corona is the botanical name for the trumpet (if it's long) or the cup (if it's shorter). At one time, it was suggested that all daffodils be classified according to their coronas — long nosed, short nosed, or snub nosed — a cute idea and certainly a simpler way of doing it than the present system.*

BULB COVERS

The baby blue eyes (Nemophila menziesii) luxuriating under the daffodils as seen at left are just one of several shallow-rooted annuals that can be sown over the tops of newly planted bulbs. They'll come into bloom faster and probably last longer, helping to hide the withering bulb foliage. Besides the baby blue eyes, a California native, try forget-me-nots (also blue), Swan River daisy (Brachycome — white and shades of blue and violet), linaria (resembling baby snapdragons in a gay mix of colors), sweet alyssum (white, rose, and purple; the dwarf kinds are best), and Virginia stock.

DAFFODILS FOR WARM CLIMATES

Because their perianths, or "petals," are actually thicker, these daffodils thrive in warm climates like Southern California's. Many are from the Jonquilla or Tazetta divisions since these seem especially suited to hot climates: Arctic Gold, Binkie, Bridal Crown, February Gold, Geranium, Jenny, Kinglet, Mabel Taylor, Martha Washington, Mount Hood, Thalia, and Trevithian. Bear in mind that in hot climates daffodils need lots *of water, at least once a week.*

The group to join is the American Daffodil Society, Tyner, North Carolina 27980. The many local societies that sponsor spectacular spring shows are good places to see daffodils in flower before deciding which ones to plant in your garden.

Grant E. Mitsch, Daffodil Haven, P.O. Box 690, Canby, Oregon 97013, and The Daffodil Mart, North, Virginia 23128, are two good sources for the unusual and new.

the daffodil season.

Daffodils bloom only a short while, but planting varieties that bloom at different times ensures a longer-flowering garden.
VERY EARLY: Brunswick, February Gold, Golden Harvest, Spellbinder, Unsurpassable.
EARLY: Beersheba, Carlton, Duke of Windsor, Dutch Master, Flower Record, Fortune, Golden Ducat, High Sierra, King Alfred, Music Hall, Rembrandt, Royal Crown, Trevithian, Twink, William the Silent.
EARLY MIDSEASON: Mabel Taylor, Mount Hood, Orangery, Rustom Pasha, Texas, World's Favorite, Yellow Sun.
MIDSEASON: Actaea, Binkie, Brougshane, Carbineer, Dick Wellband, Geranium, Ice Follies, Irene Copeland, Mary Copeland, Mols Hobby, Rosey Sunrise, Thalia, White Lion, White Marvel, Windblown, Yellow Cheerfulness.
LATE: Cheerfulness, Red Shadow.

Naturalizing Daffodils

Planting bulbs by the dozens guarantees a spectacular spring show. Just stick to one kind and one color — it's that simple. Daffodils are among the best for mass planting because they will naturalize. In gardener's jargon, "naturalizing" means scattering bulbs about by the handful and planting them where they fall, and then letting bulbs spread and grow almost on their own with only a little thinning and weeding to keep a modicum of control.

The masses of yellow daffodils seen here have a perfect home in the San Bernardino Mountain garden of Gene Bauer. She never plants fewer than a hundred at a time, and some of these plantings consist of up to a thousand of just one variety. The bulbs have center stage; in this garden not

Naturalized drifts of Rustom Pasha are in the foreground and the lighter-colored Binkie is in the background

many plants compete with the daffodils, and the landscaping is purposely kept simple. Here, the climate and situation are just right: wet and cold in winter, hot and dry in summer — just what daffodils like. They grow in the partial shade created by big pines on the property, and there is a natural mulch of pine needles.

In Southern California's lowland gardens, daffodils usually won't perform as well as this; gardeners in this area might try some of the South African bulbs that have naturalized successfully. Babianas, brodiaeas, *Gladiolus tristis*, homerias, ixias, sparaxis, and tritonias are bulbs known to grow and multiply in mild climates. Their one requirement is that they need to be kept dry all summer after their foliage fades — a particularly good idea for drought-resistant gardens in which plants won't need water in summer.

lily-flowered

peony-flowered

Tulips and Hyacinths

Spring Pearl tulips

ABOVE CENTER: Dutch hyacinth

Darwin-type

parrot

fringed

Rembrandt tulip

Lily-flowered tulips

In most of California, tulips and hyacinths last for only one season. But it really doesn't matter—just think of them as the marigolds and zinnias of the bulb world, to be planted and enjoyed and then dug up to make way for something else. They will definitely reward you for your effort.

The reason tulips are so short-lived in mild climates has to do with the chilling they're accustomed to in winter, as previously mentioned. Although many of their wild ancestors came from the Mediterranean, tulips were developed in colder locales, primarily Holland, and therefore expect a crisp, cold winter.

They can be persuaded to bloom with a little deception. In California, bulbs should be purchased in September, but not planted. Instead, put them in the refrigerator, in the *least* cold section (where you keep the lettuce) and leave them there for four to six weeks. This simulates winter. Then plant the bulbs about six inches deep.

Tulips and, to a lesser extent, hyacinths should always be planted in masses, with each bulb spaced four to eight inches apart. The flowers will last longer if they are planted where they can get a little dappled afternoon shade, but too much shade will make for long, weak stems and floppy flowers.

Tulips grown in mild climates will totally exhaust the bulb they grow from, and if you wait too long to dig them up after flowering, you'll have a hard time finding what's left. It's a good idea to pull tulips up while leaves are still green and firmly attached to the bulbs. Just toss them away. At best they'd produce only leaves if saved for next year.

Large Dutch hyacinths can't be counted on for a second year, but they do sometimes surprise us by returning for several years in a row, though the flowers get a little smaller each season. Sometimes hyacinths bloom too close to the ground, but putting a cone of paper or an upside down flower pot on top, before buds open, will encourage the stems to grow taller before blooming.

TULIP TYPES
Tulips have been grouped into categories that, though not precise, give valuable clues about when they bloom and what they look like. At nurseries, look on the box of bulbs to see if the label tells the class; in catalogues, tulips are usually listed under these categories. Here are the most common:

Darwin and Darwin hybrids *are the most popular, especially in the southern half of California. They have a distinctly square shape and come in the brightest colors. The hybrids are a little larger and brighter, and bloom a little earlier. Rembrandt tulips are "broken" Darwins; that is, they are striped with white or contrasting colors.*

cottage tulips, *though quite variable in shape, generally look like Darwins though they are more rounded and bloom later. Bizarre tulips are broken cottage tulips.*

lily-flowered tulips *are similar to cottage tulips but their petals are pointed and gracefully curved outward. Most are unusually attractive in the garden, and make a striking display even when only a few are planted.*

early tulips, *both single and double or peony-flowered forms, bloom the earliest, on short stems. They are not well suited for Southern California, where they sometimes bloom so early their flowers are practically underground.*

mendel *and* **triumph tulips** *are halfway, in height and time of bloom, between early and Darwin tulips.*

parrot tulips *have ruffled petals and bloom about the same time as Darwins. These and the following classes grow and look well in containers.*

fringed tulips *have fringed petals and different kinds bloom at different seasons.*

peony-flowered tulips *have fluffy, fully double flowers. One classification, Double Late tulips, bloom later than most.*

multiflowered tulips *have more than one flower per stem, bloom late in season.*

Freesias are fragrant

BULB CITY

South Africa's Cape Town is the center for a totally unique flora that has found a second home in California gardens. African daisies, gazanias, gerberas, coral trees, iceplants, geraniums, proteas, birds-of-paradise, aloes, cycads, and literally hundreds of other common California garden plants come from South Africa's Cape Province. But perhaps the prettiest contribution to California gardens are the Cape bulbs.

Cape Province has a climate remarkably similar to California's — mild, nearly frost-free winters and long, hot summers. The area around Cape Town, on the west coast of Cape Province, is most like California because there rain falls only in the winter and summers are long and dry. Cape Town and Los Angeles are equidistant from the equator; one is 34 degrees south, the other 34 degrees north.

Bulbs are the perfect mechanism for surviving such summers — they simply retreat underground, secure in their papery packages, until the rains come again. And for some reason, South Africa has more than its fair share of fascinating bulbs. Only a few of these can be found in California nurseries, though

collectors have discovered many more that are downright easy to grow in our similar climate. South African bulbs are unusually pretty, often petite — scaled to today's smaller garden — and so at home in California that many thrive like a native. Most need no summer irrigation and many will naturalize in a short time. They are worth searching for at plant sales or from specialists.

Two California nurseries specialize in hard-to-find bulbs, especially those that do exceptionally well here, including most of the Cape bulbs. In Northern California, try Berkeley Horticultural Nursery, 1310 McGee Avenue, Berkeley, California 94703. In Southern California, try Burkard Nurseries, 690 N. Orange Grove Boulevard, Pasadena, California 91103. Both print a yearly catalogue or list.

Cape Town

Special Bulbs for California

Tulips and daffodils are just one band on the bulb rainbow. In California, there are bulbs that do even better — for naturalizing, growing in pots, or just all-around dependability. In other parts of the country, these special bulbs are something to brag about. They are native to areas with climates similar to California's — South Africa, the Mediterranean, and one even comes from California's own hills. They have learned to grow and blossom during the mild rainy season, then lie dormant during the hot, dry summer until the rains come again. This makes them difficult to grow in other parts of the country because they don't like cold winters or wet summers. In California, they feel right at home.

Three of the best of these special bulbs grow in Eleanor Samuel's San Fernando Valley garden, shown here — ranunculus, sparaxis, and freesias. The ranunculus deserve special mention. No other bulb, and possibly no other plant, makes such a splash in California gardens. Their colors are as bright and colorful as the climate. Ranunculus are perfectly adapted and, in fact, are one of the few bulbous plants grown commercially in the state. They are superb as cut flowers, and once started require little care. The only trick is getting them started.

The tubers, which look like a clump of bananas, will rot if they get too much water at first. Plant them one inch deep and six to eight inches apart, water heavily, and then do not water again until they sprout. However, if the ground dries out completely before they sprout, water thoroughly one more time. Once they are above ground, begin regular irrigation.

The surprise in the Samuel garden is the annual return of the ranunculus. Although the scenario calls for the tubers to slowly decay from summer irrigation, more and more

Fluffy ranunculus and multicolored sparaxis come back year after year with little help

gardeners are finding that the plants return on their own the following fall, as they do here.

The sparaxis and freesias are even easier to grow. Only thinning has slowed their spread through the Samuel garden. On the following four pages they are described along with another two dozen or so special bulbs that Californians are privileged to be able to grow.

What happens when summer comes and the bulbs brown and wither? Some people carefully dig them up and store them in a cool, dark, well-ventilated place until fall. But it's easier just to leave them in the ground. In the Samuel garden, other plants — mostly summer annuals that reseed themselves — take over, but mulched bare earth could suffice as covering. Then with the first rains of winter, back to life come the bulbs, and óne can hardly wait for spring again.

Cyrtanthus mackenii

FAR RIGHT: *Moraea tripetala*

The Best Bulbs for California

allium. There are many ornamental onion relatives; the two described here are especially easy to grow. The flowers of *Allium neapolitanum* are pure white, not often found in bulbs. Good as a cut flower, it thrives in pots. It grows a foot tall and blooms in May through late summer. *Allium sphaerocephalum* is an odd bulb you'll either love or despise. Sometimes called "drumsticks," the flowers resemble corncobs, and their color changes from green to magenta-purple. It grows easily to about two feet; flowers cut well. Planting depth for both: two inches.

amaryllis. The huge-flowered bulbs commonly known as amaryllis are actually *Hippeastrum*, which grow outdoors in the California garden and look best in bold tropical plantings. More useful is the true amaryllis (*A. belladonna*), the belladonna lily or naked lady from South Africa. It forms bold clumps of foliage in fall and winter, goes dormant in spring, then bursts into bloom in August before the foliage reappears. Funnel-shaped flowers are pure pink — harder to find are pink and white strains. It is an extremely tough plant that will live forever in the garden. Planting depth: just below the soil.

babiana. Called "baboon flower" because baboons eat the corms, this South African plant is one of the best for naturalizing. The flowers are rich shades of blue, purple, and magenta, the most striking being *B. stricta rubrocyanea* with its purple flowers that have brilliant magenta throats. They grow to about twelve inches, and leaves may last well into summer before turning brown and requiring cutting. This bulb thrives in partial shade under trees. Planting depth: two inches.

Brodiaea laxa. Originally a California native, this plant has been developed by the Dutch, resulting in easy-to-grow bulbs with bigger flower heads and sturdier stems. The easiest true native variety is *Brodiaea pulchella*, the blue dicks, which naturalizes nicely in dryish gardens, even among weeds. Both kinds grow to about a foot. Planting depth: two inches.

Colchicum autumnale. This bulb looks like a large pink crocus and blooms in the fall, doing well in the ground. The bulbs will even bloom sitting on a table, without a pot. Planting depth: just below surface, with neck above ground.

crocus. Several species thrive and multiply even in Southern California. From the hillsides of southern Italy comes one tough little crocus, *Crocus imperati*. It blooms in February or March, growing about four inches tall. Another crocus worth searching for is *C. goulimeyii*, a recently discovered species from Greece. Other crocuses developed by Dutch breeders are less dependable in California but worth trying for their pretty little flowers. Planting depth: two inches.

cyrtanthus. Several species are hiding in collectors' gardens, but one is really worth searching for, *Cyrtanthus mackenii*, with nodding clusters of tubular, cream-yellow or delicate apricot flowers. Forms a grassy, foot-tall clump that stays green most of the year.

Dutch iris. These are bulbous iris, quite unlike the perennial bearded iris. Lovely blue, yellow, or white flowers marked with other colors top slender, two-and-a-half- to three-foot stems. Space bulbs only three to four inches apart for the best show. Planting depth: three inches.

freesia. Every California garden should have some freesias. They come in a variety of colors; the whites, Marie, Ballerina, and White Swan, seem to naturalize the best. Their fragrance is delightful. They have one bad characteristic — the flower spikes tend to fall over, but then they are excellent for cutting. They grow about one foot tall. Planting depth: two inches.

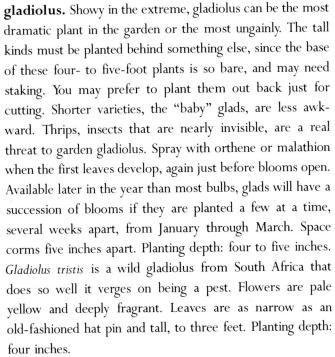

Lapeirousia laxa

gladiolus. Showy in the extreme, gladiolus can be the most dramatic plant in the garden or the most ungainly. The tall kinds must be planted behind something else, since the base of these four- to five-foot plants is so bare, and may need staking. You may prefer to plant them out back just for cutting. Shorter varieties, the "baby" glads, are less awkward. Thrips, insects that are nearly invisible, are a real threat to garden gladiolus. Spray with orthene or malathion when the first leaves develop, again just before blooms open. Available later in the year than most bulbs, glads will have a succession of blooms if they are planted a few at a time, several weeks apart, from January through March. Space corms five inches apart. Planting depth: four to five inches. *Gladiolus tristis* is a wild gladiolus from South Africa that does so well it verges on being a pest. Flowers are pale yellow and deeply fragrant. Leaves are as narrow as an old-fashioned hat pin and tall, to three feet. Planting depth: four inches.

homeria. This tall grower, with long, drooping leaves, blooms for a full three months in the spring. *Homeria breyniana aurantiaca* has apricot flowers and grows two- to three-feet tall. *H. ochroleuca* has golden flowers, growing to about one and a half feet tall. Planting depth: three inches. *Homeria lilacina* is smaller and has bright lilac flowers that open precisely at 2:30 P.M. In South Africa they say you can set your watch by it.

Ipheion uniflorum. Called "spring starflower," this Argentine plant with pale blue flowers multiplies rapidly. It grows in sun or partial shade and tops out at eight inches. Planting depth: two inches.

ixia. Tall, graceful stems give this plant its common name of wandflower. Flowers come in various shades of yellow, scarlet, and white. The rare *Ixia viridiflora* has shocking green flowers. Plants grow to two feet tall. Planting depth: three inches.

BULBS IN POTS

Pots can be handsome homes for some of nature's loveliest bulbs. They can be prominently displayed when the flowers are in bloom and simply put out of sight when the bulbs are dormant.

Caring for bulbs in containers is easy. Choose pots with straight sides — bulbs seem to do best in these. A standard potting soil works fine, especially if a little coarse silica sand is thoroughly mixed in to improve drainage. Plant the bulbs shallower than you would in the ground. Bulbs with long necks are actually left partway out of the soil so there is enough room for roots to grow beneath.

Bulbs can be put close together — in fact, almost touching — if they're planted as a clump in the center of the pot, or just an inch or so apart if they are spaced evenly around the pot. Water thoroughly once, and then whenever the soil is close to dry. Place the bulbs in full sun; this is essential since the winter sun is so weak. Fertilizing isn't required for most kinds of bulbs.

After the bulbs bloom you can move the pots to a less sunny place, but keep watering until the foliage browns naturally. Allow the pots to dry and move them to a shady, out-of-the-way spot for the summer. They shouldn't receive any water in summer (some gardeners turn the pots on their sides just to make sure). Begin watering again in September for a repeat performance.

The bulbs in the following list will all do well in pots. Those that are long-lived and especially easy to grow are marked with a dot. If your favorite bulb isn't included, it simply means that success in pots isn't as easily assured, though not impossible. Gladiolus and watsonia are easy to grow in pots, but too tall. Common varieties of daffodils, hyacinths, and tulips are usually one-season container plants and require special care at planting time. However, the wild species of these common bulbs are often among the easiest to grow.

In pots these bulbs should be planted with their necks above the soil surface:

- amaryllis   daffodil
- colchicum   • nerine
- cyrtanthus   sternbergia

In pots these bulbs should be one or two inches below the soil surface:

- allium   • lapeirousia
- babiana   • moraea
- brodiaea   muscari
- crocus   ornithogalum
- Dutch iris   • oxalis
- freesia   ranunculus
- homeria   rhodohypoxis
- hyacinth   • sparaxis
- ipheion   • streptanthera
- ixia   • tritonia
- lachenalia   tulips

LEFT TO RIGHT: ixia, *Ipheion uniflorum*, sparaxis, *Nerine bowdenii*, *Tritonia crocata*, *Ornithogalum thyrsoides*, *Sternbergia lutea*, *Allium neapolitanum*, *Allium sphaerocephalum*

lachenalia. These elegant bulbs from South Africa's Cape look difficult to grow but aren't. The one shown is sold under the name *Lachenalia pearsonii*. *L. bulbiferum* (sold as *L. pendula*) has yellow-tipped red flowers. Another, *L. tricolor* Aurea, has yellow-orange flowers. All grow to about twelve inches. Planting depth: one and a half inches.

Lapeirousia laxa. This is a weed in some gardens, but a delightful one, growing only eight inches tall with clusters of starry vermilion flowers. There is also a white variety named Alba. Planting depth: one inch.

moraea. These iris relatives have deep lilac flowers that come close to true blue. All kinds flower for weeks and all have narrow leaves that are ridiculously long. There are an amazing sixty-one species growing in South Africa but only a few have found their way to California, including the somewhat weedy *Moraea polystachya*, *M. tripetala,* and probably the prettiest, *M. villosa*, which has markings on the petals that rival a peacock's feathers. Planting depth: two inches.

muscari. Better known as grape hyacinths, there are several kinds — all basically deep shades of cobalt blue, and all staying under ten inches tall. The best for naturalizing is *Muscari armeniacum*, a wonderful contrast when planted in between daffodils. Planting depth: two inches.

narcissus. Several wilding daffodils are especially reliable. There are many forms of the hoop petticoat daffodil, *Narcissus bulbocodium*. It comes from the Mediterranean and grows to about six inches. *Narcissus jonquilla* is the true jonquil, a wild ancestor of today's fancy hybrid daffodil. It has distinctive, round, rushlike leaves and tidy fragrant flowers. It grows to eighteen inches. Planting depth: two to three inches.

Nerine bowdenii. This has exquisite, long-lasting pink blooms that are excellent cut flowers. It blooms early, in December or January, and grows about two feet tall. It may keep its foliage all year. Planting depth: three inches.

Ornithogalum thyrsoides. This sturdy bulb is especially valued for its long-lasting cut flowers. Wonder flower, its common name, refers to its lasting abilities. It grows to eighteen inches in sun or partial shade. Planting depth: two to three inches.

oxalis. Some kinds are the worst weeds in western gardens, others are delightful spring bulbs. *Oxalis purpurea* Grand Duchess, in pink or white with little shamrock leaves, only grows inches tall with flowers close to two inches across. Planting depth: one inch.

rhodohypoxis. The daintiest of bulbs with blooms in pale

LEFT TO RIGHT: *Brodiaea laxa, Lachenalia pearsonii, Babiana stricta rubrocyanea, Homeria breyniana aurantiaca, Narcissus jonquilla, Narcissus bulbocodium, Tulipa clusiana, Tulipa sylvestris, Crocus imperati*, freesia

pastel pink (*Rhodohypoxis baurii*) and white blushed with pink (*R. platypetala*), they grow only two inches tall but send up flower after flower for three or four months. They usually go dormant in winter rather than summer. Recently they have become available in pots in spring. Planting depth: one inch.

sparaxis. Called the "harlequin flower" because of its clownlike markings, this Cape bulb comes in an amazing mix of colors. A champion colonizer, it grows to one foot. Planting depth: two inches.

Sternbergia lutea. Resembling a large crocus, this Mediterranean plant should be put into the ground in late summer since it flowers in the fall. It makes a long-lasting cut flower, despite its six- to nine-inch size. Planting depth: just below surface with neck above ground.

Streptanthera cuprea. This looks like an orange sparaxis and naturalizes just as well. One landscape architect made a pleasing foot-tall meadow under an oak with just this and purple babianas, and it has returned for more than twenty years. Planting depth: two to three inches.

Tritonia crocata. Brilliantly colored flowers, usually in shades of apricot or orange, bloom for up to three months in spring. It grows twelve to eighteen inches tall and flower stalks tend to lean like a freesia, so don't plant things too close by. Planting depth: two inches.

tulip. Most tulips grow best in Southern California when treated as annuals, but the leaves of several kinds will return in following autumns. *Tulipa clusiana* (commonly called the "lady tulip") thrives here. It naturalizes in parts of the garden that get no summer water, and does well in pots. It grows twelve to eighteen inches high. Another wild tulip from the Mediterranean region, *T. sylvestris*, can be a bit shy about blooming, but it is worth a try in well-drained soil. It's from Iran and is smaller than most, six to eight inches tall. Planting depth: two to three inches.

watsonia. These gladiolus relatives bloom reliably for years in the garden. Tall, straight stems and foliage (to four feet) carry lots of large flowers in brilliant shades of red, pink, lavender, and white. One of the easiest to grow. Planting depth: four inches.

The Rock Garden

A rock garden is not a garden of rocks but of plants that like the company of rocks. These special plants typically grow in rocky soil in the wild. They are lean and hungry by nature, accustomed to eking out an existence in soil that is mostly mineral, far from what we consider good garden soil. As a result they are thrifty and compact, seldom over a foot tall. Rock plants often produce more, and bigger, flowers than their size would suggest. Rock gardeners consider them the jewels of the plant kingdom and collect them avidly. And since they are so small, a great variety can fit into a very small space.

Crowded with fascinating little plants, rock gardens can get in your blood. Before you know it, there you are on your hands and knees, squinting at some tiny gem of a plant while the rest of the garden slowly reverts to weeds. Size and variety are everything in the rock garden. The smaller the better and the more the merrier, for rock gardens are simply a means of gathering a great number of plants together in some natural fashion with the rocks providing a frame for the collection. Sometimes this scheme of things goes awry and the rocks become more important than the plants, so they are best kept to a minimum. Rock walls, embankments, or rock gardens on anything but the gentlest of slopes are not terribly practical in California because they are so difficult to water.

The classic rock garden plant is an alpine. Alpine plants grow on high mountain slopes where anything resembling soil quickly washes down to the valley floors. It is an environment difficult to duplicate in California lowland gardens, so many of the classic alpine plants made famous by English rock gardeners simply won't thrive here — though a good many gardeners have gone mad trying. Although other alpines are somewhat more amenable, the future of rock gardening in California will probably depend on the plants found on the dry hillsides surrounding the Mediterranean,

on the equally dry talus slopes of New Zealand's Southern Alps, or on the gravelly washes and plains of Australia and South Africa. Rock plants from these areas are not well known because they are difficult to grow in colder, wetter climates, where rock gardening is so popular, but the few that have been tried in California have succeeded. Be sure not to overlook succulent plants. These survive in rocky, barren soils and some don't look out of place growing next to leafier plants in the rock garden.

With several exceptions, plants suitable for a rock garden won't be found at nurseries. However, you can obtain them from specialists, whose typical catalogue may list several hundred kinds of plants, a bewildering array for even the most assured rock gardener. And, compounding the problem, if you order them from out-of-state nurseries, many plants will not perform well in your climate, especially if you live in Southern California, where water high in salts is not to the liking of plants accustomed to crystal-clear mountain water. There is a good deal of trial and error involved, but rock gardeners consider this part of the challenge.

In the Los Angeles rock garden at left, pink-flowered *Armeria maritima* is the mainstay, and it couldn't be easier to grow or find. Look for it in flats at nurseries where it's sold as ground cover. The grayish mat is common woolly thyme, and the small white star flowers are another readily available ground cover, *Isotoma fluviatilis*. Blue campanulas and a pink dianthus in bloom are just as easy to grow. Punctuating this tapestry are much rarer plants that make rock gardening a challenge, but don't forget that their more common compatriots are valuable too.

The plants described on the following pages guarantee surefire success, and even in Southern California you will be able to start a collection. Some are downright easy to grow. A good mail order source for rock garden plants is Siskiyou Plant Nursery, 2825 Cummings Rd., Medford, Oregon 97501.

Spring in a Los Angeles rock garden with armeria in bloom

GROWING ROCK PLANTS —GRAVEL AND GRIT

Rock plants require special, gritty, fast-draining soil. The quickest way to kill a choice or difficult rock plant is to let water stand around its base for even a few hours. Excess moisture is their enemy, but neither is drought to their liking. The trick is to concoct a soil and a situation between these two extremes.

Rock gardens should always be raised or mounded above soil level so excess water can drain rapidly. There is no need to create a mountainous pile of rocks—a gentle rise of a foot or two will suffice.

Normal garden soil must be improved or completely removed. Chris Rosmini's Los Angeles rock garden, seen on page 60, looks as natural as the San Gabriel River bed where she finds her stones, but she removed one foot of soil from her garden and replaced it with two-foot mounds of soil of her own making. Her blend is as follows:

2 parts pea gravel (the smallest you can find)
1 part coarse washed sand
1 part peat moss
1 part homemade compost (or packaged soil amendment)

Garden soil can be part of such a mix as long as the sand and gravel outweigh it. The proportions to strive for are equal parts of sand, gravel, and organic matter and garden soil. The sand and gravel ensure drainage and plenty of air for the roots, while the organic matter provides some nutrients and helps hold moisture so the mix doesn't get too dry, too fast.

On top of this artificial soil it is very important to place a mulch of pure gravel an inch thick. As seen in the drawing, this guarantees a dry bed for foliage to lay on and helps keep the very base of the plant, called the "crown," on the dry side. The crown is where rock plants are most vulnerable to rot caused by excess moisture.

Rock plants are easiest to water with sprinklers, early in the morning so the soil's surface dries quickly. Subsurface irrigation devices are better but difficult to design. Because the soil mix is so porous, the plants may need to be watered often. They seldom need fertilizing, but weeds can quickly overwhelm these tiny plants.

SCREE AND SAND

Natural screes, sometimes called "talus," are accumulations of broken rock at the base of mountain peaks or cliffs. They may be pure rock, but plants that have learned to grow on these otherwise vacant expanses are some of the choicest for the rock garden. They often have deep tap roots that search out moisture—snowmelt in high mountains, spring water, or trapped rainwater in lower elevations. Some surface roots search for the few nutrients they need in decayed bits of such tough plants as mosses and lichens that become trapped in cracks. Not all rock plants grow in such a severe environment, but those conditions are the basis for rock garden culture.

Sand is an important part of many planting mixes and essential to the growing of

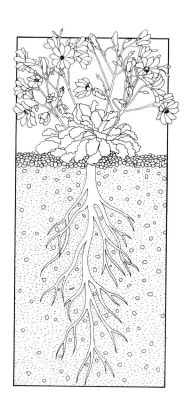

Antennaria dioica

Cheilanthes fendleri

Campanula portenschlagiana

The Best Plants for Rock Gardens

Antennaria dioica. A miniature ground cover that will make dense, spreading mats of silvery gray leaves and occasional spikes of small clusters of white flowers on short stems. Easy to grow.

aquilegia. There are tiny columbines no taller than a few inches that do well with a little shade. Some of the best, including *Aquilegia flabellata*, come from Japan. A trifle difficult to grow and short-lived.

arabis. These are traditional rock garden plants. The best kinds make dense, spreading mounds of dark green leaves. Those with white flowers, as on *Arabis sturii*, are most useful. Easy to grow.

armeria. The pink flowers that adorn the garden on page 60 are *Armeria maritima*, easy to grow and often sold as a ground cover at nurseries. *A. setacea* (*A. juncea*) is only inches tall, perfect in pots.

campanula. Some of the prettiest bellflowers are rock-garden-sized. *Campanula cochleariifolia* (*C. pusilla*) spreads to form happy colonies of nodding blue or white bells. *C. portenschlagiana* (*C. muralis*) is similar but blooms better. Easy to grow.

cheilanthes. Two western ferns that belong in the rock garden are *Cheilanthes feei*, which makes an airy, six-inch clump, and *C. fendleri*, which spreads to form large colonies. Both grow best in full sun but grow in partial shade as well. Easy to grow.

dianthus. Many small dianthus are good rock garden plants, most with a grayish foliage and flowers in shades of pink. Easy to grow but sometimes short-lived.

Erodium chamaedryoides. Another little plant often sold as a ground cover that makes a neat little dome when planted by itself in the rock garden. Lots of tiny pink flowers. Easy to grow.

rock plants. Many books call for the use of "sharp" sand, which is exactly that — viewed under a microscope, the edges would be sharp like broken glass; not rounded like a pebble. But avoid asking a salesman at a building-supply yard for sharp sand and instead ask for "washed" sand. It is inexpensive, and the smaller, siltlike particles have been washed out of the sand. Unwashed sand gets concrete-hard after it dries. Better still, and preferable for use in potting mixes, is pure "silica" sand. It is pure white, very sharp, uniform, and expensive. Pure silica sand, and sometimes other sand, is sold by the size of the individual particles. Never buy fine sand because it compacts too easily. Buy the coarsest sand available (number 12 or 16), which allows more space for air between the particles.

ROCK STRATEGY

Rocks aren't really necessary in a rock garden, but they can help. First, they provide a backdrop for the tiny plants and help give the garden a unified look. Try to find rocks that are native to your area, of neutral color, and always select the biggest stones you can get into your garden. They'll make the most impact.

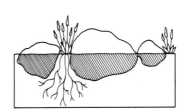

Always bury a little more than half (preferably two-thirds) of the rock underground, as seen in the drawing. After exerting so

much effort to get the rock into the garden, it seems a shame to then hide so much of it, but rocks that sit on top of the soil look unnatural.

In addition, burying so much of the rock helps the plants. They can send roots beneath the rocks where soil stays cool and moist. It's not uncommon to see the happiest plants in a rock garden huddled around a rock. Many plants do especially well planted in crevices between rocks. Consider the exposure around larger stones. The south side will be hot and dry, the north side cooler and partially shaded. Certain plants may appreciate either.

Tufa is a universally available, extremely porous, natural rock. It is so porous that roots can actually grow into it. Rock gardeners have found that it makes the perfect home for many tiny, delicate rock plants. These gardeners drill or chisel out little holes to give the plants a start, then they water the rock as they would water a garden. (Keeping the tufa in partial shade keeps them from drying out too fast.)

Rock gardeners spend an inordinate amount of time weeding on hands and knees, and they've found one tool particularly useful. It's an asparagus knife, actually designed to cut off asparagus stalks below ground, but perfect for prying weeds out of tight places, or cutting deep tap roots without disturbing much soil.

asparagus knife

Helianthemum hybrid

Hypericum yakusimana

Phlox subulata hybrid

blue fescue (*Festuca ovina* Glauca). A blue-gray grass that looks good in a rock garden and can be found at nurseries. Easy to grow.

Globularia cordifolia. Rosettes of narrow, dark green leaves that spread to form low mats. Sometimes small, blue flowers appear on short stems. Other kinds from the Mediterranean are worth searching for. Easy to grow.

sunrose (*Helianthemum*). Tough little shrublets with leathery leaves and blindingly brilliant flowers in white and shades of yellow, orange, red, and pink. These Mediterranean plants feel right at home in California. Easy to grow but sometimes short-lived.

hypericum. Several tiny relatives of the big ground covering hypericum bring bright yellow flowers to the rock garden. *Hypericum coris* is upright, gray-green; *H. cerastoides* is similar. *H. balearicum* has reddish stems, and sprawls about. Easy to grow.

blue star creeper (*Isotoma fluviatilis*). This may be sold as *Laurentia*. It has the tiniest of leaves that spread quickly to become a ground cover with little blue star flowers that bloom most of the year. Easy to grow.

leptospermum. The extreme dwarf versions of this large landscape plant from Australia make tidy shrubs in the rock garden. Most are named varieties of *Leptospermum scoparium* or *L. humifusum* with pink to deep rose or crimson flowers. Easy to grow.

lewisia. These native Western alpines are almost succulent with spectacular white, pink, or rose flowers. Varieties of *Lewisia cotyledon* are easy to grow.

Limonium minutum. A very dwarf statice with delicate sprays of tiny white flowers. Quickly makes large clumps of deep green foliage an inch high. Especially easy to grow.

Lithodora diffusa. Better known as *Lithospermum diffusum*, this is another dense shrublet with uncommon flowers that are a shocking cerulean blue. It is a little difficult to grow.

Corsican mint (*Mentha requienii*). Tiny peppermint-scented leaves spread to form a mat as flat as a layer of paint. Tiny flowers are lavender. The plant is sometimes found in the herb section at nurseries. Easy to grow.

Morisia monanthos. A real collector's plant, it is native to Sardinia, where it grows on sandy beaches. Short tufts of saw-edged leaves produce large yellow flowers. Seemingly easy to grow, though not many gardeners have tried it.

Nierembergia repens. Better known as *Nierembergia rivularis*, this South American plant spreads quickly into a little patch of spinachlike leaves. Large white flowers completely conceal the foliage. Likes more moisture than most rock plants. Easy to grow.

penstemon. Though most of the penstemons are native hereabouts, they are a challenge to grow and bloom. The easiest, *Penstemon hirsutus* Pygmaeus, is only four inches tall with large lavender and white flowers. *P. rupicola*, with rose-colored flowers, and *P. pinifolius*, with red flowers and leaves like pine needles, are more difficult.

Petrophytum caespitosum. For the collector, this ground-hugging shrub seems happiest planted between rocks. Foliage is white-gray, flowers are like little white foxgloves. Somewhat difficult to grow.

phlox. From this large group of native American plants come several choice rock garden candidates, including *Phlox bifida*, which makes a relaxed little bush of light lavender flowers, and *P. subulata*, which comes in many forms in addition to the one seen here with barrio-pink flowers and sharp, needlelike leaves. Generally easy to grow.

potentilla. A very large group of plants suitable for the rock garden. One, *Potentilla verna*, is a common ground cover with dark green leaves and bright yellow flowers. Better in the rock garden is *P. nevadensis*, from Spain, with grayish leaves and soft yellow flowers. Easy to grow.

Putoria calabrica. A little shrub from the Mediterranean with light pink flowers followed by red berries in summer. Easy to grow.

Encrusted saxifrage

Stylidium adnatum

Raoulia lutescens

raoulia. These fascinating plants from New Zealand make dense, spreading carpets of tiny leaves, usually grayish. *Raoulia hookeri* is silvery; *R. lutescens* is gray-green, forms a mat that becomes as hard as a rock, and is easiest to grow.

saxifrages (*Saxifraga*). The saxifrages fill pages in rock gardening books but are generally difficult to grow in California. They are most successful when grown in tufa, as shown here. The so-called encrusted saxifrages are grown mostly for their foliage and form. All are grayish and dusty white. Mossy saxifrages look like moss with pretty, delicate flowers. Difficult, at least, to keep going.

sisyrinchium. These grassy iris relatives are native to North and South America. Two of the best are California natives: blue-eyed grass (*Sisyrinchium bellum*), with masses of blue flowers; *Sisyrinchium californicum*, with fewer, yellow flowers (best in partial shade). *S. macounianum* Alba is a choice miniature. There are also several South American species with large yellow flowers. Easy to grow; sometimes short-lived.

Stylidium adnatum. A miniature shrub from Australia that is quite graceful and has lots of tiny white flowers. Easy to grow.

Teucrium subspinosum. A tiny bush with thornlike stems, little gray leaves, and small, crimson flowers. Moderately easy to grow.

thyme (*Thymus*). There are many creeping thymes perfect in rock gardens, and some can be found at nurseries in the herb section or are sold as ground covers. All are intensely fragrant. *Thymus lanuginosus* is gray-leaved with pink flowers. *T. serpyllum* is gray and woolly. Easy to grow.

Tunica saxifraga. Recently renamed *Petrorhagia*, this little shrub lies flat on the ground and sends up delicate pink flowers well into the fall. Easy to grow.

veronica. Many of the veronicas are small enough for the rock garden. One of the smallest, *Veronica repens*, makes flat mats with pale blue flowers. This one is easy.

In a pot: *Sisyrinchium macounianum* Alba with native polypody fern

Tunica saxifraga growing over woolly thyme

viola. Most small violets look at home in the rock garden but *Viola labradorica*, with purple-green leaves and deep purple flowers, is especially nice and easy, though seedlings may become pests.

wahlenbergia. The best come from New Zealand and Australia, including *Wahlenbergia tasmanica* (*W. saxicola*), which stays low and sends up many little blue or white bellflowers on delicate stems. May die down for the winter and need to be reseeded. Easy to grow.

The Rose Garden

Field of roses outside Wasco, California

PLANTING BARE ROOT

In January and early February nurseries sell roses without any soil around their roots. They're called "bare-root" roses, and there are two good reasons to buy them this way: roses are cheaper bare root, and there is usually a bigger selection to choose from at the nursery.

There's a third reason that many nurserymen consider debatable—roses planted bare root do better. Many people believe they do better because the roots are surrounded by garden soil after they're planted, not potting mix. This helps avoid what is called an "interface"—where two different kinds of soil meet—which sometimes acts as a barrier to root growth. Roses eventually become established planted either way but bare-root planting seems to get them off to a better start.

A word of caution: if you buy a bare-root plant, check the roots to make sure they are still plump and moist. Then, when you get the rose home, soak the roots overnight

Rose stem and thorns

Tiffany

Friendship

Roses hardly need an introduction. Despite being prickly, occasionally plagued by pests, and often ungainly in the garden, roses are the most popular of all plants — it's those flowers, of course, exquisite in bud, sumptuous in blossom. Other plants may be described as being "rose flowered" for their full blooms, but roses set the standard.

In California, roses are easy to grow, especially the newer kinds. Rose growers have inadvertently stacked the deck in California's favor because so many rose nurseries are located here. Other parts of the country may grumble about roses not being as hardy as they once were, but that never happens in California. As you'll learn, we grow roses a little differently. Because they don't have to survive cold winters (the blood of many new roses is quite thin) and because they produce wave after wave of blossoms from the first buds of April to the final flowers in November, they must be pruned less, fertilized more, and perhaps planted a little deeper.

If there is any difficulty associated with roses, it is simply that there are so many to choose from. Every year new and often startling roses are introduced, adding to the

ranks of the old, tried, and true. Today several thousand years of rose growing, selection, and hybridizing have left us with several thousand choices. Where to begin?

To organize things just a little, roses have been divided into categories: old roses, miniatures, floribundas, grandifloras, hybrid teas, and climbers. Naturally, plants being what they are, these categories at best only hint at how a rose looks.

This chapter will first examine the old roses, then the new. Old roses, one quickly finds, is the least helpful classification. It includes an amazing variety of plants. In fact, all old roses are not even old. Officially, "old" means only that the group the rose belongs to existed before 1867, when the first of the hybrid teas were introduced. So many individuals in these groups are more recent.

There are some fine landscaping roses hidden in this classification but, in the end, it's likely that the old roses that survive the ages will be grown for their flowers. These, often smaller and less complex, and blooming only once or twice each year, will never be replaced.

in a pail of water and plant immediately the next day. Bare-root roses will be severely damaged if they dry out — one reason many nurseries pot up their stock.

A NEW WAY TO PLANT

To create your rose, the commercial grower cut a bud from the parent plant and attached, or "budded," it to a short piece of stem and roots, usually belonging to a completely different rose. This bud union is where the rose was born.

Most available literature suggests planting the rose so the bud union ends up just above ground. In California this often results in lots of suckering — rapid-growing shoots that come from below the bud union and therefore not from the same plant.

Most people use that method, but here's another way: plant so the bud union ends up about two inches underground. This prevents suckering and encourages the rose to send out new roots above the bud union. These are the rose's own roots, not something it was grafted onto, and the rose seems to do dramatically better.

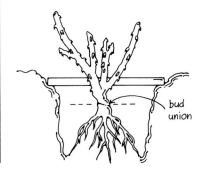

bud
union

So before planting, decide where you want the bud union to end up — above or below the ground. Now dig the hole. It should be about two feet wide by one and a half feet deep. Hybrid tea and grandiflora roses should be spaced about three to four feet apart, floribundas about two feet. Add soil amendments such as redwood or homemade compost to the excavated soil, then put some of the amended soil back into the hole, forming a cone-shaped pile. Spread the roots over this cone of soil and fill the hole. Firmly pack down the soil so there aren't any air pockets left underground.

If the rose is from a can, follow the same steps but don't form the cone of soil in the bottom of the hole. Just dig and plant. Right after planting, mound up leftover soil to form a damlike watering basin around each rose. This will help funnel water to the rose.

Give each plant a thorough soaking right away, then wait until soil is almost dry before watering again. Don't feed yet — wait until the first leaves start unfolding in early spring. This first feeding is very important, since the rose will do much of its growing in spring. Use a fertilizer that has a balance of fast-acting plant food (called "available nitrogen" or "nitric nitrogen" on the label) and slow-acting plant food (listed as "organic nitrogen"). Most commercial rose fertilizers are a good balance of both.

1 Golden Wings
2 Ballerina
3 Eglantine
4 Buff Beauty
5 Rose du Roi
6 Blush Noisette
7 Common Moss
8 Rosa Mundi
9 Safrano
10 Rosa Gallica Officinalis
11 Reine Victoria

The Old

The roses shown here are called old-fashioned, and that's a pity. The term suggests that they have no use in our gardens except as quaint museum pieces. The truth is quite the opposite. These roses are still around—some after a thousand years—because they are so good, and they'll be around long after many of the flashy new ones have had their moment of glory and then faded from the catalogues.

The painting shows the great range of color and form among these older roses, but it can't show their fragrance. Each has its distinctive perfume. Nor does the painting show the several ways in which old roses can be used in your garden. To see them in their roles and at their showiest visit the Botanical Gardens of the Huntington Library, in San Marino, in April, which has the largest collection of old roses in the country. There you'll find these roses, and many more, trained as great fountains, used as ground covers and edgings, flung over pergolas and across walls, and planted as background for bedding plants.

Very few old roses are rigid, upright growers like the hybrid teas we've become accustomed to. Some are neat and bushy but many grow in a manner that can only charitably be called "relaxed." These produce long, floppy canes that must either be supported on a trellis or fence, or pegged to the ground some distance from the plant, with bits of wire shaped like croquet wickets, to form large, ground-covering shrubs. Pegging the canes forces blooms all along the horizontal parts of the stem.

The term "shrub rose" is a further classification that principally includes descendants of *Rosa rugosa* and *R. rubiginosa* hybrids, but also some miscellany like the large, single-flowered Golden Wings seen in the painting. It's obviously not a hybrid tea, but neither is it old (1956). Some interesting roses like this seem to be hiding in the shrub classification and are usually included in any discussion of "old" roses.

The planting and care of the old rose is about the same as for the hybrid tea: give it a place in the sun, water it regularly, and feed it in March and again in August with one of the slow-release plant foods. A 14-14-14 formula is good.

Pruning deserves a special note. You don't whack into a bush the way we're accustomed to with a hybrid tea. Old roses need only a light pruning for shaping and grooming; also remove dead wood and the oldest twiggy growth. With some kinds, this can be done in summer. Remove the dead blooms to encourage flowering, except where you want a show of hips—spectacular bright orange to red seed pods, full of vitamin C.

Following are the rose groups generally referred to as old roses, and some varieties of each, with their odd and antique names, that are highly recommended for California by Huntington rose authority John C. MacGregor IV. There are, of course, many other old-rose varieties but these will prove difficult to find. While gardeners may not have forgotten the older roses, the rose business certainly has. You won't find them among the hundreds of roses at nurseries but you will find them at plant sales or in mailers from specialists. Here is one specialist:

Roses of Yesterday and Today
802 Brown's Valley Road
Watsonville, California 95076

APHIDS, MILDEW, AND MULCHES

In California, the most common problems for roses are spider mites, aphids, and mildew. You can get a head start on controlling these and other problems with a winter clean-up spray. Use what's often called a "dormant spray" that contains petroleum oil (this suffocates overwintering pests, especially mite eggs) and lime sulfur (this checks fungus and overwintering spores of mildew and rust).

In parts of Southern California, hot January weather often causes the oil in dormant sprays to burn the rose canes. Some gardeners have had good luck with a dormant spray called Calsul that does not seem to burn.

To help prevent aphids, keep ants away from roses and avoid routine spraying, which kills creatures that prey on aphids.

To get rid of aphids, first try blasting them off with water in the early morning. This should be repeated for several days. Or spray with orthene, cygon, metasystox-R, diazinon, or malathion.

To prevent mildew, plant where there is good air circulation and sun first thing in the morning. Spraying roses with the hose early in the morning also helps during the mildew season (mid-spring, late summer).

To get rid of mildew during the growing season, spray with acti-dione, benlate, or funginex. Add a spreader sticker (a wetting agent) to help spray adhere to the waxy foliage. Hosing off foliage also helps prevent mites.

Mulches go around a plant on top of the soil to help cool the soil beneath and to slow down evaporation. With a good two- to three-inch-thick mulch you can often get away with watering only once every three to four weeks in summer. The most effective mulches are probably compost, leaves, or gravel-sized volcanic rock. Many people mulch with big chunks of bark, but gaps between the chunks make an excellent hiding and breeding place for some creatures that can be a nuisance in the garden—notably snails, slugs, and earwigs.

Reve D'or, a fragrant climbing noisette

The Best Old Roses

OLD EUROPEAN ROSES

Though the ancestors of these early roses came from elsewhere in the world (mostly Asia), they were developed in Europe. Most bloom only once, at best twice a year.

Gallica roses. The greatest and oldest rose ancestors, the earliest dating back to the twelfth century B.C. and the ancient Persians. Very fragrant and used in the production of oil and perfume from the thirteenth to the eighteenth century, when it became known as the French rose. Most blooms are dark reds and dusky purples, though *Rosa* Mundi (*Rosa gallica versicolor*) has flamboyantly striped petals. Growing to a height of three to four feet, they fit handily in a small garden. They bloom just once in spring and then produce a profusion of hips. Try *Rosa gallica* Officinalis; *Rosa* Mundi; Belle de Crecy; Belle Isis; Charles de Mills.

Damask roses. Two kinds here, both ancient: *Rosa damascena* and its varieties bloom only once, in spring; *Rosa bifera*, the Autumn Damask or Rose of Castile, blooms twice. Both have a delicate fragrance and floppy pink or white flowers in clusters. They grow to about six or eight feet in an arching, half-clambering fashion. Try *Rosa damascena*; *Rosa bifera*; Mme. Hardy; York and Lancaster.

Alba roses. The White Rose, also ancient, was most popular during the Renaissance. It has flat white or pink semi-double flowers that are very fragrant, and most make fairly upright, dense, six- to eight-foot shrubs. Try Maxima; Great Maiden's Blush; Konigin von Danemark.

Centifolia or cabbage roses. Best known are the kinds with huge, nodding, multipetaled blooms that look like pink cabbages. Very fragrant, they grow fairly upright to six feet. Try *Rosa centifolia*; Bullata; Petite de Hollande.

Moss roses. Developed from the Centifolia roses, all have

Charles de Mills,
a Gallica rose

"mossy" growths on the calyx that covers the buds. A variety of flowers and habits of growth are included here, even some very modern miniatures. Some bloom once a year: try Communis (Common Moss); Crested Moss; Henri Martin (Old Red Moss); Oeillet Panaché (Striped Moss). Others bloom more than once: Salet; Deuil de Paul Fontaine; Jeanne de Montfort.

TEA AND CHINA ROSES, AND THEIR OFFSPRING

When these were introduced to Europe in the late 1700's and early 1800's they were forever to change garden roses. They brought new colors, a dwarfer habit, and, most important, "continuous" bloom.

China roses. *Rosa chinensis* was important for its contribution of a true red color and repeat blooming. Growth is bushy, two to three feet tall, though there are even more miniature kinds (the source of today's miniroses). Most have small, semi-double blooms with a peppery fragrance. Try Old Blush (Parson's Pink China); Agrippina; Archduke Charles.

Portland roses. Considered either the last of the old European roses or the first of the newer China-Tea roses, they look most like Damasks in flower. Fairly upright, they grow to five feet, and have smallish flowers that generally rebloom. Treat them as low bushes or peg them to the ground for a fountain effect. Try Rose du Roi; Comte de Chambord; Jacques Cartier.

Bourbon roses. Similar to but more successful than the Portlands, they are reliable repeat bloomers, semi-climbing, the height of charm. These will spread to eight feet pegged to the ground, or prune to keep compact. Try Reine Victoria; Souvenir de la Malmaison; Mme. Ernest Calvat.

Tea roses. Similar to the China but flowers are fuller, more fragrant, and include such colors as pale yellow and apricot. "Ever-blooming" with a tea fragrance. An important parent of today's roses. Try Monsieur Tillier; Maman Cochet; Duchesse de Brabant; Lady Hillingdon.

Noisette roses. An American class of largely rambling roses with clusters of soft pastel flowers, most notably yellow. They can be allowed to sprawl to make a fountain four or more feet wide and as tall, or can be trained up as climbers to eight feet. Fragrant and "ever-blooming." Ideal in California's climate. Try Blush Noisette; Fellemberg; Alister Stella Gray; Lamarque; Mme. Alfred Carriere; Maréchal Niel.

Hybrid Musk roses. Not terribly old (introduced in the 1920's), they are descendants of the Noisettes, with similar growth. They include a variety of flowers with some charming single blooms. Most are ramblers, perfect trained against a wall or fence or simply left to grow into a big mound. Try Buff Beauty; Newport Fairy; Prosperity; Ballerina.

Hybrid Perpetual roses. The link between old and new, they have the strong, semi-climbing growth of old roses, and double flowers that bloom nearly as often as new roses. Most grow to eight feet and come in many colors except, for some reason, yellow. Try Baronne Prevost; Ferdinand Prichard; Paul Neyron; La Reine.

Polyantha roses. Varieties of *Rosa multiflora*, most are low, extra-bushy plants with massive clusters of very small flowers. The next generation, Hybrid Polyanthas, were renamed floribunda roses, a modern class. Try Cécile Brunner; Gloria Mundi; The Fairy.

Pernetiana roses. The deep yellow and orange found in modern roses came from this group through *Rosa foetida* (Austrian Brier). Pernetianas were quickly absorbed into the modern hybrid tea classification, but some are still sold under this name.

And the New

Modern roses — mostly those you find at nurseries — fall into one of the following groups. Generally they are distinguished from the old roses by bigger and better shaped flowers, in greater quantities, with an ability to produce bloom after bloom throughout the rose season.

Hybrid tea roses are by far the most popular class of roses because their flowers are the biggest and their buds the shapeliest. Add to this sturdy, long stems, and you have one of the finest cut flowers. Since 1867, when the first, La France, made its debut, hybrid teas have set the standard for exhibition roses. Unfortunately, they are often awkward plants in the landscape. Since they seldom carry leaves all the way to the ground, they have a gawky, bare-bottomed look. Their growth is rigidly upright and, more often than not, they are planted by themselves in formal plantings. However, the awkward lower half of the plant can be disguised by putting lower growing kinds in front. Most hybrid teas should be allowed to grow to five or six feet tall.

Grandiflora is a recent, rather muddy classification. Generally, expect a rose bush as tall as or taller than a hybrid tea but with slightly smaller flowers, most often in small clusters. Several grandifloras have especially sturdy flowers that don't curl up or fade until the petals fall off.

Floribundas are graceful modern roses that are quite useful in the garden because they are bushy, only three to four feet tall. Though flowers are decidedly smaller, they come in large clusters, often covering the bush. A common practice is to plant the shorter floribundas in front of the taller hybrid teas and grandifloras. Nevertheless, they are elegant all alone. It's a pity more aren't planted.

Smaller still are the miniatures. Some miniatures are tiny plants, others grow just as big as floribundas, but all have miniature foliage and flowers, often in massive clusters. Much effort is going into the breeding of miniatures right

HOW TO PRUNE

The pruning of a rose is probably simpler than you think. And with the right tools, it's really no thorny task. What's important is knowing why you prune and how you prune. The time to prune is when roses are dormant, in January or February. In coastal Southern California, roses may never go completely dormant, so prune in early January.

Why do you prune? First, let's deal with a common misconception—that rose plants need severe pruning to produce really showy blooms. Actually, the reverse is true in California. If pruning is overzealous, the plant may be set back so that it can only bear a few blooms. This sort of misconception may be a carryover from the Northeast and the Midwest, where roses had to be cut way back to get them through the winters.

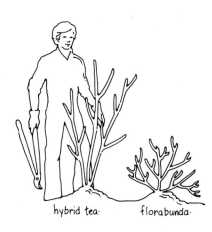

hybrid tea.   florabunda.

In California you should prune lightly—this will produce the most blooms—and prune for a pleasing shape. The illustrations here will give you some idea of what the bushes should look like after they're pruned. We've simplified things by showing fewer upright canes than most bushes have. In general, never remove more than about one-third of the growth.

After pruning, hybrid tea and grandiflora roses should end up about waist high. Leave on all healthy primary canes (canes that branch from the base) and make cuts into secondary (branching) canes. Prune off all branches thinner than a pencil and cut back all other branches so there are three or four eyes left (eyes are where leaves sprout from a stem and where future growth begins). Prune so the plant ends up with a rounded top.

Floribunda roses should end up about knee high with a round, bushy shape. It's best to leave much of the twiggy growth, but cut out the center branch that carried the last season's flowers from each cluster of branches. Trim remaining branches back to three or four eyes.

Use pruning shears for most small cuts; long-handled shears for bigger cuts. Where the shears won't reach, try a narrow-bladed keyhole saw, available at hardware stores. This skinny saw makes clean cuts in very tight spots.

Don't make cuts above just any branch, bud, or leaf. Pick one that will grow away from the center of the plant, so that the center of the plant remains open and airy.

It isn't necessary to seal pruning cuts with tarlike pruning compounds. Only the largest cuts need any protection at all, and these can be now and some of these promise to be excellent landscape plants, while the tiniest may be best as pot plants. Miniatures are not listed here because a dozen new ones seem to appear every week. It will be several years before the best can be sorted out from the rest.

The flowers on climbers may be few or many, big or small, but they always come on a clambering plant. All climbers must be attached and trained on something—a fence, wall, or trellis.

Practically all the modern roses will do well in California, and in fact most of the recent introductions were developed here, but some do better than others. In the lists that follow, the roses that are most graceful in the garden have been recommended. Some rose fanciers may be offended because certain prize exhibition roses have been left out, but if growth is ungainly, or if the rose is regularly plagued by pests or diseases, it becomes more of a burden than a blessing in the average garden.

The AARS designation that appears after some roses means that that rose is an All-American Rose Selection. Roses earning that distinction have proven themselves all across the country, but it's not a guarantee they'll be great for California. Those that are great are included in our list. These all-stars have been grouped by class, then by color. There are sixteen official color groups designated by the American Rose Society. Representative roses from fifteen of the official groups are shown on these pages. The sixteenth category—russet, a brownish-tan color—is so recent that as yet there are no exceptional examples to include in our list of the best.

Fifty years ago half of these luscious rose colors didn't exist. Even yellow roses didn't appear in gardens until the late 1800's, and the fancier kinds are more recent. The first orange roses were introduced in the 1940's and the multi-colored blends in the 1950's. Today you can choose from a rainbow of roses.

The Best New Roses

HYBRID TEAS

These are tall plants, usually with only one flower per stem. They are listed here by color.

White or Near White

Honor (AARS, 1980). Creamy white blooms on long stems. Lots of flowers all the time. Mildew resistant.

Pristine (1978). Exquisite, high-centered blooms in creamy white with pink blush. Compact, spreading plants with perfect healthy foliage. One of the best roses ever introduced.

Sweet Afton (1964). Another tall grower for the background and for cutting. Long white with slight pink blush buds open slowly, last long, and exude an ambrosial fragrance.

Medium Yellow

Allspice (1977). Large-flowered, tall grower with spicy fragrance. Sunshine yellow with abundant, semiglossy foliage.

Apollo (AARS, 1972). Large, long-lasting brilliant yellow blooms with dark foliage. Tall and vigorous.

Eclipse (1935). Tall, shapely plant produces beautifully formed, slender buds. Golden yellow.

Deep Yellow

King's Ransom (AARS, 1962). Deep yellow-gold, long-lasting blossoms on extremely long stems. Upright habit.

Oregold (AARS, 1975). Long buds of deepest yellow touched with russet in cool weather. Short plant resents pruning. Slow to become established, but worth waiting for.

Summer Sunshine (1962). Still our best deep yellow hybrid tea. Let it grow six feet high and prune lightly if you want it to be a real success. Protect from mildew.

Yellow Blend

Peace (AARS, 1946). Voted world's favorite rose. Yellow with rose-pink, profuse bloomer tops very strong stems with deep-green glossy foliage.

covered with a dab of white glue that dries invisible.

Many rose books suggest making all cuts about one-quarter inch above a bud or leaf. Don't. This little stub will only die back and invite a little boring larva to tunnel into the stem, possibly killing the entire cane. Instead, cut as close to a branch, leaf, or bud as you possibly can.

When two branches rub together, cut out the older of the two. You can usually spot the older cane by its rough bark.

Cut off (don't tear) all of last year's leaves. Rake up fallen leaves and send them all to the dump so they don't carry pests and diseases into the new year. This is also the time for a clean-up spraying.

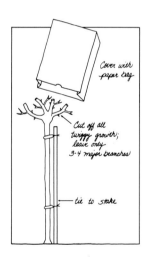

Cover with paper bag

Cut off all twiggy growth; leave only 3-4 major branches

tie to stake

TREE ROSES

Rose bushes shaped like little trees are not a separate class of roses, they're just grown differently. Most roses have two parts — the top and the roots onto which the top was budded. Tree roses have three parts: the top, the trunk, and the roots, all grafted to one another. The top can be any kind of rose, but a few varieties are known to do better as tree forms. Olé, a deep orange-red, is spectacular as a tree rose. Trumpeter looks like a smaller Olé and is usually available on shorter trunks. Other good choices are Double Delight, Iceberg, Mon Cheri, and Paradise. Many old roses are exceptional tree roses, if you can find them.

Tree roses need extra attention at planting time. Because the top is so far from the roots, the plant has a difficult time at first drawing moisture up that trunk (it's like drinking from a very long straw). As soon as you get the rose, soak the roots in water and prune off all but three or four major canes. Plant, stake the rose, and then cover the top with a big paper bag (not plastic) for a week or two before it begins to leaf out. All of these measures help conserve moisture for the top.

In following years, don't prune the tops too vigorously or the rose will slowly decline. Do prune off old woody canes and thin smaller branches. The tops of tree roses should be allowed to get big and bushy; most will easily spread three or four feet.

CLIMBING ROSES

Modern climbing roses are of two kinds. Most useful are the natural climbers. These bloom heavily in spring, quickly followed by new growth. Blooms come on short, lateral branches arising from long canes. If these canes are trained horizontally, more *flowering branches will be produced. All climbing roses need to be tied to some kind of support. Don't prune at all the first few years. Then prune after flowering, removing the oldest canes, which are unlikely to produce flowers, keeping the newer canes, which will continue flowering into winter. Good choices for the California garden include:*

America *(AARS, 1976). Soft orangey-salmon flowers with lovely fragrance. Vigorous growth. Blooms late and is slow to repeat.*

Handel *(1965). Large clusters of white blossoms edged with cerise and a touch of lemon. Lemony fragrance too. Shrubby climber to ten feet. Occasional light mildew on its glossy foliage.*

Joseph's Coat *(1964). Large, multicolored (yellow, orange, and red) flowers, off and on all year, with deep, glossy green foliage.*

Red Fountain *(1976). Semi-double, nonbluing red velvet flowers all season long. Versatile habit. Can be used as a pillar, espalier, or large arching shrub.*

Royal Gold *(1957). Perfectly formed deep yellow blooms. Repeats well if hips are removed. Moderate growth.*

Tempo *(1975). Well-formed medium red flowers. Vigorous climber to twelve feet but needs ample support. Some mildew.*

The other kind of climbing rose is simply a climbing form of another favorite rose. They have the same name, usually preceded by "climbing," and the same flowers, though they do grow differently. They also flower most of the season. As with other climbers, don't prune at all for the first few years, and train branches horizontally. Prune these in winter when dormant, removing the occasional tired old cane but mostly cutting back the side branches so only two or three buds remain on each for next year's flowers. These are two of the best for California:

Climbing First Prize *(1976). Perfect exhibition blooms if canes are trained horizontally. Long growth to twenty feet.*

Climbing Peace *(1950). A super vigorous version of the all-time great rose. Huge blossoms of delicate yellow and pink. Large, glossy, round foliage. Best in full sun, and give it room.*

FRAGRANCE TOO

On the subject of roses, fragrance closely follows beauty. We expect a rose to smell good, so it is sometimes a surprise to find out that not all roses are redolent. Following are some that definitely are:

Angel Face. *A dark mauve floribunda.*

Autumn Damask. *Very old pink rose, source of perfume.*

Command Performance. *Orange-red hybrid tea.*

Chrysler Imperial. *Dark red hybrid tea, smells of roses and cloves.*

Climbing Cecile Brunner. *Old pink polyantha.*

Double Delight. *Red and white hybrid tea, spicy.*

Fragrant Cloud. *Coral-purplish-red hybrid tea, spicy.*

Seashell (AARS, 1976). Peachy pink and yellow blend on a vigorous, resistant plant.

Apricot Blend

Antigua (1975). Clear deep apricot with fine form, substance, and fragrance on a tall plant.

Medallion (AARS, 1973). Large, long-lasting, light apricot double blooms with fruity fragrance. Leathery foliage with few thorns.

Orange and Orange Blend

Fragrant Cloud (1963). Coral-red with a heavy tea-rose fragrance. A show rose that blooms all the time with dark glossy foliage.

Mojave (AARS, 1954). Prominently veined, apricot/orange blend atop vigorous, upright stems with glossy foliage.

Orange-Red

Futura (1975). Tall, vigorous plants that produce armloads of beautifully formed, slow-opening buds in a true coral color. Superb for cutting and background planting. Fragrant.

Command Performance (AARS, 1971). Continuous blooms of orange-red. Very long-lasting, strong flowers with heavy fragrance. Upright growth.

Light Pink

Royal Highness (AARS, 1963). Double, pale pink flowers with a heavy tea-rose fragrance. Good dark, leathery foliage on upright, well-shaped plants.

Medium Pink

Bewitched (AARS, 1967). Clear medium pink, fragrant blooms on long stems. For best production, let it grow tall and plant something to cover up its long legs.

Eiffel Tower (1963). Long, pointed buds on three-foot stems from seven-foot plants. Ideal background plant. Superb cut flowers.

Sweet Surrender (AARS, 1983). Silvery pink, long-stemmed, and intensely fragrant. Blooms profusely on handsome dark foliage. Good garden rose.

Fragrant Cloud

Pink Blend

Helen Traubel (AARS, 1952). Well-formed blooms that have a pink with apricot undertone and a fruity fragrance. Vigorous.

First Prize (AARS, 1970). The top exhibition rose in the country can also be a great landscape rose. Short, spreading plants are sometimes slow to get started. Give it full sun, plenty of food, and minimum pruning.

Tiffany (AARS, 1955). Highly rated favorite. Warm pink, well-formed blossoms on tall, slender stems. Wonderful fragrance; perfect cut flower. A summer through fall bloomer.

Deep Pink

Charlotte Armstrong (AARS, 1941). An old favorite. Deep pink abundant bloomer. Very vigorous with dark, leathery foliage.

Miss All-American Beauty (AARS, 1968). One of the best landscape roses, this produces wave after wave of large, brilliant rose-pink blooms. Immune to mildew, but gets rust occasionally. Prune high.

Peter Frankenfeld (1966). Compact plant produces masses of smallish, perfectly formed, rose-pink flowers. Disease resistant, even when grown in some shade.

Medium Red

Cara Mia (1969). Very long-lasting pure red blooms, with strong growth. A favorite florist's rose, but just as good in the garden.

Ernest H. Morse (1964). Clear medium red, perfect form, long-lasting.

Mister Lincoln (AARS, 1965). Still the favorite long-stemmed, fragrant dark red cutting rose in this country. Tall and vigorous, but requires protection from mildew.

Dark Red

Chrysler Imperial (AARS, 1953). The classic blood-red rose with a heavy fragrance and dark foliage. Medium height.

Friendship. *Deep pink hybrid tea.*

Granada. *Red-yellow bicolor hybrid tea, spicy.*

Heirloom. *Deep lilac to magenta hybrid tea, lemony.*

Jadis. *Pink hybrid tea.*

Lemon Spice. *Pale yellow hybrid tea, spicy.*

Marechal Niel. *Pale yellow noisette, tea scent, climbing (use on warm wall).*

Mme. Isaac Pereire. *Rosy-bourbon colored, sweet, mounding or climbing.*

Mister Lincoln. *Deep red hybrid tea, clove aroma.*

Oklahoma. *Deep red hybrid tea, sister to Mister Lincoln, musk rose scent.*

Perfume Delight. *Bright pink hybrid tea, spicy damask scent.*

Spanish Sun. *Deep yellow floribunda, licoricelike.*

Sunsprite. *Deep, deep yellow floribunda.*

Souvenir de Mme. Boullet. *Old deep yellow hybrid tea, bush or climber, tea scent.*

Sweet Surrender. *True rose scent.*

Tiffany. *Silvery pink hybrid tea, damask scent.*

White Lightnin'. *White grandiflora, lemony.*

THE BEST FOR BOUQUETS

Some roses are distinctly better as cut flowers, but all roses can be made to last, some as long as two weeks. The trick is never to interrupt the supply of water, and to protect the cut stem from bacteria that can block the flow of water.

Roses should be cut in the early morning or late evening with very sharp shears

(crushed stems impede the flow of water). Immediately put the roses in a bucket of warm water (about 110 degrees, the hottest tap water tolerable to the hand). "Immediately" means just that—a water molecule can travel the length of a two-foot stem in just thirty seconds, so getting roses into water fast is important.

Indoors, again cut a little from the base of the stem, this time under water. Under water because when a rose is cut, it gets a sudden "gulp" of air. A bubble forms and blocks any further movement of water so even if a rose is immediately put in a pail of water, it may not be able to drink. The blockage is limited to the first half-inch of stem, solved by cutting that off under water. Hold the rose upright, keeping a drop of water over the cut, and then quickly put it in the vase.

If roses are kept in plain water, it should be changed every few days, but here's a better idea. Keep cut roses in a simple-to-make preservative solution — ¼ teaspoon household bleach and 4 teaspoons sugar per quart of water. The bleach kills bacteria and the sugar provides nutrients to the flowers. This solution will double the vase life of any rose. If roses sipping 7-Up sounds unlikely, it has been found that citrus-flavored, nondiet, carbonated drinks make a great preservative when mixed with two parts water.

Double Delight

FAR RIGHT: Sun Flare

Oklahoma (1964). Deepest purple-red blossoms. Heavy tea-rose fragrance. Dark, leathery foliage; well-branched bushes.

Red Blend

Double Delight (AARS, 1977). We're sticking out our necks on this, but if there's room for only one rose, this is it. Handsome buds unfurl into huge fluffy blooms of substance. Flowers are carmine red shaded to pink then creamy white toward the center, and color changes with the weather. Great for cutting and an endless supply.

Granada (AARS, 1964). Tricolor rose: red, pink, and yellow. Crinkled, leathery foliage.

Mauve

Blue Moon (1964). Long stems bear globular blooms of perfect form in soft bluish lavender. Protect from mildew.

Blue Nile (1981). Deep lavender flowers on thick stems. Good form and fragrance; disease resistant. Beautiful in spring.

Paradise (AARS, 1979). Vigorous plant producing really big blossoms in shades of lavender with red edging.

GRANDIFLORAS

These look a lot like hybrid teas, but their flowers are often smaller and in clusters. Expect a plant that is as tall as or taller than a hybrid tea.

Orange-Red

Olé (1964). Compact, four-foot plants that produce medium-sized, glowing fiery-red blooms in unbelievable profusion above bright green, shiny, hollylike foliage. When cut, flowers last and last and last. Lemony fragrance.

Prominent (AARS, 1977). Medium-sized, thick-petaled, perfectly formed blossoms in the most dazzling orange. Produced in great quantities, blooms on the plant or cut last more than a week.

Medium Pink

Queen Elizabeth (AARS, 1955). The grandiflora class was created for this rose, and no other has really had the exact qualities to fit the class. Shell-pink blossoms come singly or in clusters with long individual stems. Makes an excellent background hedge when pruned high. Protect from mildew.

Pink Blend

Aquarius (AARS, 1971). Light and deep pink, hot and cold colors combined on long stems. Tall, slender bushes.

Pink Parfait (AARS, 1961). Few petals, but the buds are perfect and the flowers last when cut. Clean foliage.

FLORIBUNDAS

Usually this group has smaller flowers in much more abundance. The plants are shorter, more informal, and bushy in appearance.

White or Near White

Iceberg (1958). The best white landscape rose. Exquisite buds open into large clusters. Sweet-scented and good for cutting. To five feet tall but can be kept lower.

Evening Star (1973). Fragrant, lemony-white of perfect form and excellent substance.

Ivory Fashion (AARS, 1959). Beautifully formed ivory blooms. Medium height with leathery foliage.

Medium Yellow

Golden Fleece (1955). One of the best yellow floribundas, with soft, chamois-colored blossoms. Reblooms quickly.

Sun Flare (AARS, 1983). Clear yellow blossoms in massive quantities. Perfect, disease resistant, glossy foliage. Graceful upright form. Many consider this the best yellow rose, period. An exceptional display in fall. Light anise scent.

Yellow Cushion (1966). Lowish bush with soft, creamy yellow flowers. Dead blooms must be cut off. Large, round, glossy foliage.

Deep Yellow

Sunsprite (1973). Deep, nonfading sunshine yellow with a touch of lime. Brilliant, glossy foliage. Sheds petals clean.

Yellow Blend

Redgold (AARS, 1971). Tall grower to five feet with exqui-

Matador

site buds. Flowers of deep yellow edged with orange-red. Never out of bloom. Excellent cut flower. Handsome mahogany-colored new foliage.

Apricot Blend

Cathedral (AARS, 1976). Soft salmon edging orange-red blossoms — a brilliant, changeable color. Slow to repeat bloom.

Puerto Rico (1974). A tall and wide shrub. Yellow and soft orange blooms and well-formed buds on long stems. Some mildew.

Orange and Orange Blend

Gingersnap (1977). Orangest orange. Large, ruffled, fragrant, and long-lasting flowers on glossy, abundant foliage. Good garden flower, particularly for borders.

Matador (1972). Dazzling orange-scarlet flowers with yellow on the backside of the petals. Long-lasting when cut (used by florists). Low-spreading plant.

Orangeade (1959). Tall, wide shrub with brilliant, single orange blossoms in huge clusters all season. A top landscape rose. Try it with Iceberg.

Orange Silk (1968). More double than Orangeade but similar habit and as good.

Orange-Red

Trumpeter (1976). Outstanding deep orange-red. Mildew resistant, low growing. Heavy bloomer. Looks like a miniature Olé.

Pink Blend

Bon-Bon (AARS, 1974). Luminous hot-pink blossoms with a touch of white. A good border bush. A nice cut floribunda.

Rose Parade (AARS, 1975). Low to medium in size with exquisite shell-pink buds that open to double, old-fashioned, cupped blooms. Always in flower. Great for borders planted thirty inches apart. Perfect foliage.

Medium Pink

Gene Boerner (AARS, 1968). Clear pink with darker cen-

Trumpeter as a tree rose

ter. Good garden rose. Very disease resistant with glossy foliage.

Dark Red

Interama (1981). Deep green hardy foliage produces velvety blood-red blossoms. Good garden or hedge rose. Impressive.

Merci (1975). A medium to tall bush with velvety red flowers that don't fade to blue. Mildew resistant and fairly tolerant of shade.

Red Blend (bicolor)

Eye Paint (1976). An arching four- to five-foot-high shrub with brilliant scarlet single blossoms, each with a white eye. Use it as a landscape specimen or background shrub.

Molly McGredy (1969). Brilliant red and white bicolor. Slow to repeat bloom. Immune to disease but sensitive to spray burn.

Mauve

Angel Face (AARS, 1969). Rosy-lilac tinged with cerise on the edges. Intense fragrance. Needs protection from mildew. The outstanding rose of this color range.

The Wild Garden

Spring wildflowers in this Santa Monica garden
include poppies, California gilia, and tidytips

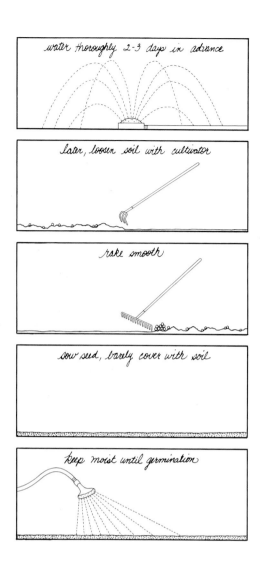

water thoroughly 2-3 days in advance

later, loosen soil with cultivator

rake smooth

sow seed, barely cover with soil

keep moist until germination

GROWING WILDFLOWERS FROM SEED

Most California wildflowers are annual plants that must be grown from seed in the fall. They survive the long, dry summers by simply disappearing, leaving lots of seed behind for the following year. The only way to grow them in the garden is from seed, following the steps shown here.

If your soil is heavy clay, spread an inch-thick layer of soil amendment over the ground and mix it into the top few inches of soil. This will make a seed bed that is easier to keep moist and less likely to compact and smother the seed.

Birds, especially white-crowned sparrows, find wildflower seeds and seedlings a treat, so it is wise to cover the seeded area with bird netting propped up on short stakes. Make sure you take it off before the seedlings become entrapped in it.

Mixtures of wildflower seed are usually available at nurseries, but purer and more interesting mixes, plus packets of seed for specific plants are available from these sources:

Moon Mountain, P.O. Box 34, Morro Bay, California 93442.

Earthside Nature Center, 3160 E. Del Mar Boulevard, Pasadena, California 91107 (many rare and unusual kinds).

The Wild Garden

Surprisingly few native plants have found their way into California gardens, considering the wealth of wild plants available just beyond the back door. They are absent because they are generally difficult to grow or short-lived, though there are the happy exceptions.

One difficulty in growing many native plants is that they need fast-draining, porous soils, since most grow on rocky hillsides in the wild. Too much water or too heavy a soil are not to the liking of most, and are fatal to many. Many natives can get by with no water at all once they are established, after the first year. Some need supplemental watering in summer; be sure to water deeply once a month at most.

Despite their being short-lived or difficult, California's native plants are just too beautiful to be omitted from the garden. So adventuresome gardeners plant them anyway and deal with the eventualities when they arise.

Hillside gardeners have good reasons to choose natives over other plants: natives are good soil binders and need little care or water — a relief to anyone who must lug sacks of soil amendment up and down a hill. Watering a hillside is almost as trying. If you garden on a hillside, definitely consider native plants. They will live longer and many will actually be easy to grow (the "happy exceptions" mentioned earlier). They'll feel right at home.

Most Californians, however, live in the valleys, and garden on level ground, where natives are less at home. Before settlement, California's valleys were grassland, peppered with trees and salted, in spring, with wildflowers. These annual wildflowers will prove the easiest to grow; success with other native plants may not be assured but certainly improved if planting beds are mounded or raised and soil amendments added to speed drainage.

Tall lupins, poppies, and red flax in the garden of Esther and Morgan Sinclaire

An all-native garden in Santa Barbara. *Yucca whipplei* point the way to the house; ceanothus and dwarf coyote brush cover the ground

It bears repeating—the trick is to keep the soil from ever becoming too wet for too long, especially in summer, when warmth and moisture encourage the root rots that are the undoing of plants accustomed to drought.

Annual wildflowers are easier to grow than other native plants because they *are* so short-lived. They grow during the wet months, so are accustomed to wet soils, then flower, set seed, and die before problems beset them. There is only one critical time in the life of a wildflower—when the seed sprouts. The easiest wildflowers, listed on the following pages, are those that sprout readily. Many wildflowers are just as easy once they germinate, but it may take considerable patience and skill to get them started because wildflowers have learned to wait for just the right set of circumstances before beginning life. They may need to wait for fire to burn the brush above them so they have the field to themselves, or they may simply be waiting for some guarantee it will be a wet year. Soaking the seeds overnight or scraping the seed coat with sandpaper triggers some of the more difficult seeds, like lupin.

Wildflowers will come back year after year from self-sown seed, but it may be a better idea to start fresh each year, saving seed, sterilizing the ground and sowing each fall. Otherwise weeds will get the upper hand, or the toughest of wildflowers, poppies in particular, will eventually dominate their smaller and daintier cousins.

The major drawback of a wildflower garden is that it is brown and bare in late summer through early winter, though irrigation can start it earlier and extend it later than one might suspect. It is possible to have something in bloom from the first poppies of February to the last clarkia in July. October is the month to plant, just before the rains begin.

Here are some reasons to include more permanent native plants in the garden despite difficulties in growing them.

They are not thirsty. Native plants can get by on very little water, which makes them a valuable part of any drought-resistant, water-saving plant palette.

They grow fast. Many native plants are sprinters, and quickly fill their roles as landscape plants. A ceanothus, for instance, can become a ten-foot shrub in just three years.

They bring sweet smells to the garden. Several native plants, prominent members of the chaparral plant community, are especially fragrant — sweet and crisp unlike any other. Their fragrance is especially powerful on mornings that promise hot days, or after rain, but they always add an aroma of wilderness.

They bring a little wilderness to the garden. Native plants are just one piece of an ecological pie, but by planting natives you might provide food or habitat for other members of the wilderness community. Birds, butterflies, lizards, and toads might suddenly turn up in a garden planted to natives. In one Los Angeles garden, clouds of metallic blue butterflies appeared after eriogonums, their favorite food, were planted. A covey of quail came to visit for several months, hiding in the dwarf coyote brush ground cover, and birds uncommon enough to require some quick research feasted on toyon berries and salvia seed. By planting a partly wild garden you help preserve what might be disappearing and create little islands of wilderness in the city.

They have native beauty. It is not difficult to appreciate native plants from the damp redwood forests or mountain meadows, but much of California's native growth is so underappreciated it is called "brush," and let go at that. But growing in the "brush," a crackling dry plant community properly known as the chaparral, are some of our most beautiful and unique native plants. These chaparral plants are short-lived, probably an adaptation to frequent fires, but while they are alive they put their all into flowering. Out of flower their dry aesthetic takes some getting used to. They

are seldom the lush green of plants from wetter climes — instead they might be silvery shades of soft green and gray, subtle colors that bring the warmth of the hills into your garden. To use these plants effectively, you must put away preconceived notions concerning what a garden should look like. Let these plants be your instructors — they will teach you much about the California you garden in.

In the lists that follow, only the more commonly available kinds have been included. Generally, these are the most available because they are the easiest to grow, but there are countless other California natives waiting to be tried. When searching for the more permanent native plants, look for named cultivars such as *Arctostaphylos* Howard McMinn. More often than not these have been chosen and named because they are either especially handsome or especially tolerant of garden conditions.

The Best Wildflowers

goldfields (*Baeria maritima*). Masses of tiny golden daisies cover these eight-inch annuals. In the wild they often cover acres. Easy to grow.

clarkia. All of the clarkias are late-blooming annuals that can extend the wildflower season in the garden clear into July (they're often called "farewell-to-spring" since they are the last to bloom). *Clarkia amoena*, most popular, is bushy with big pink to magenta flowers. Red ribbons (*C. concinna*) is not nearly so showy but grows equally low (just over a foot). *C. unguiculata* has puff-ball flowers on tall spikes to three feet. Easy to grow.

Chinese houses (*Collinsia heterophylla*). Short, tiered spikes of purple and white flowers will grow in partial shade. Prefers moist soil. Easy to grow.

Coreopsis bigelovii. This and several other annual coreopsis

Poppies and bird's-eye gilia

Clarkia amoena say a farewell to spring

Nemophila maculata

have butter yellow daisy blooms. Somewhat difficult to grow.

California poppy. Most wildflower plantings start off or end up dominated by California poppies. *Eschscholzia californica* is the common orange-flowered poppy; *E. caespitosa* is a miniature with little yellow flowers. Seed companies also sell named strains (Mission Bells) that may not look quite wild enough for a wildflower garden. Extra easy to grow.

gilia. Several gilia play perfect supporting roles for the splashier wildflowers. *Gilia tricolor*, the bird's-eye gilia, is one of the best. *G. achilleifolia*, the California gilia, is a close second with purplish flowers. Both grow about a foot tall and are great with bulbs. *G. capitata*, the globe gilia, has pleasant blue blossoms and is very easy to grow. Others are almost as easy.

tidytips (*Layia platyglossa*). One of the speediest to bloom, this foot-tall wildling has yellow daisy flowers edged with white. Very easy to grow.

blue flax (*Linum lewisii*). Best near the coast, this two-foot-tall perennial is usually grown as an annual. It has delicate funnel-shaped blue flowers. Easy to grow.

lupin. All lupins send up splendid spires of blue, lavender, pink, or white flowers. One, *Lupinus densiflorus aureus*, has yellow flowers. It and the blue-flowered *L. benthamii* stay short but like most get wide and bushy. There are many lupins worth trying, including some perennial kinds, but all are mildly difficult to grow. The hard little seeds must be soaked overnight in water before planting, or scratched with sandpaper. Snails savor the seedlings.

blazing star (*Mentzelia lindleyi*). A tall wildflower growing to three feet, it has shimmering yellow star-shaped blossoms. Almost easy to grow.

nemophila. Two nemophilas are good fillers between taller wildflowers. Both grow no taller than eight inches. *N. maculata* has white flowers with a dot on each petal (the common name is five-spot), while *N. menziesii*, the baby blue eyes, has blue flowers with white centers. Both are easy to grow.

blue bells (*Phacelia campanularia*). Though not as delicate as some wildflowers, this sturdy annual has remarkably deep magenta-blue flowers. It grows to two feet. Easy to grow.

OTHER WILDFLOWERS

There are wildflowers from other parts of the world that feel right at home in California. In an experimental planting at the UCLA Botanic Garden, Director David Verity tried many, and found the following to be the best. All returned year after year from self-sown seed, needed little supplemental irrigation, and blended well with the real thing. The photographs show sections of the garden that include genuine California wildflowers mixed in with these pretenders. Several are often included in wildflower mixes.

Swan River daisy (Brachycome iberidifolia). *Light lavender*

Cladanthus arabicus. *Soft yellow*

annual African daisy (Dimorphotheca pluvialis). *White and pastel shades*

Felicia bergerana. *Clear blue*

Helipterum roseum. *Pink*

Helipterum humboldtianum. *Yellow*

Linaria, *species and hybrids. Many colors*

scarlet flax (Linum grandiflorum *Rubrum*). *Red*

Schizanthus *hybrids. Many colors*

Silene pendula. *Pink*

Ursinia anthemoides. *Yellow*

Venidium fastuosum. *Orange*

Xeranthemum annuum. *Pink or white*

Weeds and Watering

Weeds are devastating to most wildflower plantings, but a new technique called "solar pasteurization" can help. In late summer, thoroughly soak the area to be seeded, then cover with a clear plastic tarp for several weeks. Seeds will be destroyed to depths of a foot or more by the heat of the sun.

In the garden, wildflowers need watering. They need almost constant moisture to germinate, since in the wild they won't sprout if they're not convinced of a wet winter. They'll last a lot longer in the garden with regular watering, but don't overdo it—many of these flowers will grow unrecognizably plump if they are too pampered.

Island bush poppy

FAR RIGHT: hybrid
sticky monkey flower

The Best Native Plants

PERENNIALS AND SHORT-LIVED SHRUBS

None of these should be counted on for long in the land-scape, but they grow very fast and bloom beautifully while they last. It's just their nature. In some hillside gardens they may stay for twenty years, but many won't make it past five.

bush anemone (*Carpenteria californica*). Grow it for the flowers — large and snowy white. Four-foot bush that needs summer watering.

island bush poppy (*Dendromecon harfordii*). Fast growth to at least five feet, often followed by sudden death. Masses of yellow flowers. Keep dry.

buckwheat (*Eriogonum*). Needlelike foliage and flat-topped flower clusters characterize most, including *Eriogonum fasciculatum* Theodore Payne, a good ground cover. Flowers and foliage often turn soft rusty shades for summer. Attractive to butterflies. Don't water.

Pacific Coast iris. From several wild irises have come many hybrids in shades of lavender or yellow. They bloom for months with grassy foliage in handsome clumps. Some summer water will help, and they are moderately to down-right easy to grow. Large clumps should be dug up and divided every few years in late summer or early fall before roots begin to grow.

penstemon. Tall spikes of blue, lavender, red, or rose flowers. *Penstemon heterophyllus*, *P. clevelandii*, and *P. spectabilis* perhaps the best. A touch of water in summer helps.

coreopsis. *Coreopsis gigantea*, several feet across with bright yellow daisies, makes a fascinating shrub. In summer, everything shrivels up, revealing fat, succulent stems that may grow four or more feet tall. *C. maritima* is only two feet, dies nearly to the roots in summer but is just as pretty. Both do best near the coast.

yerba buena (*Satureja douglasii*). A low mat with a minty fragrance, wonderful along paths. Likes sun or partial shade. Needs some summer watering.

sticky monkey flower (*Diplacus*). A three-foot-tall up-right bush with snapdragon flowers and sticky foliage. Common wildling is orange, hybrids range from red to yellow to white. Does best with some summer watering.

matilija poppy (*Romneya coulteri*). Huge, floppy flowers that look like fried eggs. Spreads to form large, ragged clumps with grayish foliage four or more feet tall. In the right spot it's very permanent, very aggressive. Dies back each summer. A champion hillside plant. Don't water.

sage. Two, *Salvia clevelandii* (blue flowers) and *S. leucophylla* (pink flowers), are highly aromatic — few plants smell fresher. Grayish foliage grows to three or four feet. *S. sonomensis* is greener, spreads into short, foot-tall clumps. Needs some summer watering.

wooly blue curls (*Trichostema lanatum*). Spare, shrubby growth, producing fascinating fuzzy purple flowers. As pun-gent as sage. Keep dry.

yucca. Several kinds, all with stiff, spiky, succulent foliage. *Yucca whipplei* is perhaps the most graceful — a perfect pin-cushion with tall spires of white flowers. It dies after flower-ing but new plants sprout from base. Keep dry.

California fuchsia (*Zauschneria californica*). Spreads to form loose stands of two-foot flower spikes splattered with red in late summer. Dies back by fall; should be cut back to make way for new growth. Tolerates water, blooms better.

WOODY GROUND COVERS AND SHRUBS

These can more or less be counted on in the landscape — depending on soil and situation. A few are naturally short-lived.

manzanita (*Arctostaphylos*). Many kinds, from ground covers to tree-sized shrubs. All have beautiful bark and foliage, often reddish, and clusters of tiny white bellflowers with handsome fruits. *Arctostaphylos* Howard McMinn is perhaps the most useful and tolerant of ordinary garden

Matilija poppy

soils. Others are less reliable, except on slopes or in fast-draining soils, where they excel. Many fine cultivars have recently been introduced.

dwarf coyote brush (*Baccharis pilularis*). Extremely tough two- to three-foot-tall ground cover. Shearing before new growth in early spring will keep it lower. A champion hill coverer that needs no summer watering but won't be killed if its feet get wet. Pigeon Point is the preferred variety, a little lower than the others, but Twin Peaks is fine.

California lilac (*Ceanothus*). Many kinds, from ground covers only inches tall (but yards wide) to tree-sized shrubs. All have masses of blue or white flowers. Makes a splendid show. Most will last about ten years in the garden then die suddenly. Very fast growth in the meantime. Don't water in summer. Pruning is sometimes fatal.

western redbud (*Cercis occidentalis*). A deciduous shrub or small tree with delicate round leaves and pretty magenta flowers. Does best away from coast.

flannel bush (*Fremontodendron*). Most kinds are *big* shrubs (to twenty feet) with deep yellow flowers, handsome but itchy foliage. It grows fast but dies suddenly. An exasperating plant. Don't water in summer.

toyon (*Heteromeles arbutifolia*). Usually a big, handsome shrub, growing to twenty feet, with bright red berries in time for Christmas. Stands some watering. Should be pruned when young or it gets lanky.

California holly (*Mahonia*). Several kinds, all upright growers with hollylike foliage and clusters of yellow flowers on top followed by purple fruit. Some stay two to three feet tall and spread outward; others grow to six feet and remain in narrow clumps. Appreciates summer water.

Catalina cherry (*Prunus lyonii*) and **hollyleaf cherry** (*P. ilicifolia*). Both are grown mostly for handsome shiny foliage, but have handsome fruit as well. The first grows to become a small tree, the second tops out at six feet, has hollylike leaves.

Flannel bush

Catalina cherry

Fuchsia-flowering gooseberry

Valley oak

coffeeberry (*Rhamnus californica*). A tough but handsome shrub growing to eight feet with reddish berries that slowly turn black.

sumac. Two (*Rhus integrifolia* and *R. ovata*) have handsome waxy foliage and grow to about eight feet. Both can be sheared. Good landscape plants, especially on hillsides, but flammable.

California gooseberry. Several remarkably different plants with the same first name. *Ribes sanguineum* is a four-foot deciduous shrub with lovely tassels of pink to red flowers. *R. speciosum*, the fuchsia-flowering gooseberry, makes a clump of spiny, arching branches, deciduous in summer but covered with deep red flowers in spring. *R. viburnifolium*, the Catalina perfume, spreads wide to become a three-foot-tall ground cover of dark evergreen foliage. It is unexcelled under oaks and other trees. All stand drought but appreciate some summer water.

TREES

By nature, trees are permanent plants, and all of these can be counted on for a very long time.

white alder (*Alnus rhombifolia*). One of the fastest-growing trees, it shoots straight up to forty feet, loves moisture (keep away from sewers). Looks best planted in loose groves. If you can find it, *Alnus tenuifolia* is smaller, prettier.

pine. There are a dozen or more native pines, but the most useful are the Coulter pine (*Pinus coulteri*), growing to sixty feet with huge cones; the digger pine (*P. sabiniana*) with open grayish growth to sixty feet; and the Torrey pine (*P. torreyana*), broad, gray, and smallish to only forty feet. These can go without water. The Monterey pine (*P. radiata*) is more commonly available but subject to all sorts of problems. It does best right on the coast.

California sycamore (*Platanus racemosa*). A deciduous tree growing to sixty or more feet; handsome when young, majestic in age. Large maple leaves often yellow and fall

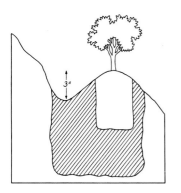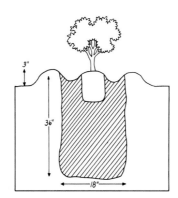

throughout the year because of anthracnose, a nonfatal disease. There are other sycamores from other countries but none grow with such grace.

oak. All native oaks are handsome, if sometimes big for garden trees. The coast live oak (*Quercus agrifolia*) is the most commonly available. It grows fast to sixty or more feet; sometimes plagued by pests in Northern California. The valley oak (*Q. lobata*) and smaller black oak (*Q. kelloggii*) are extremely handsome deciduous oaks with lobed leaves, good fall color. They don't grow well near the coast.

Coast redwood (*Sequoia sempervirens*) and **giant sequoia** (*Sequoiadendron giganteum*). The coast redwood grows fast, gets big, but still fits in most gardens. There are several named kinds that have specific shapes or foliage. It does best near the coast. Farther inland try the much slower giant sequoia if you have lots of room. Both like moisture, but will stand some drought.

California bay (*Umbellularia californica*). A handsome mid-sized tree (to forty feet) with sweet aromatic foliage. Likes moisture.

HILLSIDE AND FLATLAND PLANTING IDEAS FOR NATIVES

The people who plant along California's freeways have come up with two techniques that work especially well for native plants. One technique is for hillsides, the other for level ground, but both have this in common: the base of the plant ends up slightly higher than the surrounding soil, ensuring that after a rain or irrigation it won't be covered with silt, which is sure death for most natives, and that the sensitive upper root area dries quickly after watering. A three-inch-high ring of soil forms an ample watering basin around the plants and helps funnel water to the roots.

Note that the planting hole is deep. This helps drainage and encourages roots to go deep. On hillsides it is debatable whether adding an amendment to the soil that goes back into the planting hole (the backfill) helps or hinders the plant. It's best to add only gypsum to the backfill; if the soil is heavy clay you may wish to add some organic amendment as well. On level ground it's almost always a good idea to add gypsum and an organic amendment — both help drainage.

The time to plant is fall and winter. Plants will require regular watering at first, but by the following winter many will be able to go without. Fertilizer is unnecessary.

"Pocket planting" is a recently devised method of planting shrubs and trees from seed and is the perfect way for a native plant to begin life. Most natives have deep root systems — one way they survive drought — but if they are grown in nursery cans, their roots become thwarted. Starting them from seed sown directly in the ground lets them push deep tap roots straight down. And if seed and nursery plants are planted side by side, the seedling will quickly overtake the nursery plant.

Pocket planting works like this: dig a hole one inch wide and four inches deep. Put a pinch of slow-release fertilizer at the bottom of the hole and fill with soil to within a half-inch of the top. Plant seed at proper depth. Cut a half-gallon milk carton in half and remove the top and bottom. Use one half per hole, plunging it halfway into the ground. It will help protect seeds from creatures and will also provide a tiny watering basin. The shade it casts will help germination.

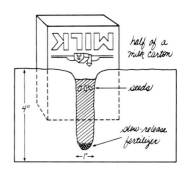

The Working Garden

A working garden is one that performs some useful task, whether it's to provide privacy, shelter, or just to fill the air with pleasant scents. Although privacy and shelter can be accomplished by using structures, plants are preferable. While structures may deteriorate or become dated, plants grow in character and grace. And as they go about their chores, they bring freshness, beauty, and color to the area.

There are a few garden jobs plants can't do: they don't, for instance, make very good seats or paths. In a new garden, structures are quickly built while trees or shrubs grow slowly into their roles. In mature gardens structures help organize, define, or pinpoint. In small gardens such structures as fences and trellises do their chores in a minimum of space.

On the following pages are several gardens that combine plants and structures in different proportions for different effects. At one extreme is a collector's garden — chock-full of fascinating plants. At the other extreme is a garden more for people and their activities than for plants: an outdoor room. All are delightful places to be.

As you look at these inventive gardens, think of what you like most about being outdoors. This will help you decide what to include in your garden scheme. Do you prefer the warmth of the sun on your back, or dappled shade? Do you like to sit in the garden with friends or by yourself, and what do you do when you're sitting there?

Notice that these gardens are complex compositions that read more like a book than a billboard. There is a strong first impression but also continuity from one end to the other, like a walk in the woods. If you stop along the way, there are details to ponder.

There are countless possibilities waiting just beyond the garden gate. You will find a world of plants that can help shape your environment while breathing life into it. This is the job of the working garden.

A place to sit in the sun, with the sound of water nearby and with interesting plants in view everywhere

A Collector's Garden

Collectors often have a hard time organizing their favorites into anything resembling a garden. This garden, designed by one plant collector for another, uses huge raised beds made from railroad ties to organize and elevate the plants. There's no reason to stoop in this garden, and it doesn't matter that no two plants are the same; the raised beds provide the necessary continuity. Here are the parts that make it work.

Height, shelter. Instead of a man-made structure, an old magnolia tree was carefully pruned to let dappled sunlight filter through. It provides the most pleasant kind of shade, appreciated by people as well as the rare ferns and begonias growing beneath. The designer was Chris Rosmini and Howard Folkman the talented contractor.

A change of level. It's impossible to garden under a magnolia because of the many surface roots, so it's a logical place for a patio. By building a deck over the roots, they won't be disturbed. Since the deck is several inches higher than the surrounding brick paving, it becomes a sort of stage. A curving edge, trimmed with header boards, is a soft contrast to the otherwise rectilinear design.

A place to sit. The benches are permanently affixed to the raised beds and flush with their top. Perched on the benches, you are just inches away from the plants. The table is movable, which makes cleaning around it easier, so it can be put in the shade or out in the sun.

Focal point, movement. The exquisite fountain was bought on vacation in Seville, Spain. Its gentle sounds disguise the noise from nearby busy streets. The pool is raised up to arm level if you're sitting on the bench beside it. Inside the railroad ties is extra-thick plastic sheeting, the kind used for large swimming pools. The pool isn't as deep as it appears; only the upper eighteen inches is water, the rest is filled with sand.

Detail. Choice little plants find a home at the base of the pool, where they soften the intersection of the railroad ties and bricks. This is one advantage of brick paving—it's easy to leave out a few for plants.

A Tasty Design

This garden has things to eat and a place where they can be eaten. The garden beds, neatly separated by paths that keep feet from getting muddy, are overflowing with vegetables. The trees, still young, are for fruit as well as privacy. This garden is unusual in that it is in a side yard. The back of the house bumps against a hill and is virtually unusable but a narrow deck continues to the left of the table along the back of the house to the other side, where it cradles a hot tub. It was designed by architects Harriet Hatch and Joseph Madda.

Height, shelter. There's not much to this overhead but its bold wedge shape establishes height, reinforces a geometric theme repeated throughout the garden, and provides just enough shelter to keep the dew off the dining table.

Storage. There's no room to waste, so hiding under the benches are storage areas that hold garden tools and accessories.

Depth and movement. An ordinary path would make this garden look small. This unusual design makes the garden seem larger than it actually is. The point of this path is depth; it moves the eye from one end to the other.

Artifacts. Little details like the odd stones near the path are fun to discover along the way. They help the eye linger so the journey becomes longer than it might.

Ground level interest. More to look at. Using big stones adds texture that can't be missed.

A Garden for People

In this garden, designed for people and their activities, structures do most of the work. There simply wasn't room for many plants—the entire space measures only 11 by 17 feet. In it there's enough room for six to soak, four to dine, and two to swing. It's a lesson on how to pack a lot into a little. Whether it's really a garden or a room without walls is beside the point—no matter what, it's a great place to spend a summer afternoon. The designer was Kenneth Goodman.

Height, shelter, color. Height is often the overlooked dimension in garden design. Here the wood overhead carries the eye up, beyond the small size of the garden, to the sky and trees beyond (which are actually in a neighbor's yard—what is called a "borrowed landscape"). The overhead also defines where the people ought to be—under its protection. The colorful canvas panels block the heat of the sun, but not its light. In winter, when the sun is once again welcome, the panels can be removed and packed away.

Detail. There are two good examples: the simple grooves on the ends of the beams overhead, cut with a hand-held router, and the hanging baskets stuffed with colorful variety.

Privacy. Since the deck is up off the ground, the fence had to be proportionately taller. In most communities fences can't exceed a certain height, but if they are set back from the property line far enough (often only five feet) as it is here, there is no limit. That's the old five-foot-tall fence just behind it.

A place to sit. Essential in every garden, the seating arrangement here is an especially nice example. There's a place for the morning cup of coffee or a complete dinner. One can lean back against the fence or the railing and the solitary table leg won't interfere with feet.

Fun. A factor too often overlooked in the garden, it ought to be fun to be outside. Here, a fanciful swing is hung from mountain climbing gear (fancy braided rope, carabiners). Another touch of whimsy is the undulating decking just to the swing's left. It is actually for potted plants, but more often than not children will be found sprawled on it.

A focal point. Every garden needs one, but this has three. Though it's not obvious from the photograph, the large hot tub is the most powerful focal point; the table and the colorful canvas panels are a close second and third.

Change in elevation; bonus seating. If you garden on flat land, some change in elevation is a relief. Here the deck is split into several levels. Functionally, this helps the house relate to the garden because the house sits up high on its foundation. Emotionally, the change makes each level feel like a different place. The steps in between can be bonus seating.

The major consideration before planting a tree is not the tree itself, but its shadow. That sapling you plant will eventually shade a large section of your property, for better or for worse. The two properties shown here show the effects of a tree's shadow. One house faces due south; that is, the sun shines through the front windows. Good places for trees on this property are in front of the house, in front of a patio, (the shadows fall on roof or paving, not plants) or in front of a fence (though shadows now fall in neighbor's yard). Though you may have no say in the matter, trees planted near the street are going to end up shading your front yard. The other house faces north, with the sun coming in the back windows. Here everything is simply reversed. Street trees work fine here because they shade the street.

The idea in both cases is to place the tree's shadow over something other than plants since there are very few plants that grow well in dark shade. Also consider this factor: a tree's shadow doubles in length in winter. In the drawings, note that the noontime shadow in the dead of winter is roughly twice as long as the

tree is tall, even longer at other times of the day. This is not as bad as it might seem. Plants growing in the tree's shadow, but not directly beneath, get the benefit of reflected light from the sky. (The deepest shade is always directly under the tree.) In the drawings, also note that plants on the south side of the tree get sun in winter, but not in summer. This extra winter sun is just enough to keep many plants happy (it's a good place for bulbs), though they may have a tendency to lean toward the sun.

Many plants grow well in what is called "partial shade." Partial shade can be found on either side of a tree. Most plants prefer sun in the morning, found on the east side of a tree. Sun in the afternoon, found on the west side of a tree, is hotter but okay. This suggests planting trees mostly along the western side of a property, as seen in the drawings, so that they will receive the full benefit of the morning sun.

Part shade also occurs naturally under some trees that let dappled sunlight through. Or it can be created by pruning. This kind of pruning is called "thinning," sometimes "lacing," or "opening a tree up." It is also the only kind of pruning that

Trees

Trees are an important part of the working garden simply because they are so visible and so permanent. Though you may not have many opportunities to plant one (most gardens come fully equipped), choosing a tree is a weighty decision. Trees can make or break a garden, and there's a lot to take into account.

First and foremost is size. Many trees are just too big for today's small gardens, though spreading trees are more of a problem than tall trees. Most gardens actually have the perfect spot for a tall tree—the south side of the house. Planted on the sunny side of the house, they will shade the roof, not the garden, and keep the house cool. Their height will bring a touch of majesty to the garden. Little can be done with large, spreading trees in the small garden.

Shade is the next consideration, discussed in detail at right. Size has a lot to do with this, but there are some trees that cast less shade than others because their growth is less dense. These are the perfect trees to sit or garden under. Careful trimming on an annual or semiannual basis can keep other kinds open and airy so they too produce only dappled shade. Deciduous trees only provide shade when it is most useful, in summer.

Roots are another consideration. Many trees have roots so close to the surface that it is impossible to grow anything underneath. If you already have a tree like this, consider building a deck or patio there so the roots are free to roam. (For patios, bricks set on sand, without mortar, are the best choice because they let water through and can be reset if disturbed by the roots.)

What you want the tree to do is the final consideration. In the lists that follow, trees are grouped into categories that should help narrow the choices from hundreds to merely dozens.

Canary Island pine

The Best Trees

There are countless choices but those listed here are special — first, because they are primarily trees that do particularly well in California and may not be found in other garden books; second, because they are anything but ordinary, and are distinguished by structure, foliage, bark, or flowers. You are lucky indeed if any of these already grows in your garden — they are not the common ashes, elms, beeches, and maples that populate most gardens. If a tree is not described in one category, it will be found in another for which it is even better suited. Trees are evergreen, unless noted.

THE FASTEST

These trees are speedy in assuming their roles in the garden. Three years after planting they are real trees; five years later they are practically full grown. Be careful here — a few of these have little else to recommend them.

Acacia baileyana, A. dealbata, and *A. decurrens.* All sprint to thirty feet in three or four years. Delightful foliage, masses of yellow flowers as early as January. Average shade.

Alnus rhombifolia.

Cassia leptophylla.

floss silk tree (*Chorisia*).

coral tree (*Erythrina caffra*).

eucalyptus.

Myoporum laetum. Grows exceptionally fast into a thirty-foot-tall ball of dark green. The toughest beach tree, boring elsewhere. Deep shade.

Canary Island pine (*Pinus canariensis*). Fast and beautiful to sixty feet. A narrow pine with soft bunches of needles. Average to deep shade.

Chinese elm (*Ulmus*).

PATIO PERFECT

You can dine or dance beneath these well-behaved trees.

preserves a tree's natural shape. It's by far the best way to prune, and it's easy to master. Follow this important rule: always remove entire branches, or cut a branch back to another major branch. Look inside the tree for branches that may duplicate others. Cut out some of the small twiggy growth but use caution here. Side branches, even small ones, help strengthen major branches and removing too many may cause others to break in winds.

The drawing shows the result of proper thinning. The tree maintains its original shape and size but lets more light through so that the area near it is better for gardening and makes a more pleasant place to sit.

Front door faces south

Front door faces north

winter   summer

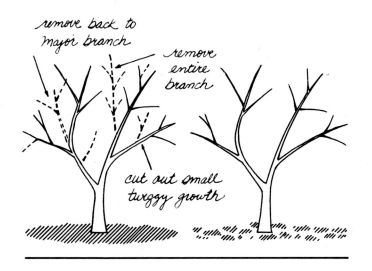

remove back to major branch

remove entire branch

cut out small twiggy growth

Jacaranda

Australian willow

Ginkgo

Their shade is not too deep, their roots not too rambunctious. Most are smallish, umbrella shaped. If they have a fault it is the occasional leaf or petal found floating in a cup of coffee.

silk tree (*Albizia julibrissin*). Grows fast, but bottom branches must be removed if you are going to stand under it. Low and flat, thirty feet tall by forty feet wide in time. Ferny foliage, masses of pink powder-puff flowers in summer. Prefers hot summer areas. Light shade.

Cassia leptophylla. Grow in Southern California only. Fast, spreading growth to about twenty-five feet. Graceful foliage, spectacular masses of golden yellow flowers that stop traffic. Easy to keep lacy and open by pruning. Briefly deciduous just before blooming in late spring. Blooms for a month or more.

Jacaranda mimosifolia. Grow in Southern California only. Graceful, feathery growth to thirty feet high, and a little wider. Masses of fragrant lavender flowers in spring. Briefly deciduous in late winter. Light shade.

mayten.

flowering cherry and plum (*Prunus*).

Chinese tallow tree (*Sapium*).

lavender trumpet tree (*Tabebuia impetiginosa*). Grow in Southern California only. Fast growth to twenty-five feet, airy foliage, spectacular masses of lavender trumpet flowers in early spring. A knockout. Deciduous. Light shade.

tipu (*Tipuana tipu*). Fast growth to thirty feet and as wide. Coarse but airy foliage, odd apricot-colored pea-shaped flowers, winged pods. Likes warm summers. Looks best if allowed to grow multiple trunks. Brittle in wind. Light shade.

brisbane box (*Tristania conferta*). Best in Northern California. Moderate growth to thirty feet, eventually spreading but upright at first. Big leaves, beautiful bark. Average shade.

Chinese elm (*Ulmus parvifolium*). Fast growth to forty feet or more. Bushy top looks best with regular thinning. Pendulous branches, small leaves, attractive mottled bark. Deciduous only in cold winter areas. Light shade with pruning.

GOOD IN LAWNS

These can coexist with a lawn. They tolerate the frequent watering, and grass at least has a fighting chance of growing beneath.

peppermint tree (*Agonis flexuosa*).

silk tree (*Albizia*).

strawberry tree (*Arbutus*).

white birch (*Betula*).

Ginkgo biloba. Starts slowly on its climb to a forty-foot-tall tree of magnificent proportions (the variety Fairmount is faster). Brilliant yellow in fall. Average shade.

jacaranda.

liquidambar.

saucer magnolia.

mayten (*Maytenus boaria*). An ethereal weeping tree with tiny light green leaves. Grows to thirty feet. Very light shade, perfect for lawns, though suckers may spring from roots.

sour gum (*Nyssa*).

palms.

Chinese tallow tree (*Sapium*).

tipu (*Tipuana*).

tristania.

NEAR HOUSE OR PAVING

These won't tear foundations or paving asunder. They can be planted close to either.

peppermint tree (*Agonis*).

orchid tree (*Bauhinia*).

bottlebrush (*Callistemon*).

Eucalyptus citriodora, E. polyanthemos.

Australian willow (*Geijera parviflora*). Leaves are willow-

Tipu

Coral gum

Weeping bottlebrush

like but growth is more upright, pendulous at tips. Moderate growth to twenty-five feet. Light shade.

cajeput (*Melaleuca*).

podocarpus.

SMALL

These trees barely qualify as such. They're good in front of taller trees or in the middle of garden beds where they provide just a touch of height. They're perfect in tiny courtyards.

Japanese maple (*Acer palmatum*). Hundreds of varieties. All are airy, delicate, topping out at fifteen to twenty feet. Leaves are often fancy, colored, give a nice fall show. In California they grow where azaleas thrive, tolerate as much shade. Tips of leaves turn brown if water is high in salts. Occasional thorough soaking helps wash salts from root zone. Average shade.

strawberry tree (*Arbutus unedo*). Grows slowly but in time becomes a most handsome small tree, to twenty feet. Reddish stems and bark, deep green leaves, pretty flowers, fruit that vaguely resembles strawberries.

bottlebrush (*Callistemon viminalis*). This species makes the best tree. Weeping growth to twenty feet. Bright red brush flowers. One named Red Cascade is a superior kind. Birds love the seed. Light shade.

bronze loquat (*Eriobotrya deflexa*). Only ten feet tall. Big bronzy leaves. Tidy plant. Average shade.

coral gum (*Eucalyptus torquata*). A beautiful small tree growing to only twelve feet. Graceful form. Lots of coral-red flowers throughout the year. Light shade.

Ficus benjamina. Grow in coastal Southern California only, or protected from frost. The familiar indoor tree makes a tidy graceful twenty-foot-tall tree outdoors. Grows in sun or part shade. Shear to keep small. May drop leaves after planting, but recovers.

Michelia doltsopa. Magnolialike form and flowers. Grows to twenty feet. Large leathery leaves are evergreen. Deep shade.

sweetshade (*Hymenosporum flavum*). Small ball of a tree to twenty feet. Grows slowly. Fragrant golden flowers in summer.

saucer magnolia (*Magnolia soulangiana*). Eventually grows to twenty feet but takes its time getting there. Loads of white to purplish goblet-shaped flowers in spring, a spectacle when mature. Deciduous. Look for named kinds. Average shade.

NARROW ENOUGH

Some trees are naturally narrow — they are good choices at the edge of the property next to fences or in side yards or other tight spots. They're perfect in front of a telephone pole. Extremely narrow trees, hardly wider than a telephone pole, are called "fastigate." Shade is seldom a concern.

pyramidal white birch (*Betula pendula* Fastigiata). Like common birch but only ten or so feet wide. Deciduous.

Italian cypress (*Cupressus sempervirens* Stricta). Fastigate in the extreme, this conifer gets sixty feet tall in time, seldom wider than six feet.

silver dollar gum (*Eucalyptus polyanthemos*).

cajeput (*Melaleuca*).

palms. Southern California specialties, deserving a book to themselves. A few hardy in Northern California. These are some commonly used as trees:

Feather palms (feathery fronds) include *Archonophoenix arecastrum* and *Phoenix reclinata*. **Fan palms** include *Erythea edulis*, livistona, and trachycarpus. All are tidy, though leaves do come down in winds. Shade is seldom a consideration.

columnar sargent cherry (*Prunus sargentii* Columnaris). Northern California only. A flowering cherry with pink blossoms that grows to thirty feet, but only ten feet wide.

Cajeput   Hong Kong orchid tree   *Podocarpus gracilior*

firewheel tree (*Stenocarpus sinuatus*). Very slow growing to twenty-five feet, only twelve feet wide. Dark green leaves are lobed, flowers fantastic, like wheels on fire. Grown mostly in Southern California. Deep shade.

TINY FORESTS
Plant these trees in groves — around decks or patios, leading up to an entry, or at the edge of the property — and they'll look like little forests. Planted close together, these trees will become dwarfed (smaller than sizes stated here).

Japanese maple (*Acer palmatum*).

white alder (*Alnus rhombifolia*). A California native that eventually gets big, to fifty feet, fast, but becomes more restrained planted in groves. Deciduous. Deep shade and greedy roots.

birch (*Betula*).

silver dollar gum (*Eucalyptus polyanthemos*). One of the best eucalyptus, it stays on the small side, to thirty feet, has round grayish leaves, attractive bark. It suggests aspens or birches. Light shade.

cajeput (*Melaleuca quinquenervia*). Looks similar to birches but grows better in Southern California. White bark is thick and spongy (kids love it). Lots of white bottlebrush flowers. Grows to thirty feet. Light shade.

coast redwood (*Sequoia sempervirens*). A handsome garden tree despite its considerable size (world's tallest tree after a few hundred years) and need of considerable water (if not watered enough there will be lots of brown branches). Tends to grow narrow and looks good in groves. Grows very fast. Look for named kinds.

PURE GRACE
These trees are unusually graceful. Many are weeping, with long, drooping branches. All have a soft effect in the landscape. Most look best set apart from other trees.

weeping acacia (*Acacia pendula*). A beautiful flowing tree to twenty-five feet with willowy gray-blue foliage, sporadic yellow bloom. Light shade.

peppermint tree (*Agonis flexuosa*). A twenty-five-foot tree with refined willowlike growth and leaves, small white flowers. It becomes massive, majestic with age, but stays small. Leaves smell minty. Light shade.

deodar cedar (*Cedrus deodara*). Planted alone or in groups, the most graceful of conifers. Too bad it's so big — grows fast to eighty feet, spreads to forty feet at base. Form depends on lower branches that touch the ground, which makes the question of shade irrelevant.

lemon gum (*Eucalyptus citriodora*). Grow in Southern California only. The most graceful of this graceful group. Tall, slender trunk, sleek pearly bark, veils of lemon-scented foliage on top. Grows fast to eighty feet after a spindly start. Very light shade.

peppermint gum (*Eucalyptus nicholii*). Billowy and willowlike. Fast growth to thirty feet.

Australian willow (*Geijera*).

mayten.

willow pittosporum (*Pittosporum phillyraeoides*). Small, weeping tree with narrow leaves. Grows slowly to twenty feet. Average shade.

Podocarpus gracilior. With patience, perhaps the prettiest greenery you can plant, once it grows out of its gawky youth. Soft and billowy, to forty feet or more. Average shade.

FABULOUS FLOWERS
Sometimes even a hard-working tree only has to look pretty. These will not disappoint.

Acacia baileyana.

Hong Kong orchid tree (*Bauhinia blakeana*). Grow in Southern California only; best in warm areas, away from coast. A small, fast-growing, usually multitrunked tree, to twenty-five feet. Spectacular orchid-colored flowers in fall, just before leaves drop. Average shade.

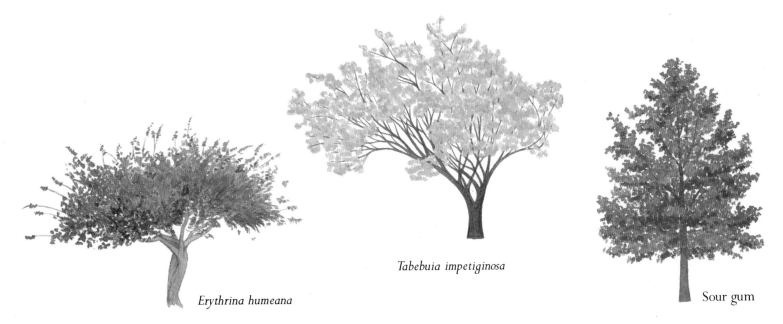

Erythrina humeana

Tabebuia impetiginosa

Sour gum

Cassia leptophylla.

floss silk tree (*Chorisia speciosa*). Grow in Southern California only. Beautiful, large pink orchidlike flowers cover the tops of this tall tree in fall. Fast growing, to sixty feet or more. Bark is green, often thorny. Not really for small gardens but people plant them anyway. Deciduous. Look for named kinds that flower reliably. Light shade.

coral tree (*Erythrina*). Grow in Southern California only. All coral trees have spectacular red or red-orange flowers. *Erythrina caffra*, the most common, is best near the coast. Grows like a weed to thirty feet with a spread of forty feet. Brittle in wind, does best with little water, pruning. More or less deciduous. Other kinds are smaller, better suited to gardens. *E. falcata* is a handsome upright tree to forty feet, nearly evergreen. *E. lysistemon* becomes a gnarly thirty-footer, goes completely deciduous. *E. humeana* has a tidy, if somewhat shrubby, habit, to twenty-five feet. Blooms in fall. *E. coralloides* has a bizarre branching pattern, grows to twenty-five feet; striking blooms come before leaves. Roots are a problem on all kinds. Average to dense shade.

red-flowering gum (*Eucalyptus ficifolia*). Grow on Southern California coast only. A small tree to thirty feet; stubby looking with age. Masses of flowers in varying shades of red in late summer and fall. Average shade.

jacaranda.

crepe myrtle (*Lagerstroemia indica*). Grow in hottest areas only, not on coast. Handsome small trees, pretty pinkish bark, slow growing to twenty feet. Late summer blooms come in many colors, including pure white, good pinks, and rosy reds. Deciduous, with nice fall color. Average shade.

flowering cherry (*Prunus*). Many kinds, best in Northern California. *Prunus campanulata*, the Taiwan cherry, with bright rose-pink flowers, is the only one that does well in Southern California. Other kinds (there are hundreds), mostly pale pink to deep rose pink, grow to twenty feet or more. Varieties of *P. serrulata*, the Japanese flowering cherry, are most common. *P. serrula* is grown for slick mahogany bark. Average to light shade.

flowering plum (*Prunus*). Not for coastal Southern California. *Prunus blireiana* is perhaps the best of many with large pinkish flowers, purplish foliage. Grows to twenty-five feet. The purple-leaf plum, *P. cerasifera* Atropurpurea, is popular for its dark purple foliage. All are deciduous. Average shade.

Tabebuia impetiginosa.

FALL COLOR

These turn vivid colors in autumn. For maximum effect, plant them in front of something dark — another non-deciduous tree, a house, a fence. Shop for them in fall as leaves turn, since individual plants are often better than others of same kind.

Japanese maple.

Ginkgo biloba.

sweet gum (*Liquidambar styraciflua*). Tall, narrow trees to sixty feet, maplelike in appearance. Many have been selected for their fall color and named. Colors range from purplish to reddish to yellow. Round prickly seed balls are an attraction and a nuisance. Average shade.

sour gum (*Nyssa sylvatica*). Not for coastal Southern California. Pyramidal growth to thirty feet, irregular with age. Pretty bark. Glossy leaves turn scarlet in fall. Average to light shade.

pistache (*Pistacia chinensis*). In autumn, the most colorful tree in California. It turns brilliant shades of gold and orange, on the same tree. Grows to fifty feet in time. Bushy if not pruned into tree shape. Average shade.

Chinese tallow tree (*Sapium sebiferum*). Not for coastal Southern California. Shrubby growth to thirty feet, must be pruned into a tree. Leaves look and flutter like an aspen's, turn brilliant red, sometimes gold. Deciduous. Light shade.

Leucospermum nutans

Shrubs

Shrubs are seldom given enough thought, yet they determine the very shape of a garden and provide a background for everything else. Too often they become more of a burden than a blessing, choking walks, blocking doorways, hiding windows, or simply growing so big that they leave space for little else.

The basic problem is usually that there is not enough space allowed for each shrub. Many of the most common shrubs simply grow too big for the average garden. In recent years, growers have introduced smaller versions of these same shrubs, more in scale to modern gardens, and these are worth searching out. The lists that begin on the following pages concentrate on naturally small shrubs or varieties that don't require constant pruning to stay in bounds. There's nothing sadder than a handsome plant hacked into some unnatural shape just to keep it a certain size — all the beauty and grace are gone. There are, however, places where sheared shrubs are appropriate, so there is a list of clippable plants that make good hedges.

Shrubs are commonly planted too close together, in the hope that they will quickly fill in. Shrubs always look best if they're given enough room to grow to their natural size and shape, but this means planting them with a lot of empty space in between. Here, patience is required. Most shrubs will take a few years to grow up. Some are faster than others, but the fastest also tend to grow the biggest, so there are few shortcuts.

Shrubs are also planted too close to walls and fences. In this case, the hope is that they'll take up less of the garden, but there are better strategies, discussed at right. Traditionally, shrubs are planted around the perimeter of the property, for privacy or to screen some objectionable view. Or, they are planted all around the house in what are called "foundation" plantings, which often involve

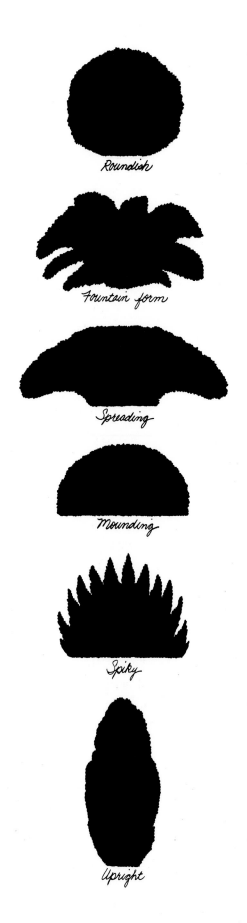

Roundish

Fountain form

Spreading

Mounding

Spiky

Upright

SHRUB STRATEGIES

Putting shrubs to work correctly requires advance planning. First decide where shrubs are really needed. Is there some view that must be hidden? This is the spot for a big shrub. How about the house? Shrubs keep houses cooler in summer if planted along south walls, or warmer in winter if insulating north walls. However, it isn't necessary to hide every square inch. Letting the house show here and there between plantings actually makes the garden appear larger. Don't plant shrubs directly under windows. Position them to one side so should they grow too big they will not obscure the view. Be careful near doors as well or you'll need a machete to get in and out of the house.

Don't plant directly under windows or too close to doors!

Don't plant in a row, plant by size. Distance from wall should be half the eventual spread of shrub!

Don't line all the shrubs up in a row. Let their eventual size determine how far apart and how far from walls or fences to space them. The distance from a wall should be half of the shrub's eventual spread, and from each other,

the sum of their half-spreads. That is, a shrub that will spread twelve feet and a shrub that will spread eight feet should be spaced ten feet apart, and six and four feet from the wall, respectively. Shrubs of course can touch, but they're most graceful if it is not by much. Shrubs are far more attractive if given the room they deserve, even if they take up more garden space in the process.

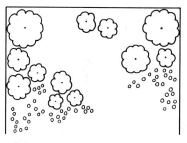

Don't fence the yard with shrubs. Use them to create a feeling of depth

The rule of never planting in a row is especially important for perimeter plantings. Shrubs planted all along the edge of your property will quickly make you feel boxed in. Plant a variety of shrubs: tall ones where privacy is needed, short ones that allow you to see all the way to the back of the property. Plant shrubs in the foreground as well, as in the drawing. It makes a neat background for flowers and also adds depth to the garden since the shrubs behind appear to be farther away than they are.

Hibiscus Brilliant

more ritual than reason. Again, at right are some better strategies for using shrubs.

In the lists that follow, shrubs that are special to California have been singled out. It's not that they can't be grown elsewhere (though some certainly can't) or that they're rare or uncommon (though a few are), it's just that they somehow seem to belong in a California garden, maybe even define it.

The Best Shrubs

PRIVACY PLUS

These grow as tall or taller than a fence. They can make a garden private or screen out unpleasant views. They also have unusually attractive foliage or flowers, a real plus. Be forewarned — all of these get as wide as they are tall, or wider, so don't plant too many or there will be little garden left.

Abelia grandiflora. Graceful, fountain-form plants with dark green foliage and white bell flowers late summer and fall. Grows to eight feet tall, six feet wide. Tolerates some shade.

Arbutus unedo Compacta. A five-foot roundish shrub with unusually handsome red-stemmed dark green leaves. Has white flowers and orange-red fruit too. Slow growing, stands some shade.

mirror plant (*Coprosma repens* Variegata). The shiniest of leaves, splashed with yellow. Grows fast, to eight feet tall, six feet wide. Upright. Easy to prune to shape and size desired.

cotoneaster. The tall kind, *Cotoneaster lacteus*, is the most common, grown for arching branches full of berries in winter. Stiffly fountain form. Foliage dull from a distance. Grows fast, to eight feet or more.

Wilson holly (*Ilex altaclarensis* Wilsonii). The best in California. Classic holly plant to six feet, lots of red berries. Upright.

pyracantha. Most kinds get big, to ten or more feet, have wicked thorns, concealed by narrow, deep green leaves. Berries, in shades of orange or red, are the reason to grow. Varieties of *Pyracantha coccinea* are best known. Upright.

Solanum rantonnetii. A big fountain-form cascading shrub growing to six feet tall and a bit wider. Looks best the first few years when it is covered with bluish flowers all the time. Fast.

marmalade bush (*Streptosolen jamesonii*). Southern California only. Grows to six feet or more in a rangy, roundish fashion. Covered with brilliant yellow and orange flowers most of summer and fall.

Xylosma congestum. Glossy foliage on arching branches make fountain form six- to ten-foot shrubs. Easily pruned into shape and size desired.

TALL AND NARROW

These too are good screens and backgrounds. They take up less space because they grow mostly up, not out.

bamboo. Many kinds grow straight up, taking up little more space than a fence. Avoid running kinds like the common golden bamboo (*Phylostachys aurea*) that can become real pests. Better bets are black bamboo (*P. nigra*, to eight feet with jet-black stems) and *Bambusa glaucescens* Alphonse Karr (to ten feet with green stripes on stems). These stay in neat clumps. Very vertical.

ginger. Southern California only. Several kinds, all vertical or leaning from fat underground stems. Exotic flowers. Shell ginger (*Alpinia sanderae*) is the most vertical, to twelve feet. *Hedychium gardneranum, H. flavum*, and the red-foliaged *H. greenei* grow to about six or eight feet, lean a lot. To keep clumps graceful, cut out stems in winter that bloomed the previous fall.

mahonia. The Oregon grape (*Mahonia aquifolium*) does best in Northern California, grows six to eight feet. The leather-leaf mahonia (*M. bealei*) grows anywhere in part shade to

The blue hibiscus,
Alyogyne huegelii

Nandina foliage in the fall

Solanum rantonnetii
cascading over a fence
and *S. jasminoides*,
a vine

Shell ginger

eight feet or more. Both have hollylike leaves, yellow flowers on top. Upright.

heavenly bamboo (*Nandina domestica*). Looks like bamboo, but much more restrained. Many kinds from eight footers to one- and two-foot dwarfs like the varieties Nana or Harbour Dwarf. Foliage changes color but doesn't fall in winter. Tolerates partial shade. Upright.

eugenia (*Syzygium paniculatum*). Does best in coastal areas. Grows upright to twenty feet tall, stays only four feet wide or less with pruning. Easy to shear into a tall hedge. Foliage reddish, turning deep green; pretty purple fruit. There are several dense, compact varieties (Newport, Globulus) even better suited as hedges.

laurustinus (*Viburnum tinus*). Upright shrubs to six feet tall by three feet wide. Dark green foliage, clusters of tiny white flowers, berries like little black pearls.

CLIPPABLE HEDGES

These can be sheared into a neat and tidy hedge. Note suggestions on how far apart to plant to get a solid hedge in a reasonably short time. Two pruning tips: clip often (once a month, even) and taper the hedge to make it narrower at the top so sun can reach the bottom. Unclipped, these are handsome, dense shrubs that tend toward vertical.

Japanese boxwood (*Buxus microphylla japonica*). Tiny oval leaves make this a hedge you can keep as low as you like, from one to four feet tall, in sun or part shade. Light almost yellow-green foliage. Space one foot apart. Roundish.

Natal plum (*Carissa grandiflora*). The variety Boxwood Beauty makes a tough two-foot-around hedge. Produces white flowers with a heady orange-blossom-like fragrance. Space eighteen inches apart. Roundish.

waxleaf privet (*Ligustrum japonicum*). The variety Rotundifolium makes a four-foot hedge (space three feet apart) while Texanum makes a six- to eight-foot hedge (space four feet apart). Glossy leaves, dense growth in time. Upright.

African boxwood (*Myrsine africana*). Small, dark green

BELOW: Feathery cassia

RIGHT: New Zealand tea tree

leaves with reddish stems. Very dense. Makes a two- to six-foot hedge. Space two to three feet apart. Roundish.

Pittosporum eugeniodes. Does best in Northern California. Makes a six- to sixteen-foot hedge. Wavy, light green leaves, not as dense as some. Space two feet apart. Upright.

ETHEREAL EVERGREENS

These have a certain light and airy look to them that sets them apart from more common shrubs that often appear as a solid chunk of green in the landscape. They are mostly from warm climates like Australia, and they grow in the casual, graceful way of plants that have never had to huddle up against the cold. Most are quite drought tolerant and are best grown with other plants that like little water. Try them with eucalyptus or melaleucas surrounded by a sea of gazanias. Or mix them with Mediterranean herbs like rosemary and lavender, or with California natives.

Acacia decora. Of the many shrubby acacias this is one of the prettiest and smallest, to eight feet tall and as wide. Fast grower with narrow, bluish leaves, spectacular yellow flowers. Roundish.

blue hibiscus (*Alyogyne huegelii*). Mostly sold as a hibiscus, but the resemblance ends with the flowers. Leaves are deeply cut, lacy. Growth is open, relaxed, and fast to six feet tall spreading to as wide as eight feet. Roundish.

feathery cassia (*Cassia artemisioides*). Graceful, spreading form, to six feet tall, eight feet wide. Silver foliage, yellow flowers. Grows fast.

Geraldtown wax flower (*Chamaelaucium uncinatum*). Grows loosely into a six-foot-tall by eight-foot-wide roundish mound of delicate, needlelike leaves. Pink flowers all winter, valued by flower arrangers.

breath of Heaven (*Coleonema*, usually sold as *Diosma*). Even wispier than the others with precious little pink or white flowers. Grows to five feet by five feet. Roundish.

Leucospermum nutans. Of the many fantastic and sometimes peculiar plants from the southern hemisphere, this is

FAR LEFT: Flame bush

Lantana Sunburst

the easiest to grow in gardens. Three feet tall by four feet wide, it blooms for months in winter, spring. Soggy soil is sure death.

LOWER THAN A WINDOW

How many windows in your neighborhood have disappeared behind a shrub that grew too tall? These will never obscure your view, though a few may peek in the bottom panes. None will grow taller than six feet, even ten years from now. This also makes them perfect in front of a fence, as a background for flower beds, or near trees. These are probably the most valuable-sized shrubs for general landscaping. Note that many are selected forms of shrubs that normally grow taller. Make sure you get these specific varieties, not the taller versions.

***Abelia grandiflora* Edward Goucher.** This variety stays under four feet tall by five feet wide. Graceful, glossy, compact, roundish. An elegant little shrub.

flame bush (*Calliandra tweedii*). Southern California only. Ferny leaves, flame red flowers most of the year. Grows to four feet tall by six or eight feet wide, but easily pruned lower. Spreading. Often looks ratty in cold winters.

Australian fuchsia (*Correa*). Several kinds with upright grayish growth to three or four feet. Pretty bell flowers in red (*C. harrisii*), chartreuse (*C. backhousiana*), pink (*C. pulchella*).

***Escallonia exoniensis*.** The variety Fraces (sold as *E. fradesii*) is a graceful, roundish, compact shrub to five feet with pretty pink flowers most of the year. Glossy, deep green foliage. Tolerates some shade. Even smaller are Red Elf and Newport Dwarf, to three feet.

***Gardenia jasminoides*.** The variety Veitchii is easiest to grow, roundish to four feet; Mystery is bigger all around, more difficult, roundish, to six feet in time. Both need a warm but not necessarily sunny spot in the garden, rich soil.

grevillea. Narrow, often prickly needlelike foliage on arching, spreading branches. Flowers unusual, some bloom in winter, others in early summer: *Grevillea* Noellii (pink and white), *G. juniperina* (yellow), and *G. rosmarinifolia* (red and cream). All grow quickly to five feet, a little wider.

hibiscus. Although most tropical hibiscus get big, these stay under six feet: Bride (white), Butterfly (yellow), Golden Dust (orange), Santana (orange-red), and Vulcan (red). All need good soil, fertilizer, ample water, some pruning.

lantana. Does best near coast. Grows two to three feet tall, spreading four or six feet. Flowers are often fascinating combinations of colors. Favorites are Confetti, Dwarf White, Dwarf Yellow, Sunburst, Tangerine. Very fast grower (full-sized in a little over a year), all bloom year-round.

New Zealand tea tree (*Leptospermum scoparium*). Soft, roundish shrubby growth, tiny black-green leaves. Small kinds like the variety Nanum (light pink flowers) grow to just two feet. Taller kinds such as Ruby Glow (deep rose) or Blossom (white with pink blush) grow to six feet. Blooms winter and spring.

pomegranate (*Punica granatum*). The ornamental kinds have spectacular waxy orange flowers, pretty fruit, and fall color. Fountain-form growth, light green leaves. Nana grows to three feet tall, Chico only two feet. The variety Wonderful is the big (ten feet) fruit producer.

***Rhapiolepsis indica*.** Most varieties stay under three to four feet, are spreading. New growth is reddish turning to dark green with clusters of white or pink flowers winter and spring. Dark berries follow. Fascination and Ballerina are two good varieties.

rosemary (*Rosmarinus officinalis*). Extremely fragrant needlelike leaves, grayish from a distance. Grows to four feet with blue flowers in winter and spring. Spiky. Looking very similar is *Westringia rosmarinus*.

LOW MOUNDS OF GREEN

Stacking flower in front of flower only works to a point, then a good green background is required to show the others off. These are low enough to plant in the flower garden with

Pittosporum crassifolium Compactum next to a full-sized *P. tobira* Variegata

annuals or perennials. As the others come and go, these remain constant. They can also break up the monotony of large expanses of low ground covers. Or they can be tall ground covers where a lot of ground needs covering.

Abelia grandiflora **Prostrata.** A variety that only grows to two feet by three feet. Mounding.

Natal plum (*Carissa grandiflora*). The variety Tuttle makes a tidy deep green mound to two feet tall by three or four feet wide. Green Carpet spreads as much, but grows to only eighteen inches.

dwarf plumbago (*Ceratostigma*). Several kinds, all low growing, to two feet, spreading. Sensitive to frost but will come back if nipped. Reddish-green foliage with blazing blue flowers in fall. Don't confuse these with the rambunctious pale blue plumbago mentioned later on.

rockrose (*Cistus*). Many species, hybrids, and varieties, all low growing to three feet, mounding. Dark green foliage, crepelike flowers in shades of purple, rose, and white. Keep on dry side for long life.

hebe (often called veronicas). Most have compact, tidy foliage and short spikes of white or purple flowers. The variety Coed (also sold as Lake) does best in Southern California, grows to three feet and as wide. Mounding.

Dwarf Burford holly (*Ilex cornuta* Dwarf Burford). Only two to three feet tall and as wide. Good berries. Leaves aren't prickly. Roundish.

Pittosporum tobira **Wheeler's Dwarf** (or Wheeleri). Dense, mounding growth that looks sheared. To three or four feet in time. New foliage light green turning to grayish green. Even denser, with a grayish cast, is *P. crassifolium* Nana or Compacta.

SHRUBS OR VINES

These three shrubs are difficult to pigeonhole. Left alone, they make big mounding shrubs. Or they can be trained like a vine against a fence or wall. All are champion chain-link fence covers.

Cape honeysuckle

pink powder puff (*Calliandra haematocephala*). Southern California only. Long, snaking branches, best trained against something. Grows fast to a ten-foot mound left alone. A very graceful plant with lovely puffy reddish-pink flowers in winter and spring. Spreading.

Cape plumbago (*Plumbago capensis*). Grows to six feet tall, sprawls to eight. Masses of pale blue flowers summer and fall. Butterflies love it. Chain-link fences will disappear beneath it in short time. Fountain form.

Cape honeysuckle (*Tecomaria capensis*). Left alone, an eight-foot-tall, and nearly as wide, shrub. Pruning will force upright growth, or train against a fence or wall. The brightest orange-red flowers, glossy, dark green foliage.

ANYTHING BUT GREEN

These have colored or variegated foliage that break up the monotony of an all-green garden.

Dodonaea viscosa **Purpurea.** Fast growing and big, to fifteen feet, with crisp purplish foliage. Roundish.

silverberry (*Elaeagnus pungens*). Wavy silvery leaves with brownish undersides. Grows to eight feet or more, but easily pruned smaller. Named kinds are best. Berries too. Roundish.

Euonymus japonica. Best in Northern California. Most kinds grown for variegated foliage. Glossy, thick leaves marked various ways with cream or gold. Most grow eight feet tall by six feet wide. Roundish.

Gold Coast juniper (*Juniperus chinensis* Gold Coast). A compact juniper growing to only two, maybe three, feet tall by four feet wide. Yellow-tipped foliage. Spreading.

lavender (*Lavandula*). Gray foliage and spikes of lavender to purple flowers. Several kinds, all to about two feet tall. Spiky.

Pittosporum tobira **Variegata.** Blue-green leaves edged with white. Grows to six feet tall by ten or twelve feet. Can be pruned smaller, but much more elegant given the space. Mounding.

LAWNS

Many grasses and one nongrass make up lawns. While each behaves differently and needs specific care, they can be divided into these groups:

Subtropical Grasses

These grasses, from subtropical climates, do their growing in warm weather, from May through October. In winter, they are dormant, and some turn quite brown in cold areas. They are generally deep rooted and need watering infrequently but thoroughly so soil is wet to one and a half feet. They should be fertilized once a month between April and October. Even if you only fertilize once, do so in May. These grasses can be planted from seed but are usually planted as sod, little chunks ("plugs"), or from bits of stolon ("sprigs"). Here are the choices:

common Bermuda grass. *If you simply want a serviceable lawn, this is it. By far the most common lawn grass in California, it is the easiest to grow. It spreads by stolons and can be quite invasive. Some people call it "devil grass." Once you've got it, it's hard to be rid of it, but you can keep it bound with edging. Where winters are cold it goes dormant and turns brown, but a common practice is to sow seeds of annual or perennial rye grass on top for winter green. Bermuda grass lawns can get by on almost no care, but they will look blotchy and rangy. To make them look their best, they need renovating every few years. Renovation is best done with a special machine that can be rented. It tears out thatch (the accumulation of dead stolons and grass) and gives grass a fresh start. Bermuda grass lawns are best cut low (one half to one inch).*

hybrid Bermuda grass. *Grown mostly in Southern California these are fancy, fine-bladed hybrids. They require more care than common Bermuda but they can be the neatest lawns of all. Santa Ana is the least refined but toughest. Tifgreen and Tifway are fine textured and low growing. All are usually cut very close to the ground, as short as one-half inch.*

St. Augustine. *Best in Southern California, this grass has wide, tall blades and stolons as thick as a pencil. It's invasive but easy to pull out of flower beds because it's shallow rooted. If it isn't, what you have is a close lookalike, Kikuyu grass, a noxious weed in coastal gardens. St. Augustine is tough and tolerates shade better than most grasses, but several pests plague it. It looks best with more frequent irrigation and it should be mowed high, to two inches. Occasional close mowing in late spring helps*

Lawns and Ground Covers

While trees provide height in the working garden, and shrubs depth, it is the role of ground covers to fill the expanses in between. In most gardens the ground cover is a grass lawn. Despite challenges from other ground covers, grass lawns remain the easiest, longest lasting, and most practical of ground covers — if you're willing to overlook a few faults.

In California, most lawns look a little ratty if they are not lavished with attention. Weeds creep in, patches don't grow as they should; in short, they never quite look like the plush lawns of wetter climates.

If you're willing to put up with this less-than-perfect state, lawns are easy to care for. All they demand is regular mowing and regular watering. They can even get by without fertilizer, but fertilizing in the spring and summer can make a lawn greener. In return for this modest care, a lawn provides a green growing ground cover that can be walked or played on. It's definitely the choice for anyone who likes to walk barefoot through the garden, or anyone with children.

So where do other ground-covering plants fit in? Here are some of their roles:

As a lawn substitute. If you are unhappy with the way your lawn looks or don't have any particular need for it, there are ground covers that look neater or prettier. They will need less water than a lawn (more about this later), but

Polygonum capitatum, Scotch moss and blue fescue

they will need just as much care. Instead of mowing, they'll require frequent weeding and in time will need replacing or cutting back because all ground covers eventually get too woody or begin to die out in patches.

For great expanses. In large gardens, there's room for a lawn and ground covers. Too much lawn makes little sense in California and is wasteful of water. This is what ground covers were developed for, and many of the best need a lot of room to roam.

On hillsides. Ground covers are the only answer here. Many are excellent soil binders and they grow low enough to protect hillside homes in brush fire areas.

For water saving. This ultimately may be the best reason to plant ground covers. Many, if not most, can get by on very little water, and some actually despise the stuff. Every year water becomes more precious in California, and in the not too distant future this may be incentive enough to plant ground covers instead of lawns.

As finishing touches. Many of the smaller ground covers can be used to fill in around other plantings or paving—wherever there might otherwise be weeds. In the small garden this is their most valuable role. The garden pictured here shows the possibilities. Several small ground covers make a gradual transition between shrubs and paving, filling all the voids. The light green patches are Scotch moss, blue fescue is the grayish grass, and the pink flowers belong to *Polygonum capitatum*.

keep thatch from building up.

Cool-season Grasses

These are grasses that make up the lush lawns of the eastern states. Because they are not fond of heat, they are difficult to grow in California, especially in the southern half of the state. They are susceptible to many pests and diseases and are easily invaded by weeds. Most are grown from seed, but they are better installed as sod (less chance of weeds getting the upper hand). They are called cool-season grasses because they do their growing fall through spring, just abiding summer.

bluegrass. Does best in Northern California, but some people in Southern California will never give up trying. There are many selected forms, usually sold mixed with other grasses—a good idea if one gets wiped out by some problem. Bluegrass has shallow roots so there's no reason to let the water run a long time, but it does need it frequently, once or twice a week. Best times to plant are fall and early spring; fertilize once a month during these seasons and mow high, about one and a half inches. In Southern California, they withstand summers better if watered every few days and mowed even higher.

perennial rye. This is tougher than bluegrass, which it is often mixed with. Selected forms, such as Manhattan, are often grown by themselves but subject to many of the same problems as bluegrass. Rust is a frequent problem. Extra easy to grow from seed. Otherwise, same culture as bluegrass.

fescue. Several kinds are usually included in seed mixes. Varieties of tall fescue, especially one called Alta, make tough, coarse lawns that need less water. Some new strains of fine-bladed fescue, Marathon is one, come close to being drought resistant, with deep root systems and blades as delicate as bluegrass. They look very promising. Mow high, to three inches.

Dichondra

Only those willing to dedicate their lives to a lawn should seriously consider this nongrass. Even though it is often found as a weed in other lawns, it is difficult to keep large areas looking good—many bugs eat it. Then again, few lawns look as lush when healthy. Plant in spring and early summer from seed, sod, or little chunks from flats. In full sun it seldom needs mowing, but requires frequent watering; needs light applications of fertilizer spring through fall. Weeds other than grasses are difficult to eradicate since selective broadleaf weed-killers also affect dichondra.

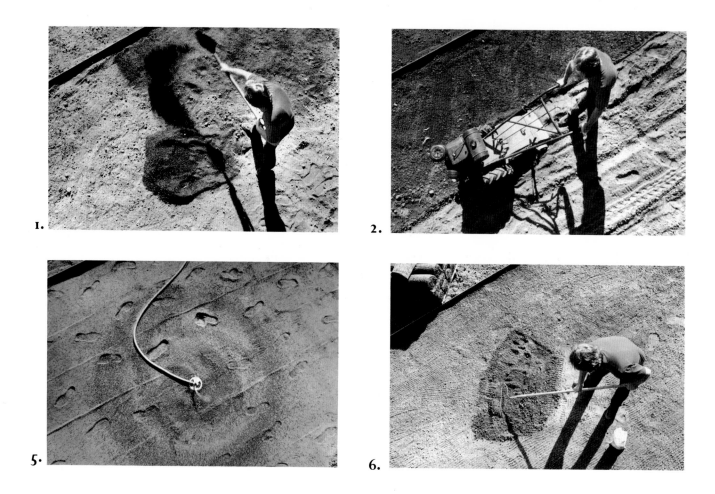

1.

2.

5.

6.

Sod: An Instant Lawn

Sod is an attractive alternative to starting a lawn from seed or stolons, and the reason is obvious: there's little or no waiting. A lawn grown in the traditional way takes at least six months before it will tolerate even a little frolicking. In the meantime, it is vulnerable to dogs, cats, weeds, children, falling leaves, erosion, and other discouraging incidents.

Sod, on the other hand, can be walked on just three weeks after being rolled out. During warm weather, when it establishes rapidly, sod will withstand a game of touch football in only six weeks.

Sod lawns are so successful it is difficult to recommend planting any other way. Lawns started from seed or stolons are less expensive than sod, but if you do the work, a new sod lawn is remarkably inexpensive. A typical lawn of one thousand square feet costs about $220 started from a box of seed. The same size sod lawn would cost around $450. The difference is the cost of the sod; soil preparation is virtually the same for both. This figure is based on an average cost of 25 cents per square foot for sod, though certain grasses can cost up to 60 cents per square foot.

Laying sod is no easier than planting seed or stolons; it's actually a little more time consuming. There are no shortcuts; sod cannot simply be laid on unprepared soil. The old lawn must be removed or the area cleared of weeds.

A sod cutter, which can be rented, makes this task easier. Sprinklers, a must in California, should be installed and drainage worked out. The new lawn must shed water away from the house. A slope of one inch per foot is desirable. It is also advisable to install edging to keep the lawn in bounds. Now follow these steps:

1. Amending the soil by adding organic matter is the most work but it is also most important. Water thoroughly the week before so dirt is easy to dig. Common soil amendments are processed rice hulls, redwood sawdust, or mushroom compost. They will open up the soil so air, water, and roots can penetrate. Best bought by the truckload, three cubic yards (cost: about $30 a yard) are required to cover one thousand square feet. Spread evenly, then sprinkle a chemical fertilizer on top. Twenty pounds cover one thousand square feet.

2. Tilling in the amendments and fertilizer is the next step. They must be worked into the soil to a depth of at least four inches, and preferably six. This requires a big, self-propelled rototiller, with cultivating tines in back. Easy to operate, one can be rented for about $65 a day including a small trailer. If the soil has been thoroughly watered the week before, it should be easy to cultivate. Make many

3.   **4.**

7.   **8.**

passes, letting the tiller dig deeper and deeper until dirt and amendments are completely blended.

3. Rake and level. Rototilled soil is fluffy and must be recompacted. Use a lawn roller or just stamp it down. Get the kids to help. Then start raking to remove stones and clods, leveling the area at the same time. The lawn should gently slope away from the house and be one inch lower than sidewalks or driveways. A large leveling rake available at rental yards for about $5 a day makes this job easier, but it can be done with an ordinary garden rake. Take your time. Be sure to get out all the rocks and clods.

4. Roll it flat with a lawn roller to compact the soil even more. A lawn roller can be rented for about $7 a day, though nurseries will sometimes lend one free of charge. Fill it with water from the garden hose to make it heavy. After rolling once, level off high or low spots with a rake, then roll again. (High spots won't get enough water and low spots will get too much.) The lawn will never look billiard-table flat, but give it a try.

5. Watering thoroughly is one way to help re-compact soil. Several days later, check for high or low spots. Then level with a rake. A thorough, deep watering is also necessary because it provides a reservoir of water that will work its way up through capillary action to nourish the new lawn. This irrigation should be done a week in advance so the soil surface isn't muddy when work commences.

6. Roughen the soil. Prior to laying the sod, scatter one more application of fertilizer, which is usually provided by the sod company. With a rake, work this into the top inch of soil. Leave the surface rough so sod can come into better contact with the soil. Sod will arrive on a wooden pallet that should be placed close to the work area. Each roll weighs about fifty pounds and is 18 by 72 inches (one square yard).

7. Roll out the sod by laying strips end to end. Push pieces together so there are no gaps between rolls, or the edges will dry out and turn yellow. Stagger the rolls, as shown, so the ends do not line up. Use a sharp knife to cut sod and never use a piece shorter than eighteen inches. It's better to split the difference and trim a little from the last rolls laid. Always finish each row with a full roll, putting the shorter pieces in the center of the lawn.

8. Quick, water! As you go, water by hand. After all the sod is down, compact with a lawn roller so it makes contact with the soil. Then turn on the sprinklers and ad-mire your handiwork. If it appears slightly yellow, don't worry. This is a temporary condition; it will turn green in a few days. Water every morning (more in hot weather) for the first ten days.

GROUND COVER GUIDE

Weeds. This is the single biggest problem with ground covers. Since it takes several years for woody kinds to completely cover, weeds are most common in plantings of these. The softer, carpeting ground covers fill in faster but tend to be more vulnerable to weeds in later years as patches die out. Two weeds in particular can be serious trouble — Bermuda grass and oxalis. If either of these are growing where ground covers are to go, get rid of them by spraying with the expensive but exceptionally effective herbicide Roundup (sometimes sold as Kleenup), or have soil fumigated.

The next step in weed prevention comes immediately after planting, even before you water. Spread a preemergent herbicide containing DCPA (dacthal) or trifluralin (treflan) on the bare soil between plants. These keep any seeds from germinating. Keep a constant eye out for weeds. Once they get started they are difficult to eliminate.

Mulches. A good thick mulch of organic material is the finishing touch, especially among shrubby ground covers (it is difficult to apply around small, closely planted ground covers). If it is three to five inches thick, it will stop most weeds, and it will prevent soil silting and compaction of soil on level or slightly sloping ground. On sloping ground, mulches are less practical.

Spacing. You can get the most mileage from woody ground covers by spacing them far enough apart so they just touch when mature. Most will have an undulating appearance when planted this way. Spaced closer together, they will cover ground more quickly and appear less bumpy, but they will also grow taller in time.

Small ground covers are usually planted from flats. Some of the smallest absolutely fill the flat and must be cut into little two- by two-inch sections; others can be separated into individual plants. Use the guide below to determine how many plants to buy. Flats usually hold sixty-four or one hundred plants. Some ground covers are sold in little plastic packs that hold six plants each. A flat of these little packs contains seventy-two plants.

Watering. Finally, watering new plants is always important, but ground covers planted from flats need extra attention because they have so few roots. Keep the ground moist for the first few weeks.

Spacing between plants	64 plants	72 plants	100 plants
6″	16 sq. ft.	18 sq. ft.	25 sq. ft.
12″	64 sq. ft.	72 sq. ft.	100 sq. ft.
18″	144 sq. ft.	162 sq. ft.	225 sq. ft.

The Best Ground Covers

WOODY GROUND COVERS

Most of these ground covers are actually very short shrubs. If you step on one it will break. What distinguishes these long-lived plants from ordinary shrubs is their ability to knit together into a homogenous mass, though some are more successful at this than others. They can cover large or small areas, and many are quite handsome planted as individuals.

manzanita (*Arctostaphylos*). There are several ground-covering kinds that are reasonably reliable, but like most native plants they do best on hillsides. Too much water will quickly kill them. All have beautiful foliage, distinctive reddish stems, and pretty clusters of bell flowers. None grows much taller than a foot. Plant them two to three feet apart. The following make denser, more weed-resistant growth than other kinds: *Arctostaphylos edmundsii* Carmel Sur, *A.* Emerald Carpet, *A.* Indian Hill, and *A. uva-ursi* Point Reyes. *A. hookeri* Monterey Carpet can be spaced as much as six feet apart.

silver spreader (*Artemisia caucasica*). Silvery foliage and fire resistant. Short-lived so best spotted between other ground covers on unrefined hillsides, little or no water. A few inches tall by two feet wide. Space a foot apart.

saltbush (*Atriplex semibaccata*). Another short-lived silvery plant best on unrefined hillsides. A foot tall spreading to several feet. Space two to three feet apart.

dwarf coyote brush (*Baccharis pilularis* Twin Peaks or Pigeon Point). Very tough, long-lived ground cover with a hint of gray. In time mounds to three feet high, but looks best if mowed or clipped back to a foot every few years. Great on hillsides, where it has some fire resistance. Space two to three feet apart.

Natal plum (*Carissa*). The variety Green Carpet makes a low, dense, dark green ground cover, to just a foot tall. Space two feet apart.

Bush iceplant growing
in rock wall

cotoneaster. Two kinds, both evergreen, do best in California. The bearberry cotoneaster (*C. dammeri*) seldom gets taller than a few inches, spreads to ten feet (space four feet apart); Lowfast, a hybrid, gets a foot tall, spreads to fifteen feet (space four to six feet apart). Both root as they spread, have nice red berries, look best in large areas.

Hypericum calycinum. Does best in Northern California. Grows a foot tall, spreads underground, can be invasive. Masses of yellow flowers. Space eighteen inches apart.

junipers. There are many spreading kinds to choose from, some growing no higher than six inches. Two six-inchers are Emerald Spreader (light green foliage) and Yukon Belle (silver gray). Popular foot-tall junipers include Sargent juniper (*Juniperus chinensis sargentii* — gray green), Shore juniper (*S. conferta* — bright green) and *Juniperus sabina* Arcadia (bright green). All can be spaced four to six feet apart, and there's nothing tougher.

parrot's beak (*Lotus berthelotii*). Best along Southern California coast. Soft silvery foliage and odd orange-red flowers. A good ground cover for large areas. Stays under a foot tall. Space two feet apart.

Myoporum parvifolium. A nice if somewhat ordinary dense, dark green ground cover that does best in coastal gardens. Grows fast, good on hillsides for fire resistance. Space three feet apart.

pyracantha. Mounding higher than other ground covers listed here, to two or three feet tall, the varieties Santa Cruz and Walderi stay the lowest. Space three to four feet apart.

dwarf rosemary (*Rosmarinus officinalis* Prostratus). Tough hillside ground cover but refined enough for gardens as well. Straggly at first, growing denser in time. A foot tall. Nice blue flowers. Space two feet apart.

lavender cotton (*Santolina chamaecyparissus*). The variety Nana is the best, stays under a foot. Most valuable for silver foliage; does well on hillsides. Yellow flowers are attractive but since they leave gaping holes in the plant when they finish, they are often sheared off before bloom. Space two feet apart.

germander (*Teucrium chamaedrys* Prostratum). A deep green, easily managed plant to six inches tall. Flowers are small, purple, on short spikes. Clip after bloom. Good on dry hillsides or in gardens. Space two feet apart.

star jasmine (*Trachelospermum jasminoides*). Viny growth that makes a loose ground cover just over a foot tall. Glossy deep green leaves, fragrant white flowers. Can be sheared after flowering. Space two to three feet apart.

SOFT GROUND COVERS

Many plants in this nonwoody group are grown primarily for their flowers; foliage is only so-so. Though most are perennials, they can't be counted on to live forever. As they die out they are simply replanted.

Ajuga reptans. Several named kinds with deep purple to deep green foliage. Just inches tall with spikes of purple flowers in spring. Mow after flowering. Watch for snails. Space six to twelve inches apart. Good in large or small areas.

Arctotheca calendula. Has gray-green leaves and masses of bright yellow flowers most of the year. Spreads by runners, grows only inches tall, gets nipped by frosts but recovers quickly. Best mowed every year in late spring, early summer. Needs little water. Space a foot apart. One of the best for covering large areas.

snow-in-summer (*Cerastium tomentosum*). Silver foliage, masses of white flowers in summer. Mow after flowering. Tough and spreading. Space one to two feet apart.

trailing African daisy (*Osteospermum fruiticosum,* also sold as *Dimorphotheca*). Has masses of flowers much of the year: try Burgundy Mound, Snow White, African Queen (purple, fading to white). Tangled stems make it best viewed from a distance. Grows a little over a foot tall, space two feet apart. Best on hillsides and over large expanses, though patches die out from root rots and need replanting.

Bush iceplant
(*Lampranthus aurantiacus*)

blue fescue (*Festuca ovina* Glauca). A blue-gray grass that makes neat ten-inch-tall clumps. Best in small areas because weeding is necessary between clumps. Space a foot apart.

wild strawberry (*Fragaria chiloensis*). The best is a hybrid: Number 25. Spreading plants with barely edible strawberries. Needs full sun, despite its woodsy appearance. Mow in spring. Space six to twelve inches apart.

iceplants. A bedazzling array of low-growing succulents. Most do best in Southern California, and the prettiest are further limited to coastal gardens. If you garden on the coast, don't miss the opportunity. Growing iceplants is as easy as falling down, just go easy on summer irrigation. They are first-rate fire resisters.

These are best for hillcovering:

white trailing iceplant (*Delosperma alba*). Foliage looks good year round, but flowers don't amount to much. Grows well inland. Space twelve to eighteen inches apart.

rosea iceplant (*Drosanthemum hispidium*). Low, spreading, sheets of glossy pink flowers. Does well inland. Space twelve to eighteen inches apart.

purple iceplant (*Lampranthus productus*). Long-lasting shimmering purple flowers. Space twelve to eighteen inches apart. Does well inland.

trailing iceplant (*Lampranthus spectabilis*). Solid flowers when in bloom; shades of pink and purple. Untidy foliage is the trade-off. Space twelve to eighteen inches apart.

These are best in smaller patches:

red spike iceplant (*Cephalophyllum*). In an imprudent shade of cerise, it makes spiky clumps that look like fat blades of grass. Does well inland. Very tolerant of cold. Space six to twelve inches apart.

yellow trailing iceplant (*Malephora luteola*). Nice foliage and flowers; tough too. Makes a happy compromise. Space a foot apart.

Trailing African daisy

Blue star creeper

bush iceplant (*Lampranthus aurantiacus*). Vivid yellow or orange flowers on foot-tall bushlets. Space a foot apart.

gazania. There are two distinct kinds. One grows in clumps; the prettiest flowers come on such gray-green plants. Aztec Queen, Copper King are favorites with big, fancy flowers. Do best in small plantings spaced a foot apart. Trailing gazanias, the other kind, make the best large-scale ground covers, have gray foliage. Flowers are smaller, less fancy though profuse, in yellow, orange, and white. Hybrids between these two groups have nice flowers, gray foliage, and are reliable in large plantings: Sungold and Sunburst are two. Space trailing kinds two feet apart. In time individual plants will die out and must be replaced.

Lantana montevidensis. This trailing lantana has lilac flowers most of the year. Mounds to a little over a foot and spreads very wide in time. A very tough plant. Space three feet apart.

knotweed (*Polygonum capitatum*). Tough enough to be a weed. Generally used in small areas. Reddish stems and leaves, pink, cloverlike flowers. Good in sun or under trees. Space twelve to eighteen inches apart.

spring cinquefoil (*Potentilla verna*). Woodsy looking but needs full sun. Bright green leaves and bright yellow flowers. One of the best ground covers for medium-sized areas that get water. Space a foot apart.

sedum. Succulent ground covers with small plump leaves and tiny flowers. *Sedum acre* is the greenest, daintiest; *S. dasyphyllum* is blue-green; *S. guatemalense* bronzy red. Used most often in small areas. Space a foot apart.

Verbena peruviana. Deep green foliage with colorful flowers in shades of red and pink all summer. Named hybrids are prettiest, stay under a foot, need regular watering. For drought tolerance, try the lilac *Verbena rigida*, which mounds to over a foot but remains graceful. Space two feet apart.

WALK-ON GROUND COVERS

None of these can actually be walked on like a lawn but they'll take occasional trodding. All are excellent between paving stones or where kids take shortcuts through the garden. A few are fragrant surprises if stepped on.

chamomile (*Chamaemelum nobile*). This is the toughest — some people have even made small lawns of it. Has fragrant, light green foliage, and tiny yellow flowers. With mowing it can be kept three inches tall. Space six to twelve inches apart.

Herniaria glabra. Very tiny bright green leaves that turn reddish in cool weather. Stays below two inches, can be mowed. Space six inches apart.

blue star creeper (*Isotoma* or *Laurentia fluviatilis*). Tiny leaves, cute light blue flowers. Stays under two inches. Looks best in sun but tolerates a little shade. Needs regular watering. Space six inches apart.

Corsican mint (*Mentha requienii*). Grows flat as a pancake with tiny light green leaves. Very fragrant. Space six inches apart.

Irish and Scotch moss (*Sagina*). Irish moss is deep green, Scotch moss almost chartreuse. Both look like moss, but aren't. Grow just inches tall, need moisture and full sun. Best in small areas. Space two- by two-inch chunks, six inches apart.

creeping thyme (*Thymus*). There are several low-growing thymes that are delightfully fragrant ground covers for small-ish spaces. *Thymus serphyllum*, most common, has dark green leaves, lavender flowers. Woolly thyme (*T. lanuginosus*) is fuzzy gray-green, a little more mounding. All grow about two inches tall, can be mowed. Space six inches apart.

Flame vine

Trumpet creeper
(*Campsis*) and
violet trumpet
vine (*Clytostoma*)

Bougainvillea
Camarillo Fiesta

Vines

Of all the plants in the working garden, vines are the most underutilized. Some people seem to fear that they will gobble up the garden when no one is looking, and there are a few that can.

But take the plunge. They can be pruned and snipped when they get out of line, even trained, but they shouldn't be too controlled because what vines do best is help a garden relax. Vines clinging to walls, blooming in the tops of trees, spilling from arbors, or twining through fences are nature at her loosest. The following vines are favorites, and are just a small fraction of those that thrive in California, especially in the southern half of the state. Unfortunately, what starts out as a bewildering selection, in theory, turns into almost none at all at the nursery. Even these vines are often difficult to find.

These will cling to anything, including stucco walls:
trumpet creeper (*Campsis tagliabuana* Mme. Galen). Big orangy-red trumpet flowers on big strong vines, deciduous in winter.
cat's-claw (*Doxantha unquis-cati* recently renamed *Macfadyena*). The name refers to the appendages it clings with. Bright yellow flowers, light green foliage, beautiful on walls. Gets big in warm areas, to thirty feet, needs cutting back.
creeping fig (*Ficus pumila*, also called *F. repens*). In youth a delicate vine that sticks flat to any surface, but in time growth changes dramatically into a house-devouring monster with large, leathery leaves. Most people pull it down before then.
Boston ivy (*Parthenocissus tricuspidata*). Glossy, maplelike leaves that turn colors in fall. Deciduous and vigorous, it can cover an entire building or fence, but doesn't get out of control. The variety Beverly Brooks is favored.

These cling by tendrils or twining so they need something narrow — a stake, fence slats, or trellis — to grab onto:

coral vine (*Antigonon leptopus*). A large vine growing to forty feet with sprays of coral pink flowers mostly in fall. Does best with heat, dies down in colder areas, but comes back.

evergreen grapes (*Cissus antarctica* and the more refined *C. rhombifolia*). Great fence coverers (especially chain link) with handsome foliage. Do best with some shade; the latter kind needs some help climbing. Both grow to fifteen feet.

Clematis armandii. This evergreen clematis does best in Northern California. Other common clematis fare less well. Pure white flowers with vigorous growth, to fifteen feet.

violet trumpet vine (*Clytostoma callistegioides*, usually sold as *Bignonia violacea*). Fast and strong, has pale purple flowers.

Distictus riversii. Grow in Southern California only. Deep green foliage and purple trumpet-shaped flowers. Grows to twenty feet by tendrils.

Carolina jessamine (*Gelsemium sempervirens*). Winter-blooming yellow flowers. Twines slowly, to twenty feet; needs tying.

Hardenbergia comptoniana. Slow grower, to ten feet. Tangling, twining, spare foliage with drooping spikes of lilac.

Guinea gold vine (*Hibbertia scandens*). Moderate, brittle growth to ten feet, handsome dark-green foliage, open-faced yellow flowers.

Mandevilla Alice du Pont. Grow in Southern California only. Has bright pink funnel flowers most of the year. Twines slowly, to fifteen feet.

bower vine (*Pandorea jasminoides*). Handsome glossy foliage. Alba has white trumpet flowers; Rosea, pink with deeper throat. Twines quickly, to twenty feet.

flame vine (*Pyrostegia venusta*). Fast growth, to twenty feet by tendrils. Orange tubular flowers in fall.

potato vine (*Solanum jasminoides*). Small white flowers all the time, lacy foliage. Fast to rampant growth, to thirty feet. Tolerates some shade.

Wisteria sinensis. Huge deciduous, woody vines, especially large and fast in Northern California, to sixty feet. Light green graceful leaves with violet flowers that hang like clusters of grapes. Twining.

These must be tied to a support or draped over something:

Bougainvillea. Many kinds but some are better vines than others. Look for long, arching stems at nursery. All need training, pruning. Very fast growth, to twenty feet. A few of the best are California Gold, James Walker, Mary Palmer's Enchantment, San Diego Red (also called Scarlet O'Hara).

lavender starflower (*Grewia occidentalis*). Best trained flat against a wall or fence. Spreads to ten feet, gets woody. Lovely little flowers most of the year.

jasmine. Several are trained as vines, including Spanish jasmine (*Jasminum grandiflorum*) and Italian jasmine (*J. humile*), but they come closer to being shrubs. Pinwheel or Angelwing jasmine (*J. nitidum*) climbs a bit. Blooms in winter and can cover a chain-link fence. The pink jasmine (*J. polyanthum*) climbs best and fastest, to twenty feet.

The Shady Garden

Azaleas and camellias find a home under a large
oak in the Glendale garden of Jack Nelson.
The azalea atop the pedestal is Redwing,
the white is Ivory Tower, and most of the
others are from the Glitters series.

UNDER A EUCALYPTUS TREE

Sometimes shade and even the fiercely competitive tree roots are not the reasons why nothing will grow. Big eucalyptus trees, for instance, actually poison the soils beneath them with a constant rain of leaves, bark, twigs, and capsules that contain a toxin designed by nature to inhibit the growth of neighbors. These toxins are washed out of the tree's debris and into the soil by rains. Tests by the University of California found that such toxins are potent enough to keep many plants from growing under, or even near, some eucalyptus — even if there is enough light, fertilizer, and water. It was also found that removing the litter helps. So a first step in gardening under a big eucalypt is to send the litter off to the dump — don't try to reuse it.

Many eucalyptus have deep roots and are no harder to garden under than any other tree, and some — E. citriodora, the lemon gum, for example — are easier. A few plants are known to grow well under big eucalyptus.

They can tolerate the competitive roots, some shade, and little water. Some of these are native to Australia (also home to the eucalyptus) and most of the rest come from a similar winter-rain, summer-dry, Mediterranean climate. All of these plants have been seen growing happily under the likes of blue gums (E. globulus), red gums (E. camaldulensis), and sugar gums (E. cladocalyx).

Two of the best plants to grow under a eucalyptus start out as shrubs but may become small trees, neatly filling the empty space beneath the tall crown of a big eucalyptus. The Victorian box (Pittosporum undulatum) and the California toyon (Heteromeles arbutifolia) will thrive with little or no care once started. Both have handsome glossy leaves and nice berries, sticky on the former. Several smaller shrubs also do well. Pittosporum tobira, Texas privet (Ligustrum japonicum), and the Australian tea tree (Leptospermum laevigatum) grow between six and eight feet and are readily available at nurseries.

Smaller still are various

Shade is inevitable in gardens. It is both a burden and a blessing; while few plants thrive in the shade, the ones that do are very pretty.

As a garden matures, trees get larger than was planned, shrubs soar and become treelike themselves, and soon there is very little sun to garden in. Many of these problems can be avoided, if trees are planted so their shadows fall on paved areas or the roof of the house, but more often they are inherited from a previous owner. Trees and shrubs can be pruned to let more light through, and some that were planted too close together should be removed, but full-grown trees and shrubs cannot be replaced quickly, so what you can do with the existing shade should be carefully thought out.

There are varying degrees of shade. Deep shade is the most difficult problem and to be avoided. Only a handful of plants will grow in dark shade, and even they would prefer more light. Deep shade is usually caused by dense trees that keep branches close to the ground. Again, thinning is one way of admitting more light, but sometimes it helps to simply cut off the lower branches so more light slips through. Deep shade is also a logical place for a patio or other paved area, which sidesteps the problem of what to plant.

Light shade is much easier to deal with, "light" meaning that some sun filters through whatever is directly above, or that if nothing is directly overhead but a plant grows in the shadow of something (as on the north side of a house), there is indirect light coming from the open sky above. Many more plants will grow in this kind of shade, and a few, famous for their flowers, actually require it.

The plants that create the all-blue color scheme pictured here thrive in this kind of shade. The daisy-flowered cinerarias, tiny blue-flowered forget-me-nots, and the pale lavender native iris grow between mature trees. They get no direct sun, but there is open sky overhead. On the previous

Cinerarias and forget-me-nots thrive in the shade

page, azaleas and camellias bloom beautifully directly under tall oak trees that are thinned every few years to admit more light. Growing with them are Japanese maples, which prefer a somewhat shady situation.

These plants and others in the lists that follow were not included in other sections of this book because growing plants in the shade is another ball game. Plants that thrive in shade — not simply tolerate it — are native to woodsy environments and require slightly different culture. Forest soils are usually full of organic matter — the decaying leaves from the trees above. As a result, woodsy soils are usually acidic, porous, and fast draining yet constantly moist. These are the keys to growing most of the plants in the shady garden.

To simulate this environment in the garden, add more than the normal amount of organic matter to the soil, so that the final mix is close to half and half. If the soil ends up higher than it was after adding all this organic matter, it will only help. Large quantities of organic matter will also help keep the soil moist and make it more acid. If plants must be fertilized, use an acid-type fertilizer. Most will need watering more often than other garden plants. Also, do not cultivate around these woodsy plants. They typically have roots very close to the surface.

rock roses (Cistus), several brooms (Cytisus and Spartium), heavenly bamboo (Nandina), rosemary (Rosmarinus), and one of the best, Australian bluebell creeper (Sollya fusiformis). And for drifts of color, try aloes, daylilies, geraniums, penstemon, and annual clarkia.

All of these plants are necessarily drought tolerant or they couldn't compete with the eucalypts' roots, but it is still important to carefully water for the first few years. Water often enough to compensate for what the eucalypt takes and thoroughly enough to encourage plants to send roots deep.

After a year or two, most of the plants listed above can do without irrigation but they'll grow and compete better if they have irrigations several times a year. Feeding occasionally also helps. And, most important, rake up and dispose of all leaf-bark-twig litter from the eucalyptus before rains or irrigations can wash toxins into the soil.

For the Beginner:

Swingtime. *Waxy red and milky white double blooms. Can be trained as an upright bush or grown as a trailing plant. Consistently voted the most popular of all fuchsias grown.*

Display. *Never-fail, saucer-shaped luminous pink single. Trailer or upright. Tolerates much sun and heat.*

Marinka. *Free-blooming, wine-red single trailer.*

Gay Fandango. *Lovely rose and soft pink semi-double. Can be shaped into perfect trailer or trained to cover a large trellis. Vigorous.*

Red Spider. *Crimson and rose single trailer with long recurved sepals. Profuse bloomer.*

Luscious Big Double Flowers:

Pink Marshmallow. *Huge pale pink blooms with a double skirted effect. Very showy trailer. Second only to Swingtime in popularity.*

Hula Girl. *Dazzling cream and rose-red blooms. Natural trailer. Best color in cool weather. Grows very well.*

Voodoo. *Deep purple and dark red upright (but can be trained for basket). Exceptionally striking pistil and stamens. Old favorite.*

Applause. *Huge blooms of waxy white and coral pink. Vigorous trailer.*

Quasar. *Stunning violet and snow white trailer. Free blooming.*

Personality. *Very large blooms of spirea red and bright rose. Trailer or upright. Old-timer.*

Lisa. *Breathtaking rich lavender and bright rose*

blooms. Prize winner.

Blue Ribbon. *Pink and cream large blooms. Trailer or upright. Dependable.*

Outstanding Midsize Blooms:

Pink Galore. *Candy pink. Best color with more than average light. Old favorite.*

Blush of Dawn. *Exquisite lavender and white ruffled flowers with very long pistils. Grow in basket or upright. Greatly admired.*

First Love. *Venerable orchid and white semi-double. Popular among fuchsia growers.*

Fan Dancer. *Orchid blue and waxy red semi-double. Easy to grow.*

Jack Shahan. *Prolific single rose-colored trailer. Heat resistant. Excellent.*

Small Flowers, Compact Growth:

Christmas Elf. *White and red single blooms. Miniature trailer. Perfect for small pots.*

Pink Jade. *Orchid pink with distinctive dark rose border. Upright or trailer. Very low-growing single.*

Papoose. *Dark purple and bright red semi-double. Trailer. Profuse bloomer. Heat resistant and easy to grow.*

Bluette. *Lavender blue and red small double upright. Oldie but goodie.*

Little Jewel. *Light purple and dark carmine. Upright single. New favorite.*

Sun-tolerant Fuchsias:

Gartenmeister Bonstedt. *Orange and scarlet single with tubular blooms in large clusters at ends of branches. Very vigorous upright.*

Amy Lye. *Coral orange and waxy white small single blooms. Upright.*

Fuchsias and Begonias

Fuchsias and begonias are considered together here because in many ways they are so alike. Looks alone suggest they should be planted together. Their colors, a little richer, a little deeper than other plants, are harmonious. The ancestors of today's fancy hybrids of both fuchsias and begonias originated in the cool moist mountains of South America, so both plants prefer similar conditions. They are grown in few places outside California, and even here they are grown mostly along the coast, where they thrive on the moist ocean air. Of the two, tuberous begonias are the more versatile in this respect, standing more heat and sun, but there are varieties of fuchsias that grow fine farther inland. There are also cultural practices that can help less sturdy varieties succeed.

Both plants do best in strong light but not direct sun, like that found under a tall tree, or on the north side of a house. They will also grow against an east-facing wall if a small projection of lath is added to the roof overhang. Serious growers build lath or shade-cloth covered enclosures that provide just the right amount of light. Inland gardeners often use mist nozzles controlled by a timer to provide the necessary humidity.

Fuchsias are usually planted in spring. They will bloom most of the summer, peaking in August, and into fall. Begonias are grown from round tubers purchased during the winter, or from plants found at nurseries in the spring. Begonia tubers are usually planted in flats of potting soil. They are barely covered with soil and kept moist, then planted outside in the ground or in baskets after they have grown some roots and several leaves. Begonias bloom from June until Thanksgiving.

Plants should be watered well and then allowed to dry out (but not wilt) before the next watering. Good drainage is essential for plants grown in the ground or in pots. Humidity can be increased by misting the plants and their surroundings early in the day, but be sure to allow begonia leaves to dry before evening.

A regular feeding program ensures continuous bloom

Tuberous begonia

and is absolutely essential if plants are grown in pots. The results can be startling. At least once a month apply an acid-based fertilizer formulated at full strength, or every two weeks use the fertilizer at half strength. Many growers use fertilizers high in nitrogen before buds appear, then switch to fertilizers high in potash and phosphorus with little nitrogen.

The worst pests of fuchsias are whiteflies and spider mites, both of which can be controlled with an all-purpose insect spray such as orthene. Begonias are occasionally affected by powdery mildew, which can be halted if caught early. Simply spray them with a captan-based fungicide such as karathane or funginex.

In late fall, as leaves yellow, slowly dry out begonias, then break off the top growth and store tubers in a cool, dark place until February planting time. Plants in pots can be stored away, pot and all.

In late winter or early spring, fuchsia growth made during the past year should be pruned back by as much as half, removing the twiggiest growth and branches that have become tangled. As new growth begins, pinch off the very tips to force branching and a bushier shape.

Fuchsias and begonias have one other thing in common — both are frequently grown in hanging baskets. Begonia tubers are usually labeled as hanging basket types or upright growers, and one cannot do the job of the other. Many fuchsia varieties can be grown in baskets or in the ground. These cascading types sometimes trail flowers in the dirt when planted in the ground but this can be discouraged at pruning time by concentrating on these lower branches. In hanging baskets, do just the opposite, pruning out branches that are too upright (if branches do not cascade enough, put clothespins on the ends until flowers weigh them down).

Tuberous begonias are seldom sold by name, only by color and purpose. For this reason they are not listed here. Fuchsias, available in far more variety, are always sold by name and are listed at right under some useful headings suggested by fuchsia fancier Mary Ellen Guffey and members of the Fuchsias Society. Under each heading the best are listed first, though there are no dullards here.

Fuchsia Blush of Dawn

Checkerboard. *Bright red and white single blooms. Upright. Favorite among fuchsia growers.*
Mephisto. *Small waxy crimson blooms borne in clusters. Tolerates sun except in warmest climates.*
Tangerine. *Orange and pink single upright. Best color develops in sun.*
Heat-resistant Fuchsias:
South Gate. *Pale pink doubles. Upright. Dainty but hardy.*
Mrs. Rundle. *Orange and cream singles. Trailer. Old-timer.*
Don Peralta. *Rose and dark red semi-double upright with large foliage. Vigorous.*
Indian Maid. *Royal purple and scarlet. Double trailer. Sepals long and recurved.*
Novato. *Salmon and white single trailer.*
Nonpariel (Lena). *Bluish purple and ivory pink semi-double. Good for espalier.*
Novelty Varieties:
Trumpeter. *Beautiful, large, orange and pink blooms with very long tube. Borne in clusters. Free blooming, striking.*
Mission Bells. *Rich deep purple and red blooms shaped like bells. Very attractive single upright.*
Nettala. *Dark red single upright. Distinctive spoon-shaped petals. Hardy grower withstanding heat, sun, and breezes.*
Golden Marinka. *Wine-red blooms. Prized for its variegated gold leaves with red veins. Trailer.*
Star Gazer. *Small rose flowers that face upward. Lovely small bush.*

New Guinea
impatiens

The Best Plants for Shade Gardens

BEDDING PLANTS

The list isn't long, but there are bedding plants that will grow in shade. Like most shade plants, these need light but not direct sun (don't count on them in dark entries, for instance). All are bread-and-butter nursery items or easy to grow from seed. Not all are annuals, but they're treated that way and replanted each year.

For Spring and Summer Planting:

bedding begonia. Newer kinds are unsurpassed for neat looks, handsome foliage (often reddish or flecked with white), and masses of flowers. Near the coast they are almost never out of bloom and can be counted on for color in the fall, and even into winter. Like impatiens, they are best replanted each spring.

coleus. Since they're grown for their multicolored leaves, pinch back tips to force more branching and cut off flowers to prolong the life of the plant. Most kinds grow two to three feet tall.

impatiens. In the last few years, exciting things have been happening to impatiens. Flowers are bigger and colors brighter on plants that are denser and more compact. Impatiens will last through the winter, but are best planted anew each spring. One of the best shade plants. New Guinea impatiens are a little different. Grown for fanciful foliage, they do best with a half-day of sun in the morning, light shade in the afternoon. They'll last several years in pots.

monkey flower. Sold as *Mimulus tigrinus*, but actually a cross between a Chilean monkey flower and a streamside California species, this has bright yellow flowers spotted with brown along foot-tall stems. Likes shade and moisture.

wishbone flower (*Torinea fournieri*). A bushy little foot-tall plant with purplish-blue pea-shaped flowers. Occasionally found at nurseries, or grown easily from seed.

LEFT TO RIGHT: *Scilla hispanica, Allium triquetrum, clivia, Aristea ecklonii, Iris japonica*

For Fall and Winter Planting:

Chinese houses (*Collinsia heterophylla*). This California native should be tried. Spikes of whitish snapdragonlike flowers on one- to two-foot stems have an airy, graceful look. Must be started from seed.

cineraria. Frosts will damage cinerarias, so they're best near the coast. They grow one to two feet tall with large flat-topped clusters of daisylike flowers in shades of purple and white. Inland, they are sometimes planted in March so they miss the frostiest weather and bloom before heat.

forget-me-not. The flowers are tiny but a perfect shade of sky blue. The foot-tall plants die down by summer but come back each fall from seed to nicely fill vacant ground.

Johnny-jump-up. While most pansies and violas like sun, this one (*Viola tricolor*) will grow in shade that is not too dark. It becomes six to twelve inches tall and has puckish little faces of purple and yellow.

primulas. In California, three kinds are commonly grown. Polyanthus or English primroses have clusters of multicolored flowers on one-foot stems. In the right soil, carefully guarded from slugs and snails, they'll last for years. Otherwise, plan on replanting yearly. The fairy primrose (*Primula malacoides*) is best for mass planting. It has airy clusters of white, pink, or lavender flowers on one-foot stems. *P. obconica* is less common. It blooms almost constantly through winter and spring in shades of white and lavender.

BULBS

Most of the bold and brilliant bulbs need full sun, but there are others, more delicate in appearance and color, that will thrive in the shade. The following can grow year round in shade under trees or man-made overheads, or on the difficult north side of a house. Botanically they're not all genuine bulbs, but their foliage is bulblike in appearance, with a similar tufty texture in the landscape.

Allium triquetrum. This member of the onion family not only survives in the shade, but also proliferates. Some call it a pest, though it's not really troublesome. The clusters of dainty half-inch flowers on sturdy eighteen-inch stems are china white. Leaves are narrow and willowy, and it dies back for the summer. Remove some of the bulbs in summer to keep planting from getting too dense.

Aristea ecklonii. True blue—not purplish—flowers are a rarity in the plant world, but aristeas have them on eighteen to twenty-four-inch branching stems. Flowers are about one inch wide. Not a true bulb, it forms large clumps of one- to two-foot pointed leaves, which last year round. It reseeds around the garden but isn't a nuisance.

Bletilla striata. It is actually an easy-to-grow terrestrial orchid from Japan, but so bulblike it's included here. Leaves—wide, pleated, and quite striking—die down for the winter, leaving only fat, tuberlike stems underground. The flowers are orchid or white on eighteen-inch stems.

Clivia miniata. The undisputed champion in the shade, it has been said clivias will grow in a cave. Year round, clumps of substantial straplike leaves; bold clusters of orange flowers in spring.

cyclamen. There are many but the best known is the florist's cyclamen (*C. persicum*) with large, almost coarse swept-back flowers in shades of lavender, pink, and white. The leaves are attractive, often mottled in shades of green. They wither in summer but resprout from fat tubers in winter. Other kinds are daintier, less reliable in the ground (safer in pots), but worth trying, especially *C. hederifolium* better known as *C. neapolitanum*. Some new intermediate types from Europe look very promising and more at home in the garden.

Haemanthus katherinae. A regal and expensive plant when it can be found, it has large wavy-edged leaves and spectacular reddish-salmon flowers on two-foot spikes. Haemanthus are most often grown in pots, dying down in winter when they should be kept on the dry side, and growing in summer.

Iris japonica. It is a mystery why this showy and reliable iris is so often unavailable at nurseries. Fans of sword-shaped

Japanese anemone

leaves lasting year round spread by stolons into large stands. Branching flower spikes are tipped with intricate flowers of white or faint blue with markings of bright yellow.

lily. Most lilies are better suited to colder climates, but every now and then a magnificent specimen in a garden here disproves this generalization. In the ground they seem to prefer high bright shade and a very rich and well-drained soil. A better place for lilies in Southern California is in pots, where they will return reliably for at least a few years. One word of caution: never let them dry out completely, even when dormant in the summer.

Scilla hispanica. While resembling the woodsy English bluebells, this scilla is much tougher. Short fountains of pointed leaves sprout from white bulbs. The flowers are blue, rose, or white on stocky stems about twelve to twenty inches tall. Just a few bulbs will produce a good colony in several years. It is most often sold as *Scilla campanulata*.

calla lily (*Zantedeschia aethiopica*). Often overlooked in the search for a shade-tolerant plant is the almost indestructible calla lily. It is considerably larger and more tropical in feel than the other bulblike plants mentioned here. Leaves are broad and arrow-shaped, eighteen inches long or more. Foliage lasts year round. The cup-shaped flowers are white, and appear throughout the year on stems up to three feet long.

PERENNIALS

Some of these are classic, die-down-for-the-winter perennials, but most are fairly permanent in the garden. Those that can stand dense shade are noted.

Acanthus mollis. Shiny dark green leaves are the attraction. Big, to two feet. White flower spikes to several feet, may die back temporarily after flowering. Very tough and good under trees.

Japanese anemone (*Anemone hybrida* or *A. japonica*). An unusually pretty plant with wispy white or rose flowers on three- to four-foot stems in fall and winter. Dark green

foliage spreads to form low clumps. Can be divided in winter after it dies back.

Aspidistra elatior. The common name of "cast-iron plant" is no joke. An extremely tough plant that shrugs off deep shade, minimum care. Long dark green leaves make clumps two feet tall.

astilbe. Best in Northern California. Has feathery flower spikes in shades of pink or white and delicate foliage spreading to form airy clumps. Divide every few years. Most kinds are hybrids from one to three feet tall.

begonia. Most are collectors' plants but common kinds of angel-wing and cane-stemmed begonias, or one named Richmondensis, are good, reliable, upright (to three feet) plants that do well near the coast. Most bloom year round, have pinkish flowers, reddish foliage.

bleeding heart (*Dicentra*). Graceful ferny foliage, little heartlike flowers, usually pink or white. Hybrids named Luxuriant and *D. spectabilis* are most used. Both grow to about two feet tall. Foliage dies back in winter. May last only one year in Southern California.

foxglove (*Digitalis*). A few are biennials, but others may persist for years in gardens. Tall spikes of spotted pastel flowers. Foxy is a good strain to grow from seed. Reaches three feet, blooms first year.

leopard's bane (*Doronicum*). Best in Northern California. Yellow daisy flowers on tall stems above spreading clumps of foliage. Divide every few years.

hellebore (*Helleborus*). The Corsican hellebore (*H. corsicus*) is the strongest grower, especially in Southern California. Fanlike leaves, odd clusters of greenish-white flowers. Most kinds grow under two feet tall, spread. Look elegant when not eaten by snails.

leopard plant (*Ligularia tussilaginea* Aureo-maculata). Large round leaves speckled with gold make a clump to two feet tall and as wide. Takes dense shade. Snail prone.

Rehmannia elata. Looks similar to foxgloves. Tall (to three

Foxglove Foxy

feet) spikes of rose or white flowers from a spreading clump. Should be divided every few years.

Cape primrose (*Streptocarpus*). Best along Southern California coast. Leaves form low primroselike clumps, produce many spikes of blue, lavender, or white tubular flowers. Easiest in pots, need very good drainage.

Vancouveria planipetala. Looks somewhat like a maidenhair fern, with lots of small leaves on dark, delicate stems and sprays of tiny flowers.

GROUND COVERS

Most of these will compete with tree roots, where ground covers that tolerate shade are most needed. Perform best in small areas.

Ajuga reptans. Several named kinds with deep purple to deep green foliage. Just inches tall with spikes of purple flowers in spring. Mow after flowering, watch for snails. Space six to twelve inches apart. Good for large or small areas.

spider plant (*Chlorophytum comosum*). This popular house plant is a tough ground cover with a grassy appearance. Space one to two feet apart.

Duchesnia indica. Looks like a strawberry, fruit and all. Great under trees, even oaks. Tough, but, alas, inedible. Space one foot apart. Good for large areas.

English ivy (*Hedera helix*). A tough, reliable ground cover, if uninteresting. Good under trees, for large or small areas. Space one foot apart.

Lamium maculatum **Variegatum.** Attractive light green leaves splashed with cream and silver. Space one to two feet apart. Best in small areas.

liriope and **ophiopogon.** Two groups of grasslike plants that are actually lily relatives. Grow as tufts with nice flower spikes. Several kinds from six inches to two feet tall, including black-leaved and variegated forms. Space six to twelve inches apart.

Pachysandra terminalis. Best in Northern California. Hand-

A big bird's nest fern grows with black bamboo and the equally black mondo grass (*Ophiopogon planiscapus* Nigricans)

some green foliage, small fragrant flowers. Stays under a foot tall. Space six to twelve inches apart.

strawberry geranium (*Saxifraga stolonifera*). Round variegated leaves with spikes of tiny starry flowers. Best in small areas. Space one foot apart.

baby's tears (*Soleirolia soleirolii*). Tiny leaves form cushiony mounds or solid mass. Crushes easily but nice between paving stones or other small areas. Space chunks six inches apart.

piggyback plant (*Tolmiea menziesii*). More often used as a houseplant, this native is also good in the garden. Hairy bright green leaves will cover small areas. Grows a foot tall. Plant two feet apart.

Vinca major. A weed in Northern California, slow to become established in Southern California. Trailing stems of dark green leaves, light blue flowers. Good on slopes, sometimes invasive. *Vinca minor* is a miniature version that is less rambunctious. Space one foot apart.

Australian violet (*Viola hederacea*). Tiny round leaves stand about three inches high with little white flowers held higher. Spreads fast in good soil to become a dense ground cover.

FERNS

The shady garden wouldn't look right without ferns, though most actually grow fine out in the sun. There is endless variety but here are some of the best, because they are among the easiest to grow. Most actually prefer bright light — dense shade is not to their liking. They also prefer a loose, airy soil that is moist but not soggy, though some stand drought.

maidenhair (*Adiantum*). The most graceful with a filmy, breezy appearance. One, *Adiantum raddianum*, also sold as *A. cuneatum*, is surprisingly tough, thriving along concrete walks where it seems to draw something it needs from the cement. It does best in Southern California, while a look alike, *A. capillus-veneris*, does fine in the north. *A. hispidulum* looks like

the cherished five-finger fern of the redwood forests, but is much easier to grow. All grow about one foot tall.

mother fern (*Asplenium bulbiferum*). A lacy, light green clump to about three feet. Many fernlets grow along fronds.

bird's nest fern (*Asplenium nidus*). In its native tropics, this elegant fern grows in treetops. In coastal Southern California, it does very well in loose, airy ground, growing to four or five feet tall.

hammock fern (*Blechnum occidentale*). Forms a foot-tall ground cover in moist soil. New growth is reddish. Nice among other shade plants because fronds grow upright.

holly fern (*Cyrtomium falcatum*). Glossy, leathery leaves look like holly. Grows two to three feet tall.

lace fern (*Microlepia strigosa*). Bright green ferny growth to three feet tall, spreading to form large clumps. Tough enough to be a ground cover.

sword fern (*Nephrolepis exaltata* or *N. cordifolia*). Rampant growth in good soil, but easy to pull out. Three-foot fronds grow mostly upright. Similar but stiffer in appearance is *Polystichum monitum*, growing to four feet and best in Northern California.

Japanese lace fern (*Polystichum setosum* or *P. polyblepharum*). Fuzzy fronds with a rusty cast make a two- to three-foot clump. Tidy appearance.

Australian brake (*Pteris tremula*). Forms a typical bracken thicket of handsome foliage with fronds two to three feet long. Very tough.

leather fern (*Rumohra adiantiformis* or *Aspidium capense*). A tough, durable fine-textured fern, growing two or three feet as a slowly spreading clump.

chain fern (*Woodwardia fimbriata*). A big wild-looking fern to four or more feet. Tough but very graceful in a woodsy setting.

tree ferns. The Tasmanian tree fern (*Dicksonia antarctica*) takes years to become tree sized, though it can reach ten feet tall. In the meantime its fronds reach wide, need ten or

Abutilon hybrid with bamboo

BELOW: Kurume azalea Rose
Glitters

twelve feet to grow in. The Australian tree fern (*Sphaerop-teris cooperi* or *Alsophila australis*) grows much faster, to twenty feet in as many years, with lighter green, even longer fronds (each one can be eight, even ten feet long). Young plants are deceptively small. Both need lots of room, though in time they are tall enough to plant under.

SHRUBS AND SHRUB-SIZED PLANTS

Some very pretty and popular shrubs grow in the shade, including camellias and azaleas. Don't overlook fuchsias, many are first-rate shrubs on the coast. Most of these are especially useful against the north or east side of a house.

abutilon. Some are handsome upright shrubs, others are rangy, can be trained against a fence or wall, even into a little tree. Most kinds are hybrids with very pretty hanging hibis-cuslike flowers, maplelike leaves. Can grow to six or more feet. Bloom in spring, early summer, then again in fall and winter. Rose systemic insecticides can control whiteflies; watch for scale insects.

Aucuba japonica. Grows slowly in deep shade to six or more feet. Handsome large glossy leaves. There are green-leaved varieties and variegated kinds.

azalea. The evergreen kinds do best in California. There is a limitless selection, though named varieties from these groups are most common: Belgian Indica and Rutherfor-diana azaleas bloom the earliest (October to March), are

sold as florists' plants and may have large double flowers. Next come Kurume azaleas (March to May), more graceful plants with smaller flowers in greater quantities, and the giant-flowered Southern Indicas, sometimes called "sun azaleas" but best in some shade—the favorites in Southern California. Finally, from May to June come the Macrantha or Satsuki azaleas, with mid-sized flowers and unusually low growth. Even more than most shade plants, azaleas need a fluffy soil that is at least half organic amendments and half existing soil. Peat moss is the preferred amendment because it holds water longer and is acid. In Southern California it's a good idea to mound or raise azalea beds several inches to speed drainage. Most azaleas will spread to three or four feet, and as high. Cut off errant, overly long branches. They should be fertilized several times between end of flowering and fall with an acid-type fertilizer.

Brunfelsia pauciflora. The variety Floribunda is common-ly called "yesterday-today-and-tomorrow" because purple flowers quickly change to white. Handsome glossy dark green foliage grows to ten feet. The variety Macrantha is much smaller but with bigger leaves, lax growth, and large lavender flowers.

camellia. Unquestionably the best shrub to plant against a north or east-facing wall, and one of the best shrubs to grow under tall trees. The first to bloom are the Sasanqua camel-

Sasanqua camellia Misty Moon

lias (fall and early winter), generally with smaller, less complex flowers, stiffer growth. There are some valuable ground-covering kinds that grow to just several feet but spread; some varieties are easy to train against walls. Japonica camellias bloom next (early spring). These have large, complex, usually double flowers. Most grow upright, eventually into little trees. Overlapping but trailing a little later in the season are the huge-flowered, lanky, and less densely foliaged Reticulata camellias. All camellias require care similar to that for azaleas, though they're not so fussy once established. Amend soils with organic matter, then plant so the top of the root ball is a little higher than surrounding soil. Fertilize several times between end of flowering and fall.

Cantua buxifolia. A good plant to trellis since growth is straggly. Flowers are spectacular, cerise striped with yellow, blooming most of the year. Grows to six feet tall.

cocculus. Thick shiny dark green leaves on a large slow-growing fifteen-foot shrub. Pruning keeps it small. Tolerates dense shade.

Daphne odora. Stubbornly difficult plant, nearly impossible in Southern California, but sultry fragrance keeps people trying. Tidy but brittle growth to four feet. Thick, glossy, sometimes variegated foliage, pink flowers. Needs fluffy, fast-draining soil. Little water in summer.

Japanese aralia (*Fatsia japonica*). A tough plant with large, lush, tropical-appearing leaves. Grows to six feet.

Griselinia lucida. Large deep green leaves on a six- to ten-foot shrub. There is a variegated variety with white markings on leaves.

heliotrope (*Heliotropium arborescens*). Soft sweet fragrance is the reason to grow. Otherwise a rangy grower to four feet tall by six feet wide in time. Purplish leaves, deep violet flower clusters.

hydrangea. The common garden kind (*H. macrophylla*)

makes a big round bush to eight feet but is usually pruned yearly to a four-foot ball. Most have pink or pinkish white flowers that turn blue in acid soil. Spread aluminum sulfate around plant as buds form to turn them blue. In Northern California nurseries carry other, more graceful hydrangeas, including the airy lace-caps. All are deciduous. Prune in winter, water well in summer.

Loropetalum chinense. A tidy elegant shrub to five feet in time. Nice white flowers that look curled. Needs lots of water.

Osmanthus fragrans. A versatile plant that can be clipped or trained into any shape or use. Good green foliage, tiny fragrant flowers. Can grow to ten feet.

Philodendron selloum. Big three-foot glossy leaves on a plant that eventually tries to climb, leaving bare stems behind. Can be trained up trees for a decidedly tropical look.

TREES OR TREE-SIZED PLANTS

There's often room under tall trees for a second-story tree, which of necessity must be small (this role is often filled by shrubs that have grown up with the tree to be tree-sized themselves). Another role for these few shade-tolerant trees is in narrow spaces between buildings where the sun seldom shines. Japanese maples, *Arbutus unedo*, and *Ficus benjamina* are three of the best in either role. They are described on page 105. New Zealand laurel (*Corynocarpus laevigata*), best near the coast, makes a neat ball of green to twenty or thirty feet in time. It should be purchased as a small tree with trunk or it will stay bushy for years. Of similar size and shape, but with hollylike leaves, is manzanote (*Olmediella betschlerana*).

Three tree-sized plants that grow very vertically and look tropical are *Pseudopanax lessonii* (to twelve feet), *Schefflera actinophylla* (to twenty feet, Southern California only), and the very similar *Tupidanthus calyptratus.*

Garden hydrangea

Australian violet

139

RADISH

5¢

LOS ANGELES SEED CO.

EGGPLANT

10¢

LOS ANGELES SEED CO.

LOS ANGELES MARKET

LETTUCE

10¢

Seeds

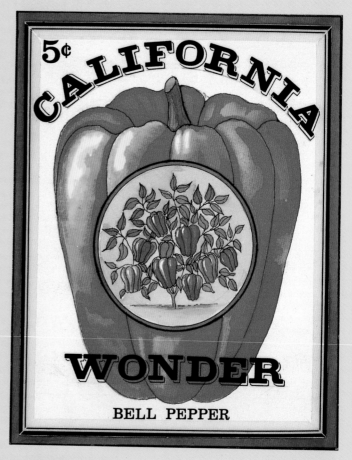

5¢

CALIFORNIA

WONDER

BELL PEPPER

The Kitchen Garden

The Kitchen Garden

In the kitchen garden you can eat what you grow, when it's at its sweetest and absolute freshest. When you pull that first carrot from the ground and the soil falls away to reveal a crunchy orange root, you have just begun . . . you can then go on to raise seasonings that make that carrot come alive in the kitchen. You can grow fruits and berries to juicy-ripe perfection. You can plant only the most savory varieties and harvest nothing before its time. And you can do it all in surprisingly little space.

The adventure begins when you choose what to grow. In this chapter many fruits and vegetables for starters are suggested, but more important we list the specific varieties of each we have found to be best, in the garden and on the table. These specific varieties won't be found at markets, nor are you likely to find them on seed racks at nurseries. You will probably have to order from one of the catalogues listed at right if it's a vegetable, or visit several nurseries to find just the right fruit tree. Some varieties are distinctly superior to others, first because they are better suited to California's climate and soils, and second because they are simply more savory. Sometimes the best is also the newest, maybe one that has received the coveted All-America Award after proving itself in test gardens around the country, but often it is an older, almost forgotten variety that comes out tastiest and on top.

Singled out are those varieties that are "early" or are space-savers. Early varieties of vegetables mature faster so they spend more time producing and less simply getting there. Early varieties of fruit trees produce crops earlier in the season, so if you plant an early variety, one that ripens mid-season, and one that ripens late, you have fruit over a longer period of time.

Early varieties of vegetables conserve space since they occupy the ground for a shorter period of time but there are also varieties that produce more in the same amount of space, or actually occupy less space. There are space-saving fruit trees too that grow much smaller than normal.

You can also save space by starting certain vegetables in small pots or in flats and then transplanting them into the garden. While they're getting started in life, other vegetables have a chance to finish up. Generally, vegetables should be started four to six weeks prior to when they are to be planted out into the garden. You can start them indoors from seed in a sunny window but they'll be sturdier started outdoors in a mostly sunny location. Raised indoors seedlings will be a little lanky and pale, and when it comes time to move them outside you must do so gradually, first setting them in partial shade and then giving them a little more sun every few days until they can stand a full day's worth. Outdoors the principal problem is making sure they are kept watered.

If there is simply no space in your garden for traditional vegetable beds or orchardlike rows of fruit trees, don't overlook the ornamental value of fruits and vegetables. Peppers, eggplants, and chard can hold their own and be grown right in there with flowers. And there are fruit and nut trees, like apricots and macadamias, that can double as respectable shade trees.

The Perfect Plot

Space is undoubtedly the most important consideration in gardens today. This complicated little garden plan packs a lot of vegetables, and even a few annual herbs, into a small area — only twelve by twenty feet. Followed literally, it is a nearly perfect plan, but it also contains lots of good planning and planting ideas that can be applied to any size garden.

In it vegetables are much closer than is normally recommended because the soil is intensively improved. And it uses some special vegetable varieties that consume less space. For instance, the Dusky Hybrid eggplant produces as many as thirty fat fruits; older varieties may only produce five or six. And the Sweet 'n Early cantaloupes produce lots of small fruits that are light enough to be trained up in the air on a trellis, which saves as much as thirty square feet, the space they'd take if they sprawled on the ground.

This garden must be located where it gets a full day of sun, year round — it simply won't work if it gets more than one hour of shade per day. You may have to cut down a tree or tall bush, but find or create that sunny place. Note that the garden is oriented to the south, with most rows running east to west and all of the tall vegetables planted along the north edge so they don't shade the smaller ones.

The garden is shown in two seasons: fall-winter and spring-summer. These are the two major planting times in California, and each has its own distinctive vegetables that grow best during one season or another (though there are a few vegetables that grow year round). The garden is divided into seven separate raised beds — the best way to grow vegetables in a small area. They are not raised very high, only a few inches, but they are much easier to work in and to water. By planting vegetables with similar watering needs in each bed, you can better control how much each kind gets. Lettuce for example needs frequent shallow irrigations,

SEED SOURCES
These seed companies carry a general assortment of vegetable seed, including most of the varieties recommended in this chapter:
W. Atlee Burpee Co., *Warminster, Pennsylvania 18974*
Gurney's Seed and Nursery Co., *Yankton, South Dakota 57079*
Geo. W. Park Seed Co., *Greenwood, South Carolina 29647*
R. H. Shumway Seedsman, *Box 777, Rockford, Illinois 61101*
Stokes Seeds, Inc., *Box 548 Buffalo, New York 14240*
Otis Twilley Seed Co., *Box 65, Trevose, Pennsylvania 19047*
These seed companies specialize in certain hard-to-find vegetables or varieties mentioned in this chapter:
Exotica Seed Co. *1742 Laurel Canyon Blvd., Los Angeles, California 90046 (Mexican and South American vegetables and fruits, tropicals)*
Farmer Seed and Nursery Co., *818 NW Fourth St., Faribault, Minnesota 55021 (vegetables and varieties for northern climates)*
H. G. Hastings Co., *Box 4247, Atlanta, Georgia 30302 (vegetables and varieties for southern climates)*
Kitzawa Seed Co., *356 W. Taylor St., San Jose, California 95116 (Chinese and Japanese vegetables)*
Le Jardin Gourmet, *Box 139, West Danville, Vermont 05873 (French vegetables and varieties)*
Nichols Garden Nursery, *1190 N. Pacific Coast Hwy., Albany, Oregon 97321 (herbs and rare vegetable varieties)*
Redwood City Seed Co., *Box 361, Redwood City, California 94064 (vegetables from Europe, the orient, old-fashioned American varieties, Southwest Indian varieties, and herbs)*
Taylor's Garden, Inc., *1535 Lone Oak Road, Vista, California 92083 (herbs — live plants and seeds)*
Tsang and Ma, Inc., *1306 Old County Road, Belmont, California 94002 (Chinese vegetables)*

while tomatoes, with roots up to five feet in the soil, must be watered more thoroughly but also less often. With vegetables planted this close together, it is also a good idea to feed a little more frequently.

You can use two- by six-inch redwood or pressure-treated lumber to enclose the beds, leaving three inches above the ground. The narrow paths in between are just large enough to give you easy access to every row of vegetables so there is no need to step inside the bed and get your feet muddy. Cover the paths with leaves or garden debris, or leave the paths plain dirt.

Raised beds aren't as practical for large gardens because they are expensive to build and relatively inflexible, but in small spaces they let you garden intensively and are worth the investment. Thoroughly prepare the soil *before* building the beds, remembering that the roots will grow under the paths. Then construct the beds and steal a little improved soil from the paths to add inside the beds, so the soil is a trifle higher inside than outside. This helps drainage.

Build the tomato cages as described later under tomatoes, then build the two trellises using the same wire mesh material. Use ten-foot-tall, four-by-four redwood or pressure-treated posts, burying them three feet underground. Then nail on eighty-four-inch-wide (seven foot) concrete reinforcing screen (available at building-supply yards). This mesh is very sturdy and has six-inch openings between the wires, which makes it easy to reach through when picking vegetables.

It's now time to plant. This garden will last for years, but remember to improve the soil a little each time you replant and to move some of the crops to different beds from time to time so diseases that may build up in the soil don't become a problem. Tomatoes and broccoli should never be planted two years in a row in the same spot.

SCARECROWS?

Some people insist they work, others are just as convinced they don't, but most likely it depends on how lifelike a scarecrow looks. This one, by Dawn and Max Navarro, worked. It kept sparrows, jays, and crows away from fruits and vegetables that had been plagued the year before, probably because it looks so human. In fact, it was modeled after the Navarro's daughter, Heather.

The frame for the scarecrow is a simple cross made from 2- by 4-inch lumber. An outgrown pair of size 8 overalls was the inspiration for the body and the head is a pillowcase stuffed with straw. Pigtails were braided from sea grass, the bangs are more hay. The hat was nailed on top to keep everything else in place.

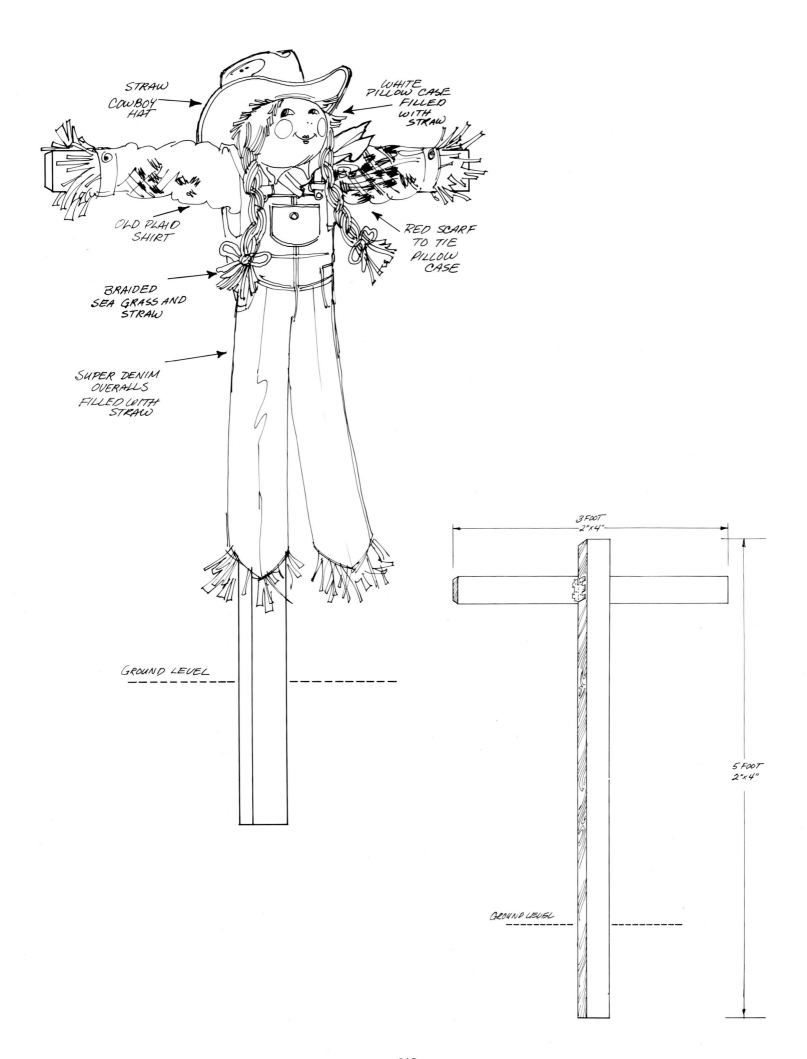

STRAW
COWBOY
HAT

WHITE
PILLOW CASE
FILLED
WITH
STRAW

OLD PLAID
SHIRT

RED SCARF
TO TIE
PILLOW
CASE

BRAIDED
SEA GRASS AND
STRAW

SUPER DENIM
OVERALLS
FILLED WITH
STRAW

GROUND LEVEL

3 FOOT
2"x4"

5 FOOT
2"x4"

GROUND LEVEL

THE FALL-WINTER GARDEN

Most of these vegetables prefer to grow during cool weather and are planted as the summer garden fades, from mid-September through February or even March.

Bed 1. Few cool-season vegetables can be considered tall, but Brussels sprouts come close, growing to at least three feet. Here the best variety, Jade Cross E, grows on the north edge with room for six plants spaced eighteen inches apart, which can yield as many as five hundred sprouts.

Bed 2. Broccoli and cauliflower grow together here; there are seven of each, spaced about eighteen inches apart. The De Cicco variety of broccoli was chosen because it continues to produce side shoots after the main crop.

Bed 3. Four cabbages spaced eighteen inches apart, and six plants of pak choy spaced a foot apart grow together in this bed. There are two kinds of cabbage, Ruby Ball, which resists hot spells, and the extra tasty Early Jersey Wakefield. Both require lots of water.

Bed 4. A bed of thirsty greens contains five collard plants and five of kale, all spaced ten inches apart. Spinach gets a row to itself, since it doesn't go too far when cooked. There are eighteen plants spaced just six inches apart.

Bed 5. Peas of various kinds grow on the trellisés. In back is a row of forty-eight garden peas spaced two inches apart. Green Arrow and Lincoln have a few more peas per pod, yielding about one and a half pounds of shelled peas total. In front, the versatile Sugar Snap pea gets half the trellis, and Oregon Sugar Pod snow peas get the other half. There are twenty-four of each, spaced two inches apart. Expect about twelve pounds from Sugar Snap, since they are eaten pods and all, and about twelve quarts from the snow peas (they don't weigh much). In between the trellises, grow a quick row of fifty radishes, which will mature before the peas shade them out.

Bed 6. If you're going to try a crispy head lettuce, give it a bed to itself and lots of space so those big heads have room to develop. Space plants eighteen inches apart. A new type named Mission looks to be easier to grow than others.

Bed 7. Everything growing here is a root or bulb crop. Rows are about a foot apart, and there are leeks and garlic in the back row (sixteen of each spaced two inches apart), then onions (thirty-five, spaced three inches apart), carrots (fifty, spaced two inches apart), and finally parsnips (twenty-five, spaced four inches apart).

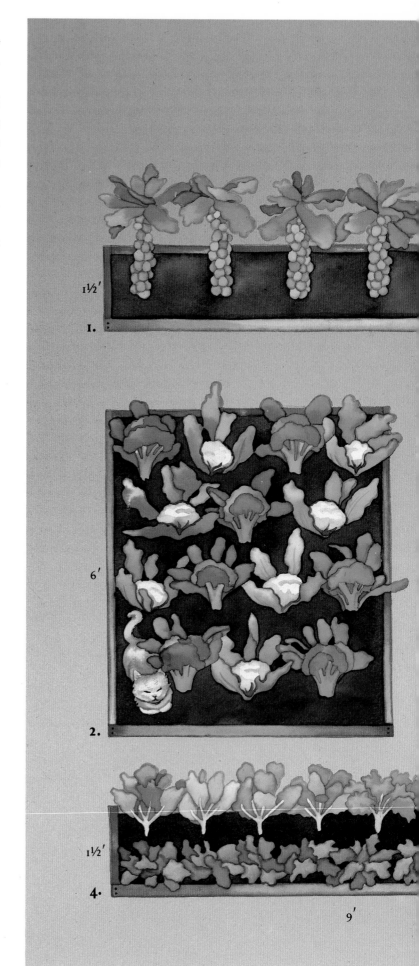

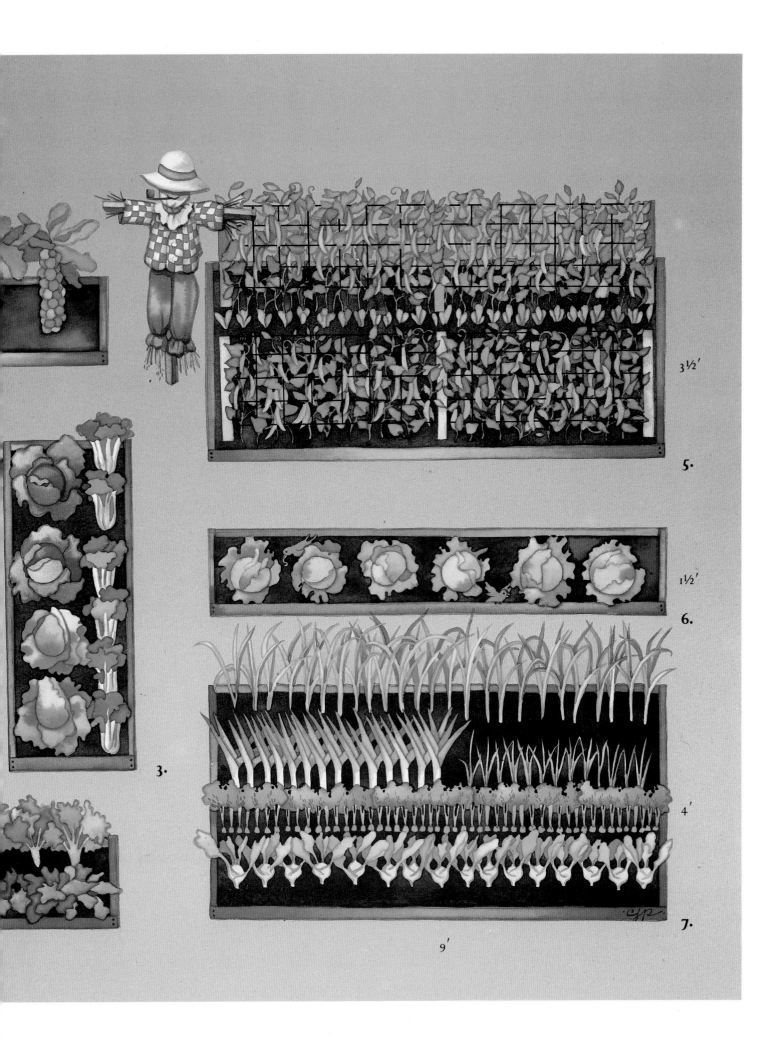

3½′

5.

1½′

6.

3.

4′

7.

9′

THE SPRING-SUMMER GARDEN

Most of these vegetables can be planted as early as March, but a few should wait until the weather warms in May.

Bed 1. Three big sunflowers spaced three feet apart should keep you in seed for a year. They also act as supports for lima beans. Plant six lima bean seeds around each sunflower after it is a foot tall, then thin to only four strong vines. The best choices are King of the Garden or Prizetaker. Twelve plants will produce twelve pounds of beans.

Bed 2. Corn must be grown in blocks for proper pollination. This plot holds eighteen plants of midget varieties like Early Sunglow or White Midget spaced a foot apart in rows eighteen inches apart, which yields about three dozen ears. Or plant only three rows spaced two feet apart for normal-sized corn.

Bed 3. Three seven-foot-tall tomato cages made from concrete reinforcing screen accommodate one standard tomato, one paste-type tomato, and a tomatillo for variety. In front, try a row of basil and cilantro.

Bed 4. Three big growers occupy this ground. They are planted in pairs, spaced three feet apart. First, there are two zucchini; Burpee Hybrid, Seneca, or Gourmet are good varieties, each producing forty fruits. Early Summer is a very productive variety, with as many as thirty-five fruits. Finally, try the equally productive Patti Green Tint squash.

Bed 5. On the back trellis, try a pole bean like Blue Lake, spaced four inches apart. From twenty-four plants expect twenty-five pounds of string beans. On the other trellis, train four cucumbers like Sweet Success and four small-fruited cantaloupes like Sweet 'n Early for a total of fifty cukes and twenty-five melons. Both plants should be spaced a foot apart and will have to be tied to the trellis.

Bed 6. Two summer specialties go here. There's room for five pepper plants, spaced a foot apart. Try two bell peppers (for fifty peppers if you plant Yolo Wonder), a mild ancho, a hotter Anaheim, and a torrid jalapeño. These will produce as many as a hundred peppers apiece, which ought to enliven summer substantially. There's even room for two eggplants spaced two feet apart. Black Bell or Dusky Hybrid produce fifteen fruit each.

Bed 7. This plot is for small things. With rows a foot apart, there's room for a row of romaine lettuce and chard, a row of leaf lettuce, all spaced six inches apart; a row of beets, spaced three inches apart, and a row of carrots, spaced an inch apart. This will produce fifty carrots, thirty-five beets, twenty-four plants of lettuce, and eight of Swiss chard. Anyone still hungry?

1.

2.

4.

3.

5.

6.

7.

The Kitchen Garden Compendium

Here are some likely candidates for the kitchen garden, including the best varieties of each. Before planting, the garden should be prepared as described in the first chapter of this book. All vegetables, and most herbs, do best in good soil. With only one exception, all of these vegetables and herbs need a full day of sun. They also need regular watering, and many should not be sprinkled from overhead or they will mildew. Most can be fertilized with an all-purpose granular fertilizer that is simply raked into the soil around the plants, then watered in. A few, however, do better with regular applications of a liquid fertilizer that goes to work a little faster.

Where it applies, how to plant in rows is described, though vegetables can obviously be planted in containers, in circles, or just here and there. Row planting is the conventional method, and often the most efficient.

How deep to plant seed appears on seed packets. Seed packets also recommend how far apart to space plants, but the suggestions given here often differ. In the backyard vegetable garden most vegetables can be planted closer because they grow in better soil and receive better care. You might experiment with even closer spacing, though there are a few vegetables where this is not recommended.

When planting seed, sow three times as much as you need, then thin to the recommended spacing, removing the weakest growers. A common mistake is to sow too much seed in the hope that some will come up. But it is the nature of seed that if some come up, all will. Also, by sowing more than one seed per space, you cover yourself if an occasional seedling gets nibbled off by a cutworm or snail.

You might also wish to experiment with other varieties of vegetables, especially the odd or unusual. That's how we

Artichokes

Asparagus

discovered that an ugly old beet called Lutz is better than any sophisticated modern beet. Our suggestions, however, are tried and true. We know. Through the years, Los Angeles *Times* columnists Bill Sidnam and Teddy Colbert have tried hundreds of vegetable varieties and our suggestions are based on what they found to be best in the garden and best on the table. Most of the recommended varieties are available from major seed companies (listed on page 143), and we give sources for the exceptions.

ARTICHOKE

This Mediterranean delicacy can be grown in few places other than California. Even here it does best in the cool, foggy coastal areas, though it can be persuaded to grow farther inland given a half-day of shade. It is the immature flower bud of this thistle that we eat—left to develop it turns into a pretty purple flower. The plants get large, up to four feet tall and as much as six feet across.

They are most often planted as root divisions, available at nurseries in fall and winter. Green Globe is the common variety. Plants require a full year in the ground before buds can be harvested. Harvest buds after the first year, when they are three to four inches in diameter and still tightly closed.

Four to six plants produce enough buds to satisfy a family. Peak production occurs when the plant is about three or four years old. When five or six years old, plants should be restarted by removing a sideshoot with roots attached and replanting in the fall.

plant: seeds or root divisions in fall or winter.

space: 3 to 4 feet apart.

fertilize: in early spring, again in fall.

ASPARAGUS

This perennial requires extra effort at planting time but a properly prepared bed will produce for twenty years. Asparagus may be grown from seed, but you will save a year of growing time by planting roots available at nurseries in late fall and winter. Forty roots will be more than enough for the average family.

Asparagus is best planted in specially prepared trenches. For forty roots, dig two twenty-foot-long trenches spaced three feet apart. They should be one foot wide and ten inches deep. Put four inches of planting mix or compost on the bottom and add a general purpose vegetable fertilizer at the rate of one pound for each twenty feet of row (one pound fills half of a one-pound coffee can). Water thoroughly.

Place roots along the length of the trench about a foot apart with the crowns up and the roots spread outward. Cover with two inches of soil and tamp firmly. Water again, then once every week. As the shoots appear, rake in more soil, but never cover the tips of the shoots. Do this every three weeks until the trenches are filled.

Do not harvest any spears the first season because the plant needs all its foliage to establish strong roots for future production. Let the plants grow through summer until foliage turns yellow in early winter, then cut it to the ground.

About the first of April the first spears will be ready to harvest but cut only one spear from each plant. The following year you may harvest most of the spears over a four-week period. Let the rest develop into foliage. The next year and each additional year thereafter, you can harvest the spears for a six-week period, but after six weeks, stop all harvesting and let the plants build up energy for the next season's crop. To harvest properly, cut the spears about an inch below the soil level when they are five to eight inches long. A forked asparagus knife is a handy tool.

Be certain to harvest daily in late spring, as the spears make phenomenal growth during warm weather. If any of the spear tips have started to open into fern-producing shoots, leave them to produce foliage.

plant: seeds or roots in fall or winter.

space: a foot apart in special trenches, rows 3 feet apart.

Haricots verts:
Royalnel (left),
Aiguille vert (right),
Regalfin (below)

Lima beans

fertilize: in early spring as growth begins.
best varieties: Martha Washington (most common); Brock's Imperial; California U.C. 66 (or 72).

BASIL

Basil (*Ocimum basilicum*) is an annual usually planted at the same time as tomatoes, in early May or June, a happy coincidence since this herb is a traditional addition to tomato dishes. It is also the basis of pesto.

Basil is easy to grow. Be sure to pinch out top growth when the first few leaves appear to encourage bushiness. If flower spikes are pinched off, plants produce into winter, then wither in the first frost, or just fade away.

Sweet basil, the most common variety, can be found as seedlings in the herb section at nurseries. It can be planted about six inches apart in neat rows or plant here and there. Quite a few plants are required if you're planning on pesto. Exotic varieties such as Persian anise-scented or lettuce-leaf basil can be grown from seed.

BEANS—SNAP BEAN, HARICOT VERT, LIMA BEAN

Snap beans are ordinary string or green beans, though the best varieties nowadays don't have that characteristic string that runs the length of the bean. Snap beans are available in bush forms that need no support and pole forms that definitely do. We recommend planting the pole kinds because in California's long growing season they produce over a longer period, and in less space, than the bush varieties.

Beans are best planted early in the season before spider mites, powdery mildew, and root rots arrive in late summer. Adding fertilizer to the soil before planting is very important, and the soil should be improved with amendments so it does not crust, which impedes germination. Regular irrigation is also very important—don't let beans dry out, they won't recover.

Pick before beans swell inside the pods. If a few get too ripe before you get around to picking them, pick anyway, or they will slow production.
plant: seeds, from March through July, pole types on trellis at least 7 feet tall.
space: pole types, 4 inches apart in rows 3 feet apart; bush types, 2 inches apart in rows 18 inches apart.
fertilize: before planting, again when first beans mature.
best varieties: Blue Lake (pole, stringless); Burpee's Tenderpod (bush, stringless); Royalty, Purple Pod (bush, burgundy pods turn green when cooked).

Haricots verts are slim, select beans prized by gourmets and restaurateurs for their succulent meaty flesh. They are bush beans and need no support. It is handy as well as traditional to grow summer savory next to them. Their flavor is also enhanced with fresh minced dill or a small amount of lemon juice added to butter.

Harvest when beans are still immature, before the seeds reveal a prominent shape through the skin. Depending on variety, beans are about four to six inches long at this stage. They should be firm, snap easily, and contain only sliverlike seeds. Pick the beans regularly since they remain at their best for only two or three days. Seeds are available from Le Jardin Gourmet.
plant: seeds, from March through July.
space: 3 inches apart, in rows 18 inches apart.
fertilize: before planting, again as flowers open.
best varieties: *Aiguille vert* (the most slender); Regalfin; Royalnel.

Most people have never sampled the rich, nutty flavor of fresh lima beans. They are almost impossible to locate in markets, and even vegetable stands surrounded by fields of limas in Oxnard, where much of California's lima bean production is located, rarely sell them. They are so good that children who wince when frozen limas are set before them

Lutz beet

will greedily consume the fresh version.

Limas, like snap beans, are available in bush and pole forms. The pole-climbing varieties produce best and use the least space. Pole types also seem less prone to attacks by various pests. If you have problems with spider mite in your area, bush limas will be a risky crop; they are quite susceptible. Pole limas, on the other hand, seem to have little trouble.

For a higher germination rate, cover the soil with a mulch of newspapers that is kept damp to prevent the soil from crusting over. Check under the papers daily and remove them immediately when the plants have emerged through the soil. Like all beans, they need frequent irrigation, at least once a week.

plant: seeds, from April through June, on 7-foot-tall trellis.
space: pole limas: 6 inches apart, in rows 3 feet apart; bush types: 4 inches, in rows 2 feet apart.
fertilize: before planting.
best varieties: King of the Garden (an old pole variety but still the best); Prizetaker (pole, huge beans); Burpee's Improved (bush, large beans, profuse, only 20 inches tall); Fordhook No. 242 (good in hot inland areas).

BEETS—LUTZ AND OTHERS
On a scale of ugliness ranging from one to ten, Lutz beets would rate a solid ten. Who would plant this huge, rough-skinned old-fashioned beet, when those small, round smooth-skinned beets are available? We would. Also known as Long Season or Winter Keeper beets, they have survived all these years because they have superior taste. They grow to three times the size of standard beets without becoming pithy or losing their flavor—their fine-textured flesh has a high sugar content that accounts for its sweetness. The foliage is of a lighter green than regular beets and makes succulent eating when prepared as you would other greens.

Lutz beets will keep for several months without loss of flavor. There are, of course, many other beets, but try this one first.

When planting Lutz or other beets, keep in mind that the root is what counts. The soil should be as loose as possible so add extra amendments. Don't use manure; it will cause the beets to split.

Each beet seed actually consists of a cluster of two or three seeds that germinate in clumps and need to be thinned to one plant per seed. When the young plants are two inches high, it is very important to thin them to the distance recommended below.

You should harvest most beets when two to three inches in diameter, before they get too large and pithy. Since Lutz beets don't become tough you can let some grow large. Don't forget that all beet tops are nutritious and an excellent substitute for spinach.

plant: seeds, any time of the year.
space: 3 inches apart, in rows a foot apart (Lutz should be 4 inches apart).
fertilize: before planting.
best varieties: Lutz (the best); Pacemaker (very sweet, sugar beet ancestry); Earlisweet (early and sweet); Mono King Explorer (labor saving, one beet per seed); Burpee's Golden (orange flesh, good flavor).

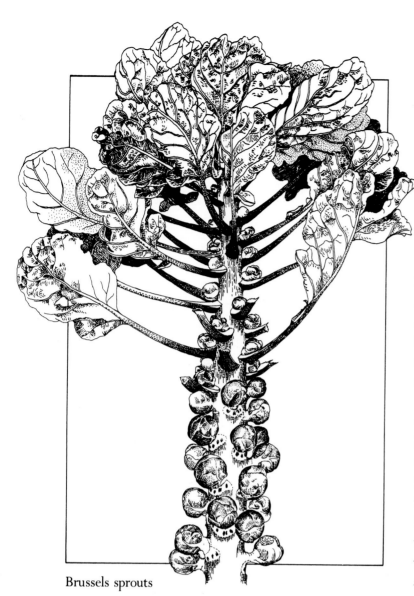

Brussels sprouts

cauliflower —
tie leaves over head

BRUSSELS SPROUTS

A fascinating and sometimes frustrating crop, Brussels sprouts are produced along the stalks of large, unusual-looking plants. They develop from the bottom of the stalk upward, produced at the base of the leaves. It is not unusual for each plant to produce more than a hundred sprouts.

It is easiest to start Brussels sprouts from transplants, which are readily available at local nurseries. They may also be started from seed in pots for later transplanting, but you will save four to six weeks growing time by purchasing transplants. Six transplants will easily feed a family. When transplanting Brussels sprouts, keep the following in mind. Like other cole crops, they should be planted deeper, right up to their first set of leaves, otherwise the weak stems will topple later on. Also, watch the base of the stems, right above the ground, for cutworms and sowbugs, which nibble just enough to topple plants. If they get even one plant, protect others for a week or two with a short tube of paper or a cat food can with both ends cut out.

When the sprouts appear, remove the lower leaves and continue this process as the sprouts grow upward on the stem. Brussels sprouts should be harvested when they are approximately one inch in diameter. If allowed to grow larger, they begin to turn bitter. Once in the kitchen, be careful not to overcook this vegetable. Boil rapidly for seven or eight minutes, so the sprouts retain a rich green color.

plant: transplants from a nursery, or seed, from September through January.

space: 18 to 24 inches apart, in rows 3 feet apart.

fertilize: before planting, monthly.

best varieties: Jade Cross E (twice as many sprouts as other varieties).

Broccoli

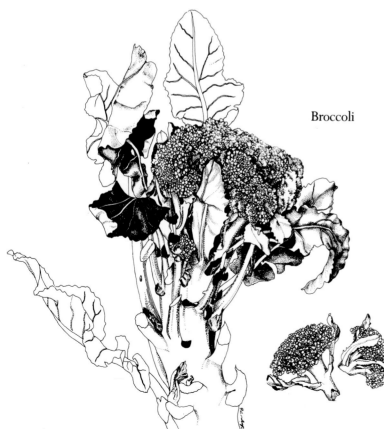

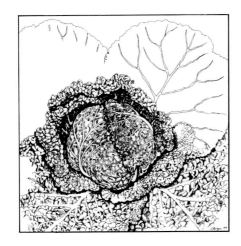

Savoy cabbage

BROCCOLI AND CAULIFLOWER

These cool-season favorites require nearly identical culture. Both are grown for their flowers, which are harvested in dense heads before buds mature. Broccoli is the easier of the two. Cauliflower isn't that much more difficult, though it may not form perfect heads if a hot spell comes at the wrong time, and the curds (heads) must be blanched.

Transplants of these two vegetables are available at nurseries, but to grow some of the better varieties you must order seeds to plant directly in the garden, or in pots for later transplanting. Broccoli is easy to transplant; cauliflower is not, as it is very susceptible to transplant shock. Plant deeper than they were in the pot, up to their first leaves, or they'll topple. Set out plants in the early evening when it is cooler, and check them the next day. If they look droopy, you may need to shade them for a few days. Use a wood shingle stuck in the ground to shade each plant.

Harvest the central head of broccoli when the buds are small and tight, before they begin opening into tiny yellow flowers. After cutting the central head of most varieties, small side sprouts will form that can be eaten.

Most cauliflower varieties require blanching. After the heads begin to form (when they are first visible through the leaves), tie the leaves over the heads to keep them white. Harvest cauliflower when the heads are tight and smooth.

plant: transplants, or seeds, from September through February.

space: 18 inches apart in rows 3 feet apart.

fertilize: before planting, then when six inches tall.

best varieties of broccoli: Green Comet Hybrid (the earliest, seven-inch heads); Premium Crop (All-America winner, 10-inch heads); Di Cicco (slower to mature but produces longer).

best varieties of cauliflower: Snow Crown Hybrid (All-America winner, immense two-pound heads); Snow King (earliest and most heat tolerant); Purple Head (the easiest, delicate broccoli taste, no need to blanch).

CABBAGES—
GREEN, RED, SAVOY, CHINESE

Though there are an astronomical five hundred distinct cabbages listed in various seed catalogues, each can be put in one of four major groups. Green cabbages, the main constituent of cole slaw, cabbage rolls, and sauerkraut, are the commonest. Red cabbages are preferred in salads; they also add color to the garden. Savoy cabbages have crinkled foliage and the heads never become really hard. Many gardeners consider them sweeter, more delicate. Chinese cabbages have a subtle flavor and no odor when cooked. They're equally good raw. They are sometimes called Napa or Tientsin cabbage.

Although cabbages may be directly seeded in the soil, chances are you will experience better results by sowing the seeds in pots (indoors or out) for later transplanting. They may also be grown in large containers. A half whiskey barrel will accommodate three plants.

Cabbages require a good deal of water; the soil should always be moist. Watch for slugs and snails. Otherwise, they're remarkably easy to grow, especially if planted early in the season to avoid hot spring weather.

plant: transplants, or seeds, from October to March (Chinese, October and November only).

space: 15 inches apart in rows 2 feet apart.

fertilize: before planting, again when 6 inches tall.

best varieties of green cabbage: Early Jersey Wakefield (fast, three-pound pointed heads); Copenhagen Market (round, solid); Early Flat Dutch (flat, large leaves for cabbage rolls); Emerald Cross Hybrid (round five pounders, superb); Stonehead Hybrid (extra solid and compact).

best varieties of red cabbage: Ruby Ball Hybrid (maybe the best cabbage, period; weathers hot spells).

best varieties of savoy: Savoy Ace (All-America winner, six pound, olive-green heads).

best varieties of Chinese cabbage: Michili (spicy flavor); Burpee Hybrid (shorter and more oval).

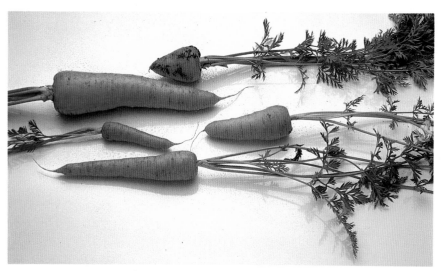

Carrot varieties (top to bottom): Short 'n Sweet, Red Cored Chantenay, Royal Cross, Frubund, Dominator

Swiss chard

CARROT

With their worth hidden underground, carrots seldom get the attention they deserve. They are among the easiest vegetables to grow and the most productive for the space they occupy.

They can be grown year round in California but produce best during the cooler months of fall and early spring. In summer, seed may need a little temporary shade to germinate (one trick is to dig an inch-deep narrow slit that shades the seed planted in the bottom). Since you harvest the roots, good soil is their one demand. It should be loose and fluffy so the roots don't run into any obstructions. The more organic matter added to the soil, the better, but don't use manure — it causes roots to split. If you've had trouble growing carrots with long roots, try the shorter varieties.

plant: seeds, at any time.

space: 2 to 3 inches apart in rows a foot apart.

fertilize: before planting

best varieties: Danvers (Our favorite. Excellent taste, crunchy); Short 'n Sweet (good choice in hard soils, early); Nantes (cylindrical shape, good for cutting crossways); Dominator (long, slender, and tasty); Parks Munchy (one of the longest, good flavor).

CHARD

Swiss chard produces bountiful crops that require very little attention. It is quite nutritious and is a good substitute for spinach and beet greens. In addition, Swiss chard is an ideal container crop — neat, compact, even colorful if you choose the ruby red varieties.

Belonging to the beet family, Swiss chard is indeed a type of beet, minus the edible root. A single planting may be harvested over many months. Cut only the outer leaves and leave the rest of the plant to continue growing. It is easy to freeze any excess.

plant: seeds, all year.

space: 8 inches apart, in rows one foot apart.

fertilize: before planting.

best varieties: Rhubarb Chard (just because it's pretty); Fordhook Giant (tall, vigorous, white stalks); Lucullus (scaled for smaller gardens).

CHAYOTE

Chayote (chi-yo-tay) is a squashlike vegetable from Mexico with a delicate, sweet, rather nutty flavor. They are easy to grow, and produce masses of fruit. To grow chayotes, plant the whole fruit, which can be purchased during the winter at supermarkets. Store the fruit in a cool area, but not your refrigerator, until planting time.

Plant chayotes March through June in a sunny area where it will have lots of room to spread. The huge vines grow to fifty feet in all directions, and an ideal location for them would be on a trellis up the south side of a building. When planting chayotes, lay them horizontally in a shallow trench with the large end slanted slightly down and the small end barely exposed above the soil line. Two chayotes must be planted about six feet apart to assure pollination and fruit production.

Do not water chayotes much when you first plant them or they will rot. Once the vines start growing, water weekly, feed monthly. Chayotes are perennials. Cold weather will slow growth and a heavy frost will kill the foliage, but the plants will come back next year.

Another form, known as perlita or chestnut chayote, has even nuttier, more solid fruits. Though the fruits are half

Four kinds of corn (left to right): Golden Cross Bantam, Early Sunglow, Honey and Cream, Platinum Lady

the size of the standard kind, a single plant can produce as many as five hundred, from early May until frost (it also shows better resistance to cold). This variety is available from Exotica Seed Co.

Chayotes are ripe when a thumbnail can easily pierce the skin. Steam, boil, or bake chayotes until soft and serve sliced or cubed with a simple butter sauce, or scoop out the insides. They can be used in soups, stews, and fritters. In Mexico they are often used in desserts, as well as in salads or egg dishes, and can be stuffed as for chayotes rellenos.

CORN

There is simply no comparison between the corn you buy and the corn you grow. The sugar content of most sweet corn varieties starts changing to starch soon after the ears are picked. Within hours, what was sweet is now just starch. So, if possible, cook corn just seconds after it's cut.

In recent years plant breeders have made tremendous strides in developing superior varieties, but few of these will be found at markets. Besides the traditional yellow kerneled kinds, there are those with white kernels, some with both white and yellow kernels on the same ear, and special hybrids that have been developed to be supersweet. These supersweet varieties hold their flavor longer because the sugar is converted to starch at a slower rate, but they are not necessarily the sweetest — that distinction belongs to the white-kerneled corns.

To ensure proper pollination and the development of a full set of kernels on each ear, corn should be planted in blocks of at least three to four rows standing side by side (rows don't have to be long). Never plant in a single row. Sweet corn should be watered deeply on a weekly basis. Keep the corn patch weeded or use a mulch.

To test corn for ripeness, puncture several kernels. If there's a spurt of milky juice, the ear is ready for picking. Most varieties take around eighty-five to ninety days from planting to harvest, but a few are decidedly faster.

Pesky corn earworms can be controlled with a light application of a few drops of mineral oil applied to silks when they start to turn brown.

Best Yellow Varieties

Golden Cross Bantam (reliable, good for the beginning gardener), **Early Sunglow** (for the impatient gardener. Matures in just 63 days. Small four-foot stalks), **Iochief** (for the hot weather regions of Southern California because it tolerates extreme heat), **Barbecue** (thick husks protect ears from the coals), **Golden Beauty** (All-America winner, early, very tender).

Best White Varieties

Silver Queen (strictly gourmet, the best. Tall, slow to mature), **Platinum Lady** (delicious unique purple and green husks), **Country Gentleman Hybrid** (a superior cream-style corn), **White Sunglow** (the earliest of the white corns).

Best Bicolored Varieties

Honey and Cream (rich and creamy), **Bi-Queen** (similar to Silver Queen, sugary-sweet).

Best Supersweet Varieties

Kandy Korn E.G. (aptly named), **Mainliner E.G.** (slightly longer ears), **Burpee's Sugar Sweet** (the sweetest of the supersweet types with a unique crunchy texture), **Early Xtra-Sweet** (the earliest).

plant: seeds, from March through July.

space: 10 to 12 inches apart, in rows 30 inches apart.

fertilize: before planting, again when a foot tall.

Four kinds of cucumbers (clockwise from top left): Armenian, West Indian Gherkin, Liberty Hybrid, Lemon cucumber

CUCUMBER

Shown here is a sampling of a few of the odd but delicious cucumbers you won't find at the market that can be grown in your kitchen garden. There are both slicing cucumbers, meant to be eaten fresh in salads and such, and pickling cucumbers, designed to spend some time in the brine.

Many seed packets recommend that you plant cucumbers on "hills." This is misleading. The soil should not be mounded, as this impedes irrigation. Most varieties are easy to trellis, or simply grow in rows or clumps. Since cucumbers are 94 percent water, the plants need ample irrigation. Avoid overhead watering as this promotes mildew. Cucumbers are somewhat heat sensitive. In very hot inland areas they are often planted on the north side of corn rows for the shade, or dried corn stalks are laid across the plants.

plant: seeds, from April through June.

space: 12 inches apart in rows 60 inches apart, or in groups of 3, spaced 3 feet apart.

fertilize: before planting, again when vines are 6 inches long.

best slicing varieties: Armenian (beautiful, huge, grow on trellis); lemon (tiny, tart, but "burpless"); Sweet Slice (the sweetest); Burpless Hybrid (mild); Kyoto (slim, sweet); Pot

Luck (for containers); Bush Champion; Bush Whopper.

best pickling varieties: West Indian gherkin (chubby, little, splendid taste. Pick young; big vine); Liberty Hybrid (All-America Selection); Peppi (very early, small vine); Pioneer Hybrid (huge crop in short time. Can get two plantings into one season); Tiny Dill (for containers).

EGGPLANT

Eggplant is perhaps the prettiest vegetable in the kitchen garden. The name seems a mite mysterious until you've seen the variety named Easter Egg. Its fruit is bright white and the size and shape of an egg, much like the original plants from India.

Nurseries carry the more standard varieties as small plants but there are much better, newer varieties that out-produce the old. These must be planted from seed. Eggplants may be seeded directly in the ground but they fare better when planted in pots for later transplanting. Be careful with the transplanting procedure — plants have a delicate root system and are quite susceptible to transplant shock.

Eggplant bear fruit all summer and even into November or December. The fruit of purple eggplants are ready to harvest when they are a glossy dark purple. When they lose their glossy appearance, they are past their prime and will taste bitter. The white varieties should be harvested when they are shiny white before they lose their luster. Seeds of Easter Egg and Imperial are available from Otis Twilley Seed Co.

plant: seeds in small pots, then transplant; from April through June.

space: 24 inches apart in rows 30 inches apart.

fertilize: every three weeks with liquid fertilizer.

best varieties: Black Bell Hybrid (huge, productive), Dusky Hybrid (mid-sized, very productive, good in containers), Ichiban (a slim Japanese variety, pretty, productive), Imperial (slim, delicious), Easter Egg (good in containers).

Jícama

An eggplant called Easter Egg

JÍCAMA

Jícama (hé-ka-mah) is a delicious tuberous root with the texture of a potato and the flavor of a sweet water chestnut. These large, flat, turnip-shaped vegetables are produced on underground stems of showy vines bearing beautiful white or purple flowers. It takes about six months from seed for the vines to produce tubers. Let sprawl or trained on a trellis, the vines will grow to twenty feet before tubers are ready to dig. Keep the flowers picked so they do not form seed pods, which causes small and misshapen tubers. Jícama seeds are also *extremely* poisonous.

Jícama has a fairly low water requirement. Water at the time you plant the seeds. After they germinate, irrigate the vines every two weeks.

Jícama can be cooked, but is most often eaten raw, and is especially delicious in salads. In Mexico it is often served raw with lemon, chili powder, and salt as an appetizer or snack. Seeds are available from Exotica Seed Co.

plant: seeds, in April or May.

space: 2 feet apart.

fertilize: before planting.

KOHLRABI

A curious-looking vegetable, kohlrabi is a crunchy, low-calorie treat that looks a bit like a small green apple with long fluted leaves. It grows quickly and should be harvested before that swollen base is much larger than three inches in diameter. After they exceed that size, unpalatable woody fibers develop within the bulb. Most people who turn down kohlrabi have eaten it when it is too old. Kohlrabi keeps with refrigeration for exceptionally long periods.

Roots are very near the surface. At harvest, cut off the plant at the soil surface so it won't jostle its neighbor's delicate root system.

Peeled and cut in slivers it is a healthful dunker for dips. Chopped in cubes and tossed into salads it can dupe

Kohlrabi

Lemon grass

the uninitiated into thinking water chestnuts come in squares.

For better flavor as a cooked vegetable, leave the skin on, slice and serve with butter, salt, and pepper. Or embellish it by adding a cream sauce or a dollop of sour cream. Chopped fresh parsley sprinkled on top before serving helps brighten the sober color.

plant: seeds, September through March.

space: 6 inches apart, in rows 16 inches apart.

fertilize: before planting.

best variety: Early White Vienna.

LEMON GRASS

Lemon grass makes a striking garden plant, a pleasant tea with few rivals, and the basal stem is an exotic, mildly flavored vegetable. The origin of this tropical perennial is believed to be Southeast Asia. When the Spaniards introduced it to Mexico, lemon grass (*Cymbopogon citratus*) became naturalized there.

Single plants can be found in the herb section at nurseries. Planted in a sunny warm spot (they are handsome against a wall), they quickly grow into a four-foot clump of rough-textured, sharp-edged, aromatic leaves. Lemon grass will withstand light frost but not much more.

Either fresh or dried leaves, cut in one-inch lengths, brew a soothing, gentle, lemon-flavored tea that requires no sweetening. A tablespoon of fresh leaves and a lesser amount of dried leaves to a cup of boiling water is a good proportion. In Mexico it is called *té dé limón* and is frequently served with a stick of cinnamon.

The fibrous leaves of lemon grass can also be used in the cooking of fish, chicken, baked bananas, and to flavor liquors, but the leaves should be removed before serving.

The basal portion of the lemon grass stalk is sold in oriental markets as a vegetable. It is usually sliced thin and eaten raw in salads, chutneys, or fresh vegetable marinades.

To prepare the stem, peel off the fibrous outer layers of leaves and set them aside for the teapot, leaving the tender center section.

LETTUCE

The trick with lettuce is to keep it coming year round. Since it is basically a cool-season crop, if it gets too warm it "bolts" — it sends up seed stalks and the leaves become bitter and rapidly wilt. But there are varieties that will grow into or through the summer, so you still have lettuce in the garden when tomatoes are ripe. With lettuce, everything depends on the variety you plant.

Lettuce is divided into four broad categories. There are the looseleaf kinds that never form a head but can be grown and harvested year round, romaine with its distinctive tall oval shape, crisphead or "iceberg" lettuce, and butterhead or "Bibb" lettuces, the tastiest of the bunch.

A good growing strategy would go like this: in the fall, plant crisphead and butterhead varieties; in early spring, switch to looseleaf kinds and romaine. In late spring and early summer, try Buttercrunch for sure, Salad Bowl and maybe one last planting of romaine, if you live near the coast. In summer, you might try some other looseleaf varieties in partial shade. They seem to get by on just five hours of sunlight a day in summer. Otherwise, lettuce should be grown in full sun. Lettuce tends to mature all at once, so make small plantings at ten-day intervals rather than multiple plantings.

Gardeners and gourmets are convinced that the butterhead varieties have the best flavor of all lettuces. They are frequently called Boston, Bibb, or Limestone lettuce but these are actually names of specific varieties. Butterhead lettuce varieties are soft and fragile in texture, containing a butter-colored heart surrounded by vivid green outer leaves. The spongy leaves have a delicate, sweet, buttery flavor, and the heads never become solid. Most kinds grow best from

Lettuce varieties (left to right):
Buttercrunch, Prizehead,
White Boston

October through March but one, Buttercrunch, does just fine all year round and should be in every summer garden. Bibb, the most popular variety, turns out to be the least reliable.

Buttercrunch (heat-tolerant, reliable, delicious; the best lettuce, period), **Dark Green Boston** (excellent flavor, but does poorly in hot weather), **White Boston** (strictly gourmet flavor, early).

Crisphead is what most people call "iceberg." It is a finicky, difficult crop for the home gardener, not impossible but risky. It's better left to the commercial growers of the Imperial Valley, where bright sunny days and cool, crisp nights provide ideal growing conditions. Knowing its limitations, the home gardener might try two varieties: Great Lakes and Iceberg. Plant these from mid-fall to late winter, and be sure to space plants far apart so they can produce heads without having to compete with neighbors for room.

There may be an exception to our advice not to try crispheads — Mission, a brand new variety. It reputedly tolerates heat and is easy to grow into tight round heads.

Looseleaf lettuce is the easiest kind to grow and the fastest to reach maturity. As the name implies, they do not form heads of any sort. This group also contains the most variety with crinkled, frilled, wavy, or curled foliage. Colors range from lime green to deep burgundy. They can be kept in production from fall through early summer. They will produce in midsummer, but the quality often deteriorates when they mature in hot weather. If harvested young, they all have a mild sweet flavor.

Black Seeded Simpson (mild, reliable), **Grand Rapids** (stands a long time without bolting), **Oakleaf** (fascinating leaves, delicious), **Prizehead** (perhaps the sweetest flavor), **Ruby** (red-tipped, with great flavor), **Salad Bowl** (the most heat-resistant), **Red Salad Bowl** (not as heat-resistant as Salad Bowl).

Romaine takes its name from Roman lettuce grown by fourteenth-century popes in the Vatican gardens. Sometimes referred to as Cos, it is the lettuce made famous in Caesar salads. Its flavor is not delicate but bold and hearty if properly grown. The tall oval heads are bright green on the outside, blanching to a greenish white at the heart. Romaine is crisper than other lettuces, and if rapidly grown to maturity, the leaves have a piquant, yet sweet taste. Romaine prefers cool weather but will produce satisfactorily most of the year in all but the warmest areas. Ideal plantings should be made in winter and early spring, then in late summer and early fall. Most need about eighty days to mature.

Parris Island Cos (dependable with good flavor), **Parris White Cos** (lighter green).

Lettuce needs lots of water. There should be no weed competition. A mulch of straw or similar material between plants can retard weed growth and preserve moisture. It will also keep lettuce leaves clean during the rainy season. Feeding brings dramatic results.

Lettuce is best harvested early in the morning, then crisped in the refrigerator until salad time. Pick the butterhead types while they are slightly immature, as they tend to lose their sweet buttery flavor if allowed to stand too long. With looseleaf, harvest a few outer leaves at a time as needed.

plant: seeds or transplant; head types from September through February, looseleaf from September through June.
space: head types, 12 inches apart in rows 16 inches apart; looseleaf, 6 inches apart in rows a foot apart.
fertilize: every two to four weeks with a liquid fertilizer.
MELON

Melons take a lot of space, true, but if you have ever tasted a vine-ripened cantaloupe, you'll find the room — few things in the garden are so luscious. To keep these sprawling vines from consuming your entire garden, there is a planting

Melon family portrait

method that allows a bountiful harvest within a three- by twelve-foot area. And there are several new varieties that grow more like a bush, and some that can be trained on a trellis.

The bush varieties are the newest wrinkle. They may only produce two to six fruit, but most only use about four feet of garden. Most bush varieties also ripen earlier than full-sized vines, so they are good in coastal gardens which sometimes just don't get enough heat to satisfy a melon. Melons are gluttons for heat and should be planted in the hottest part of the garden. If you live where lettuce won't grow in the summer, melons are your compensation. (Honeydew and crenshaw melons are only recommended where summers are scorching.)

If you want lots of melons but still don't have space, try this method: mark off a plot three feet wide by twelve feet long. Down the center, plant a row of melon seeds every six inches. After germination, thin them to about twenty inches apart, so you are left with seven plants. As these grow just keep tucking the vines back into their allotted space until they form a mounded maze in which the melons mingle like eggs in a nest. Plots like this will produce about thirty cantaloupes or fifteen watermelons.

Most melons are too heavy to be grown on a trellis, but there are a few exceptions. One we've tried is the Sweet 'n Early cantaloupe. It will grow to the top of a seven-foot trellis and each plant bears about six 4½-inch melons. This variety is also good near the coast, and it is mildew resistant. Space plants eight inches apart along a trellis.

Never water melons from overhead—this promotes mildew. Covering the ground with a black plastic mulch speeds up the ripening process, keeps weeds in check, and keeps melons clean. Make sure you cut slits in the plastic so water gets through.

Cantaloupes are ready for harvest when the fruit breaks away from the stem with the tiniest of tugs. Water-melon ripeness is more difficult to determine. Generally, watermelons are ready for harvest when the first tendril on the stem next to the melon dries and turns brown, and when the color of the bottom surface of the melon changes from a straw color to yellow.

plant: seeds, April through June.

space: in groups of three, spaced about 5 feet apart (or see alternatives discussed above).

fertilize: before planting, again when vines are a foot long.

best cantaloupe varieties: Chaca No. 1 (small, but tops in taste); Classic Hybrid (orange sherbet flesh); Alaska Hybrid (early, good near coast); Honeybush; Musketeer (bush-type); Sweet n' Early (good on trellis).

best watermelon varieties: Crimson Sweet (the tastiest, huge to 25 pounds); Yellow Doll (small, yellow flesh); Sugar Doll (similar but red); Bushbaby; Sugar Bush.

ONIONS AND CLOSE KIN

Full-sized slicing onions are easy to grow once you plant the right kinds in the proper season. There are two main groups: the sweet, mild ones, good fresh or for slicing; and the stronger-flavored onions, preferred for cooking or storing.

Seeds are the least expensive way of growing onions, or you may plant onions from sets (small bulbs) for faster results, but only the stronger, cooking types are available this way. Green onions or scallions are obtained from most onion varieties by harvesting the plant while the bulb is still immature. Or you can grow one of the bunching varieties, such as Evergreen Long, which do not form bulbs but put their substance into crops of leaves.

Onions are ready for harvesting when the bulbs grow large and the tops begin to yellow and fall over—usually in late spring. When the majority of the tops fall over, bend the rest of them, as this hastens the ripening process.

Dig them up when tops have withered and let them cure in the sun for five days. Then cut off the tops about an

inch from the bulb. Onions may be stored in a mesh bag in a cool, well-ventilated place.

plant: seeds, from October to January; sets, from January to March; green onions, anytime.

space: 3 inches apart in rows a foot apart; green onions, ½-inch apart.

fertilize: before planting.

best mild varieties: California Red Flat (easy, enormous, hamburger-sized); Texas Grano (the Maui onion, sweet, big); Crystal White Wax (exceptionally sweet); Italian Red Torpedo (conversation piece).

best strong varieties: Early Yellow Globe; Ebenezer.

Shallots, outrageously expensive at markets, are ridiculously easy to grow, easier than ordinary onions — a pleasant surprise for the gourmet cook. They thrive in poor soil, need little care, and multiply year after year. They're grown and harvested just like onions. When they start to topple, they're ready to dig and dry, but be sure to leave a few bulbs in the ground to produce more plants. You can plant bulbs purchased at markets, or order from a seed catalogue.

For the uninitiated, shallot bulbs lend a mild garlic-onion flavor to meats, sauces, and other dishes. A new shallot variety, Fresh Green, lets you cut the tops and eat them like chives, and the whole plants can also be used in an immature state, when they taste like a sophisticated green onion.

plant: bulbs, from October through February.

space: 2 inches apart in rows a foot apart.

fertilize: before planting.

Garlic (*Allium sativum*) is just about the easiest member of the onion family to grow. Buy a garlic bulb at the grocery, pull it apart and plant. These will multiply and form bulbs which may be harvested in about three months.

Elephant garlic (*Allium ampeloprasum*) lives up to its name and is more fun to grow. Each clove usually yields a massive bulb of five cloves the following summer that can weigh as much as a pound. Mature bulbs drying in the sun waft a buttery garlic aroma. Because of its mild flavor, there is no need to remove the chopped cloves when cooking vegetables and sauces or braising meats.

plant: bulbs, September through December.

space: 2 inches apart, in rows a foot apart.

fertilize: before planting.

Chives (*Allium schoenoprasum*) are also onion kin and extra easy to grow. The foot-tall plants are unusually attractive, with pretty pink flowers and thin tubular leaves. They can be planted anytime and harvested anytime. The chopped green leaves give color and a subtle onion flavor to fresh-cooked dishes. Since the volatile oils disperse quickly, add after cooking.

Chinese chives (*Allium tuberosum*), also known as oriental garlic or garlic chives, grow like chives but their leaves are flat and gray green. The flowers, which can be used like garlic, are white. Snipped and added to eggs, stir-fried vegetables, broths, or salads, they transform the ordinary into the extraordinary.

plant: seeds or small plants, anytime in fall or spring.

space: several clumps a foot apart will do.

fertilize: don't.

Pak choy

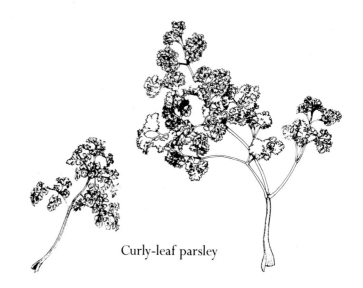

Curly-leaf parsley

and the pieces of white celerylike stalks common in these dishes are frequently the ribs or stalks. It is a good substitute for spinach, Swiss chard, or beet, turnip, and mustard greens, as well, and the leaf ribs and stalks are an excellent substitute for celery.

Pak choy is a cool-season vegetable and is easy to grow. To reach perfection, pak choy must grow rapidly. It needs constant moisture and regular fertilizing or it will lose its tenderness and flavor. Harvest by picking the outer stems and leaves, allowing the plant to continue growing, or by cutting the entire plant at the base.

plant: seeds, from mid-September through February.
space: 6 inches apart in rows a foot apart.
fertilize: every three weeks with a liquid fertilizer.
best varieties: Lei-choi (larger, less likely to bolt); Crispy Choy.

PARSLEY AND SEVERAL PALS

Curly-leaf parsley (*Petroselinum crispum*) is the most popularly grown garden herb. Usually used as a garnish, it is probably the most neglected edible on the plate. It has a delicate flavor and is high in vitamins A and C. No competition for beauty but high in flavor is another variety, the flat-leaf or Italian parsley (*P. neopolitan*). Parsley is a biennial, going to seed in the second year, but is usually treated as an annual and planted anew each year. It will take full sun but appreciates some shade during the hot months.

Chervil (*Anthriscus cerefolium*) has the hint of tarragon and anise, dear to the heart of fine salad fanciers. The plant is lacy and fernlike and, like ferns, chervil needs some shade and a lot of moisture. An annual, chervil must be resown each year. Left to go to seed in the summer, it usually resprouts after the first heavy autumn rain.

If you don't remember whether you've tasted cilantro—also called Chinese parsley (*Coriandrum sativum*)—you haven't. The flavor has a bang, pungent in taste and aroma. It lends itself to highly seasoned Mexican

OREGANO AND MARJORAM

These closely related Mediterranean herbs grow quite differently but have a similar taste. Oregano (*Origanum vulgare*) spreads by underground stems into a two-foot-tall mass of lax stems, though there are some varieties that grow only a foot tall. Give it lots of sun and fast drainage. Just a small amount supplies the zest to pizza and other Italian dishes. It's a pronounced taste, so be sure you like it before adding it to stews, vegetables, and soups.

Sweet marjoram (*Origanum majorana*) has tiny dense leaves with a gray-blue cast and velvety texture. It grows to two feet, making it an attractive and fragrant low hedge. Like most herbs, the flavor is best just before flowering. Use leaves in cheese dishes, casseroles, soups, and stews.

PAK CHOY

Also known as bok choy and, incorrectly, Chinese cabbage, pak choy resembles Swiss chard with white celerylike stalks topped with dark green spoon-shaped leaves. The dark green leafy ingredient in many Chinese dishes is often pak choy,

164

Garden peas

and Far Eastern dishes. When you shop for cilantro seeds you won't find them under that name; the seeds are called coriander, and the handiest place to find them is on your own spice shelf. Cilantro is an annual that can tolerate some shade. It thrives in rich well-drained soil and because of its delicate root system should be planted right where it will grow. Harvest the young leaves when the plants are approximately five inches tall. Snip them off right at the base so the root system of the adjacent plant is not disturbed.

PARSNIP

Of all the root vegetables, parsnips are probably the most neglected by home gardeners, perhaps because they require a meticulously prepared soil and a lengthy growing season. But their sweet nutty flavor makes them worth the effort.

Proper soil preparation is a must — it must be loose and well drained. They will fail miserably in a heavy clay soil. Improve the soil to a depth of at least eighteen inches since some varieties will grow to fifteen inches in length. Work in huge amounts of organic matter.

Soak parsnip seeds overnight before planting to facilitate germination. Plant the seeds one-quarter-inch deep in a moist soil. Always plant fresh seeds since parsnips lose their germination ability rapidly. It will probably take three or more weeks for the seeds to germinate.

This vegetable requires four to six months to reach maturity. They may be hard to dig from the ground so be sure not to break the roots. After harvest they also require special treatment. The roots have a high starch content, which will change to sugar only after being exposed to cold temperatures for several days, so store parsnips in the coldest section of the refrigerator where the temperature is about 36 degrees.

plant: seeds, from September through December.

space: 6 inches apart in rows 15 inches apart.

fertilize: before planting, special soil preparation required.

best varieties: Hollow Crown; All American.

GARDEN PEA

Like corn, the sugar content of a fresh pea changes rapidly to starch after picking. The fresh pea you buy in the market has a bland, starchy taste, but the one you pick from the vine in your garden will be sweet and tender — the kind that literally melts in your mouth.

There are three kinds of green peas: early, mid-season, and late-maturing. For a continuous supply of fresh peas, plant all three types at the same time, rather than make successive plantings of only one variety.

Early varieties usually grow on dwarf vines about eighteen inches tall and do not need staking or other means of support. Four good choices are Little Marvel, Blue Bantam, Novella, and Maestro. Mid-season varieties grow on vines about thirty inches tall and don't require support, though it doesn't hurt. Two excellent varieties are Green Arrow and Lincoln. Green Arrow is a prolific producer of sweet, tender peas and is quite disease-resistant. Lincoln is probably the finest-quality pea ever developed. Then there is Alderman, a late-maturing variety that grows on vines four to five feet tall. These require a trellis. Alderman is productive over a longer period of time than the others.

Harvest early varieties about two months after planting. Then come the mid-season and late varieties. Pea pods develop from the bottom of the plant upward. Make several test pickings when the pods begin to plump. Your taste buds will indicate when peas are ready to harvest — a raw pea is ripe when it tastes sweet and tender. If it's starchy and bland, it's been too long on the vine. Keep peas picked just as fast as they ripen so the vine's energy will go into making more pods. Seeds of the Lincoln variety are available from Stokes Seeds.

plant: seeds, from August through March.

space: 2 inches apart, in rows 18 inches apart; space trellised peas in rows 30 inches apart.

fertilize: before planting.

Pasilla pepper

Anaheim chile

SNOW PEA

Snow peas, sometimes called "sugar peas," are edible-podded peas—you eat the crisp pods that contain tiny immature peas. There are two types: tall climbing varieties that need support, and bush types that don't. You should try both if you have the space. The bush form will mature before the climbing variety, thus assuring a continuous supply of snow peas throughout spring. Harvest snow peas when the pods are a bright green, still flattened but slightly bumpy with the immature peas in the formation stage. Mature pods may be shelled and the peas eaten, but the pods will be too tough.

In the kitchen, stir-fry in a wok or boil like snap beans. Do not overcook them; three minutes will render them tender but still crisp.

Sugar Snap is an all-new kind of climbing pea that falls halfway between a snow pea and a green pea. One of the tastiest of all peas, it can be used like a snow pea (though pod walls are thicker) when young. As pod matures, remove the string that runs down one side and use like a string bean. Fully mature, shell like a green pea.

plant: seeds, from August through March.

space: bush types, 2 inches apart in rows 2 feet apart; climbing types, 2 inches apart in rows 6 inches on either side of a 7-foot trellis.

fertilize: before planting.

best bush varieties: Oregon Sugar (prolific); Dwarf Gray Sugar (bears earliest); Snowbird.

best climbing variety: Sweetpod.

PEPPER

Sweet or hot, peppers are extremely productive, attractive, and easy to grow. It doesn't take more than a few plants to keep you in peppers for a year. Some varieties will produce as many as one hundred fifty per plant.

Sweet peppers are the least productive, so plan on

Perilla

166

planting several. The exception is Gypsy Hybrid, which produces as many as sixty greenish-yellow peppers that are three to four inches long and about half as wide on a twenty-inch-tall plant. Sweet and crisp, they are perfect for salads and cooking, but not stuffing.

Narrower still and a little longer is Sweet Banana, a colorful pepper that turns yellow, then orange, and finally red. It's also a good slicing and salad variety.

For stuffed peppers or for slicing, plant a block-shaped bell pepper. Big Bertha, the biggest, produces huge (up to nine inches) peppers on a two-foot-tall plant. Two other bell peppers easy to grow in California are Yolo Wonder and Calwonder (California Wonder). Golden Bell Hybrid is a yellow bell pepper.

Aconcagua and Cubanelle are two mild peppers that are not bells but are fine for stuffing.

Sweet peppers also include those grown for pickling. Good choices include Pepperoncini (the famous mild Italian pickling pepper), Sweet Cherry, and Pimiento.

Hot peppers are the most prolific and unless you are a glutton for punishment, one plant of each kind will provide plenty. Jalapeños (hah-lah-pain-yos) are the most torrid, used in hot sauces or pickled for relish. You don't know the meaning of hot until you've tried one fresh off the plant. The plant grows about thirty inches tall.

Much more mild, but still hot, are the California chiles, or Anaheim chiles, that provide the long green chiles used in chiles rellenos. They can also be combined with tomatoes and onions for a semimild chile salsa. The plant stands three feet tall, and this is the pepper that can produce over one hundred fifty fruits.

Ancho chiles (also called Pasilla or Poblano) are almost as large as bell peppers, and are the ones most often dried and ground to become chili powder. They are also used fresh in soups and meat or vegetable dishes. They are hotter than a bell pepper, but still the mildest of the hot peppers. Plants grow about thirty inches tall. Seed must be ordered from Exotica Seed Co.

Peppers can be harvested in the green (or yellow) stage, or they can be left on the vine until they turn red (all peppers eventually turn red). As they turn from green to red, they will become sweeter. Never leave the peppers on so long that they start to soften.

plant: seeds in pots, then transplant into the garden from April through June.

space: bell and other small pepper plants, a foot apart; hot peppers, 2 feet apart. Leave 30 inches between rows.

fertilize: before planting, then monthly.

PERILLA OR SHISO

The fresh leaves, seeds, and flowers of perilla, with a peppery but not overpowering flavor, play a prominent role in oriental cooking. Two varieties available here are green perilla (*Perilla frutescens*), which is preferred for cooking, and purple perilla (*P. frutescens var. crispa*), whose sharper flavor and color are best for pickling. The latter is called "beefsteak plant" in the United States and is often planted as an ornamental.

Minced and added to eggs, broths, salads, and vegetables, green perilla leaves can be used copiously. Known in Japan as shiso (shee-so), it provides an indispensible flavor to many types of sushi. The intensely aromatic and flavorful dried seeds of the perilla can be used over rice, eggs, or creamed foods. The mild crunch of the seeds is similar to poppy seeds. Even the flowers are used as a garnish. Leaves of the purple perilla add flavor and a red tint when pickling.

Perilla should be started from seed, March through June. The plants can grow about three feet tall and need two feet of space between them. Purple perilla seeds are listed with most seed companies and are easier to find than green perilla, which may be found at oriental groceries, or ordered from Tsang and Ma, Inc.

Radishes (left to right): White Icicle,
Crimson Giant, Burpee White, Champion

PUMPKIN

You can grow pumpkins for pies, seeds, or jack-o-lanterns. Most varieties do all three jobs rather well, but there are also specific varieties that are better at one or another. Triple Treat is a new variety that excels in all three fields (probably the best choice if you have room for only one plant). Lady Godiva is favored for seeds since it makes seed with no hulls, easy to roast. For pies, try Small Sugar, and for Halloween, the enormous Big Max or Big Moon varieties that can weigh over two hundred pounds each (but are usually a lot lighter).

Big pumpkins need an area of at least sixteen square feet in full sun. Prepare the entire plot to a depth of twelve inches, since little roots will strike down under each leaf wherever they contact soil.

For a giant jack-o-lantern select the best immature pumpkin that is closest to the main stem. Clip off all remaining blossoms and immature pumpkins. Of course, if you'll settle for smaller pumpkins, you can leave several. If you are growing kinds for pies or seeds, leave all pumpkins on the vine. To prevent mildew, the most common problem on pumpkins, don't water from overhead.

When the vines die naturally and the skin is hard to the press of a thumbnail it is time for harvest. Always leave the stem on the pumpkin to prevent rotting. Pumpkins will store for months in a cool dark place like the garage.

plant: seeds, from April through June (by June 15th for Halloween harvest).

space: 4 feet apart.

fertilize: before planting.

RADISH

Ordinary radishes are so quick and so easy to grow they are almost foolproof. Because radishes mature rapidly, they can be planted in between rows of other vegetables and be ready to harvest before the other crops shade them out. Some are

Big Max pumpkin

Winter radishes:
Black Spanish and Hybrid Daikon

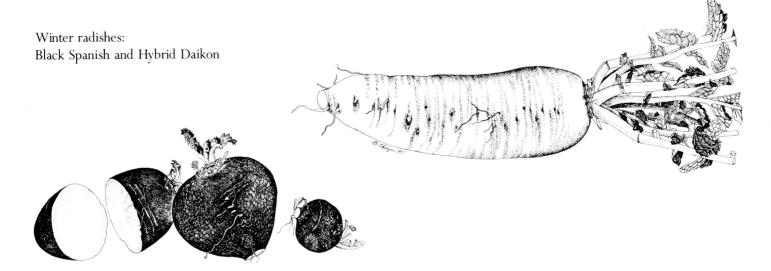

ready to eat in just twenty days. All they need is good soil and fairly constant moisture.

plant: seeds, anytime.

space: an inch apart in rows a foot apart.

fertilize: before planting.

best varieties: Scarlet White-Tipped (crisp refreshing flavor, good looks); Burpee White (big enough to pass for a turnip, crisp, juicy, and sweet); Champion (excellent flavor, pretty shape); Cherry Bell (a tiny tasty radish, very regular in shape); French Breakfast (unusual oblong shape, very fast); Crimson Giant (very large); Sparkler (extra hot); White Icicle (crisp, sometimes hot).

Winter radishes are different from their common radish cousins. They grow much larger and require a considerably longer growing period, from fifty to seventy-five days. They are sometimes called daikons, but daikons are actually a distinct variety of winter radish. In the Orient, these radishes have major culinary uses. They are pickled, eaten in tempura and are an important ingredient in stir-fry dishes. In fact, in Japan nearly 20 percent of the total vegetable crop is winter radishes. Winter radishes have about the same cultural requirements as common radishes though the soil must be worked deeper and they must be spaced much farther apart because they grow quite large. They may be harvested at varying stages of maturity, but unlike ordinary radishes, they store well in the ground for up to a month after fully mature. Seed is available from Gurney Seed Co. or R. H. Shumway Seeds.

plant: seeds, from September through December.

space: varies, from 6 inches to a foot apart, in rows 18 inches apart.

fertilize: before planting.

best varieties: Sakurajima (giant 10 pounder, pungent, looks like a volleyball with foliage, for pickling, tempura); Chinese White Celestial (mild raw or cooked, looks like a big white carrot); Hybrid Daikon (long, slim to 20 inches, mild); China Rose (pinkish-white skin, crisp, pungent); Black Spanish (black skin, pungent white flesh).

ROCKET

Rocket is a popular salad herb in many areas of Europe and the Middle East but is seldom grown by gardeners in this country. The French call it *roquette*, the British know it as rocket-salad, and in Italy it is referred to as *rucola*.

A relative of mustard, this herb is grown for its distinctively pungent leaves. Rocket should be grown during the cool season; if grown during the warm season, the leaves develop a very strong unpleasant flavor.

The leaves are ready to harvest when the plants are about ten inches tall. This will probably occur six to eight weeks after planting. Keep them harvested regularly so the plant continues to develop new foliage; the older leaves tend to get bitter.

plant: seeds, from October through March.

space: 8 inches apart, in rows 18 inches apart.

fertilize: before planting.

SAGE

Common sage (*Salvia officinalis*) has many uses. Try this herb's bracing flavor in tea, a helpful digestive aid, or use it to add flavor to poultry stuffing. Its digestive qualities make it a natural and delicious addition to fatty meats and wild game. Holt's Mammoth is the preferred variety; pick choice leaves just before flowering.

Pineapple sage (*S. elegans*) is well named—the flavor is unexpected but decided. Moreover, the slender succulent leaves and spikes of red flowers are fragrant additions to bouquets. The minced leaves, best harvested before flowering, add unmistakable flavor to punch, tea, cakes, gelatin, and fruit cups.

Both make two-foot plants but after the fourth year become woody, decline in flavor, and should be replanted.

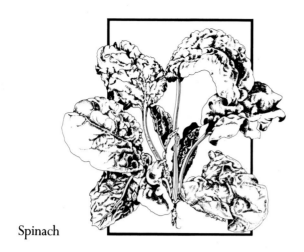

Spinach

SPINACH

In the past ten years, inventive cooks have developed myriad uses for spinach. A vegetable that was once relegated to the boiling pot is now found in a variety of dishes, ranging from crepes to lasagna. And most important, spinach is also eaten raw in salads, fully realizing its rich vitamin A and mineral content.

Indigenous to southwestern Asia, spinach has been cultivated for hundreds of years. Although fresh spinach found in supermarkets is usually in tolerable condition, it is often waterlogged, laced with sand, and lacking in flavor. True connoisseurs of raw-spinach salads should definitely include this green in their kitchen gardens.

Spinach is relatively easy to grow, but it demands cool weather and will rapidly bolt to seed if grown during the warm season. To harvest, either pull up the entire spinach plant, or make continuous harvests of the outer leaves while allowing the plants to continue to grow and produce.

plant: seeds, from September through February.

space: 4 inches apart in rows a foot apart.

fertilize: before planting, then every two weeks with liquid fertilizer.

best varieties: Melody Hybrid (All-America winner, very productive); Bloomsdale Longstanding; America; Avon Hybrid.

SQUASH

Squash come in an amazing array, and are worth growing for their good looks alone. There are summer squash and winter squash. Both are planted in the spring and grown through the summer, but summer squash are picked young and consumed immediately. Winter squash are picked when fully mature and, because of their thick skins, can be stored into the winter. Summer squash require about 50 days to reach maturity; winter varieties require between 85 and 110.

Squash are easy vegetables to grow. Because they are considered warm season vegetables they should be planted from April through early summer in a sunny part of the yard. Squash need lots of water but overhead watering promotes mildew and should be avoided.

Harvesting at the correct stage is probably the most crucial step in growing squash, especially summer squash. To assure peak flavor, all summer varieties should be harvested when they are small and immature. Zucchini should be harvested when four to eight inches long, yellow crookneck when four to six inches long, and scallop squash when no larger than a silver dollar. Scallopini should be harvested when about twice the size of a silver dollar.

Winter squash should be harvested when the leaves start to yellow and dry up and the outer skin is quite hard. Leave three inches of stem on each squash and let them cure in the sun for several days before storing in a cool, dry area.

Summer Squash

zucchini. The gardener's favorite. So prolific, most plants produce far more than a family can consume. One hint — try planting variety. There are some exotic zucchini out there just waiting to be tried. Good choices:

Clarita Hybrid (super prolific, thin tender skin), **Ambassador Hybrid, Black Jack, Chefini Hybrid, Gold Rush Hybrid** (award-winning golden variety), **Gourmet Globe Hybrid** (round with a sweet, delicate flavor on a compact plant).

yellow crookneck. Distinguished by its golden color and crooked necks, it is early maturing and an abundant producer. Some newer varieties have straight necks, despite the name. Don't overcook crookneck or the sweet flavor will be lost. Good choices: **Early Yellow Summer Crookneck** (old variety, still tastes best), **Sundance Hybrid, Goldbar Hybrid, Dixie Hybrid** (compact for containers).

scallop squash. Also called patty pan squash, it has a

Acorn squash

Winter Squash

acorn squash. Deeply ribbed with a dark green skin and orange flesh, all are delicious, but two compact varieties stand out: **Table Queen** (excellent taste), **Table Ace** (quicker maturing).

buttercup squash. Probably the tastiest, most productive of the winter squash. It is turban-shaped with dark green skin and orange flesh, and has a flavor similar to a sweet potato. Fruit averages about four pounds each and is produced in copious quantity. Best bets: **Buttercup** (the original, still great), **Sweet Mama Hybrid** (compact).

butternut squash. The popular pear-shaped squash with tan skin and flesh similar to a pumpkin (it can be used to make pumpkin pie). Try these: **Waltham Butternut, Butter Boy Hybrid.**

hubbard and banana. Huge, old-fashioned winter squash. Both keep extremely well and are tasty enough (they can be carved like pumpkins into humorous oblong jack-o-lanterns), but they grow on huge, sprawling vines too big for most gardens.

spaghetti squash. A unique winter squash. When properly cooked, it separates into long fibers that look like pasta. Even the taste is similar except for a trace of sweetness.

plant: Summer kinds, March through August; winter kinds April through June.

space: Summer squash 18 inches apart in rows 3 feet apart, or in groups of three spaced 6 feet apart; Winter squash 12 inches apart in rows 6 feet apart, or in groups of three spaced 8 feet apart. Bush types may be spaced 3 to 4 feet apart.

fertilize: before planting, then monthly.

Tahitian Squash

If you've never heard of Tahitian squash, don't be surprised. It's new to the United States. But because of its versatility in the kitchen and its prodigious production, it may become

Tahitian squash

distinctive shape with a somewhat less-than-distinctive taste, typified by White Bush Scallop, the market variety. Our remedy: **Patty Green Tint Hybrid** (superb sweet flavor).

scallopini. Scallopini Hybrid is a recent cross between a scallop squash and a zucchini. With a dark green color and a slightly scalloped shape, it is sweet and delicate when cooked or eaten raw in salads.

kuta squash. A new squash that falls somewhere between a summer and a winter variety. Picked small (when light green), it can be used like zucchini. Picked at maturity (when yellow) it develops a hard skin and can be used or stored like winter squash. It has a fine nutty flavor.

one of our most important new vegetable introductions in recent years.

Although it resembles a huge crescent-shaped butternut squash, the flavor and fragrance of this import from Tahiti are more like that of a sweet melon. And it may be eaten raw like a melon or cooked like a squash. The deep orange flesh has a high sugar content.

The sprawling twenty-five-foot vines are loaded with fruit which is deep green in color, turning to a golden yellow when ripe. It can be picked green and allowed to ripen indoors, if desired.

Tahitian squash is easy to grow. The culture is similar to other squash, although the growing period is longer, with maturity occurring about 160 days after planting. Seeds may be planted from March through June. Plant the seeds in a sunny spot one inch deep.

After harvest, the fruit may be stored in a cool dry area up to six months. The flesh may also be frozen for months and still retain its delicious flavor. In addition to being eaten raw, it is delightful cut into sticks and sautéed in butter for eight minutes. When baked for thirty minutes and served with butter or honey, it tastes like a yam. Because of its high sugar content, it makes a scrumptious pie. And it may also be dried. Seeds for this unique vegetable may be obtained from Exotica Seed Company.

SUNFLOWER

Sunflowers, a North American original, are more fun than food, but who can resist those huge showy flowers atop stems sturdy enough to act as bean poles (a good secondary use while you're waiting for the seeds to ripen).

Children are fascinated by sunflower growth. From the bud stage until almost ready for harvest, flowers turn their heads daily, following the sun from east to west like a

Sunflowers

satellite-tracking antenna. Fast growth, huge size, and spectacular color make sunflowers ideal for introducing children to the pleasures of gardening.

Allow seeds to dry naturally on the plant. Nylon netting or paper bags placed over the flowers will protect them from birds and catch the seeds as they drop. The seeds may be dry- or oil-roasted in the oven. To dry roast, spread one layer of seeds in a shallow pan. Place in a 350-degree oven for fifteen minutes or until the seeds crack. To oil roast, cover one layer of seeds with oil and roast at 350 degrees until they pop.

plant: seeds, from late March through June.

space: two feet apart in rows three feet apart.

fertilize: before planting.

best varieties: Mammoth (the biggest); Sunbird Hybrid (early, shorter, to 6 feet).

TARRAGON

The narrow, slivered leaves of French tarragon harbor a touch of anise and mint, plus an elusive flavor that disappears when it is dried. Gourmet cooks despair when this perennial herb goes completely dormant in the winter.

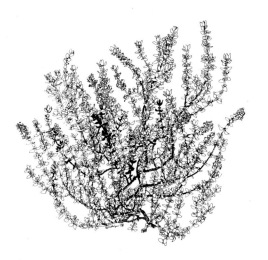

English thyme

Lemon thyme

Tomatillo

True tarragon (*Artemisia dracunculus*) must be grown from plants purchased at nurseries. It slowly spreads by underground stems to form a foot-tall clump, and it should be dug and divided every few years.

A close tastealike, the Mexican marigold (*Tagetes lucida*) doesn't go dormant in winter in California and has pretty little marigold flowers as well. Plants are available from Taylor's Herb Gardens, seed from Redwood Seed Co.

THYME

Of the many thymes, three are the favorites of cooks: the pungent and agreeably peppery English thyme (*Thymus vulgaris*) and its varieties, the milder fragrant lemon thyme (*T. citrodorus*), and the unlikely flavored caraway thyme (*T. herba-barona*).

In the garden the lemon thyme stands eighteen inches tall. Plant them that far apart and clip off the branches at the base to maintain the fountainlike shape.

English, or common, thyme forms compact tufts one foot high. Spaced a foot apart, they are neat border plants. In late summer their lavender whorled flowers contrast with pointed dark green leaves.

In addition to a unique flavor, caraway thyme has an unusual branching pattern similar to a small cobweb. The graceful four-inch plants growing between flagstones look wonderful.

A key to the successful culture of thymes is to simulate the sun and drainage of their native Mediterranean rocky mountain shores . . . no rich heavy soil for these spunky plants, or their flavorful oils diminish.

Thyme plants become woody with age and will eventually need to be replaced. Using thyme in cooking calls for tact. A little bit enhances; too much destroys the balance of muted natural flavors. A pinch of fresh crushed thyme adds such a delightful flavor to boiled or scrambled eggs that, for many salt-conscious dieters, no other seasoning is necessary. English thyme, a standard addition to seafood chowders and chicken and turkey stuffing, adds a new flavor to mashed potatoes and pea soup. Delicate, fragrant lemon thyme brightens the flavors of veal, chicken, and seafood. One sprig added to canned soup releases an aroma that dupes a sensitive nose into thinking, "Ah, homemade!"

Thymus herba-barona refers to an old English custom of rubbing branches of the herb on the sides of huge barons of beef in preparation for banquets. It still lends a festive touch to less grandiose cuts of meat. For new flavor, add a pinch of fresh crushed caraway thyme to tomato juice or stir a teaspoon into cooked carrots, beets, or boiled potatoes.

TOMATILLO

Tomatillos (tow-mah-tee-yos) resemble golf-ball-sized green tomatoes that are covered with a paper-thin husk. Closely related to tomatoes, their flavor could be described as a blend of mild chile and tomatoes. They make a delicious green sauce for tacos and enchiladas or can be used in braising chopped meats.

Tomatillo seeds can be saved from fruit bought at the market or they may be ordered from Exotica Seed Co. Remove the seeds from the fruit and allow them to dry for several days. Plant them one-quarter-inch deep in pots for later transplanting, or sow them directly in the soil. Tomatillo plants sprawl like tomato plants and you may want to give them support. A tomato cage works fine for tomatillos too.

plant: April through June.

space: 12 inches apart in rows 5 feet apart, or in cages as for tomatoes.

fertilize: before planting.

Some top tomatoes (left to right): the gnarly giant Ponderosa, Golden Boy, the huge Beefmaster, Golden Jubilee, Big Girl, and another Ponderosa in front

TOMATO

In our mind, there's only one way to grow tomatoes — in a wire cage. Described at left, it is bigger than you might expect (seven feet tall), but in our experience most tomato varieties will easily clamber all the way to the top before the season is done.

Building this contraption takes some effort, but it can be used for years, even in winter, since it is just about the right height for pole peas. Three cylinders, each planted with a different variety, will bury you in tomatoes.

And there's also only one way to plant tomatoes — as transplants buried deeper than they were in the pot. This too is discussed at left. A tomato's roots go very deep in the soil so watering is critical. Build a watering basin around each cylinder and flood it repeatedly each time you water. Don't water too often. A thorough irrigation should last at least a week, several weeks in coastal areas.

Tomatoes often drop blossoms early in the season when it is still cool (and later when temperatures go over 100 degrees). This is normal, but if it persists try using special hormones sold by nurseries to prevent blossom drop. Also normal early in the season is a tendency for leaves to curl. If this persists it is caused by a virus, not cool weather, and there is nothing you can do about it.

These are the best tomato varieties for the garden. All grow well in a tall cage. Gurney Girl and Rushmore are from Gurney Seed Co.

Better Boy Hybrid (the most foolproof, large fruit in any climate), **Gurney Girl Hybrid** (just as good), **Champion Hybrid** (excellent flavor, size), **Burpee's Supersteak Hybrid** (huge, beefsteak-type tomato that outproduces all others), **Beefmaster Hybrid** (another good biggie), **Golden Jubilee** (orange-red, excellent taste, a favorite in Southern California), **Golden Boy, Sweet 100 Hybrid** (cherry tomato that produces huge clusters on a big plant), **Ace Hybrid** (practically coreless fruit), **Rushmore Hybrid** (early, prolific, high-quality tomato), **Long-Keeper** (plant in June, tomatoes ripen in September, store for months at room temperature), **San Marzano** (best pear-shaped, paste-type tomato).

Royal Globe turnips

Tomatoes can also be grown in big containers. For this purpose, these varieties are best:

Pixie Hybrid (prolific golf-ball-sized fruits with big flavor on a two-foot-tall plant), **Patio Hybrid** (fruits and plants are bigger), **Small Fry Hybrid** (small cherry tomatoes on a smallish plant, superb flavor).

plant: May 15 through July (early kinds can go in late March).

space: one plant per cage, cages 3 feet apart.

fertilize: before planting, again as blossoms begin.

TURNIP

Supermarket turnips lack the sweet flavor and crispness of fresh turnips, especially if the tops have been removed, indicating they may have been in cold storage for several weeks. Speaking of tops, turnips are dual-purpose vegetables. Many people enjoy the succulent root but ignore the foliage, which is loaded with vitamins and minerals. Turnip greens may be prepared in a variety of ways, but they are quite good simply chopped and boiled like spinach with butter, lemon, and a few bacon bits. The roots are a delightful addition to stews or browned and served around a roast as a substitute for potatoes. French recipes work wonders with them.

Turnips taste their best grown in the cooler months, but can be grown year round. They're fast, ready to harvest in five to ten weeks. The plant is most tender when the root is two to three inches in diameter.

plant: year round, but best from September through March.

space: 3 inches apart in rows a foot apart.

fertilize: before planting.

best varieties: Royal Globe Hybrid (good greens, pretty purple coloring); Tokyo Cross Hybrid (All-America winner, very early); Shogoin (best for greens).

TOMATO TRAINING, PLANTING

Most varieties of tomatoes need training of some kind or they'll sprawl everywhere. Up in the air is our suggestion, where they use little space and where fruit is safe from rot and pests that inhabit the ground. Build a cage like the one shown, from seven-foot-wide welded wire screening sold for reinforcing concrete at building supply yards. The wires are spaced six inches apart which makes it easy to pick the tomatoes inside. You'll need five feet to form a one-and-a-half-foot-diameter circle. Use two stakes tied to either side to support the cage and plant one tomato dead center.

Here's how to plant small tomato plants bought at nurseries or that you raised yourself: dig a fairly deep hole and put fertilizer in the bottom, cover with a little soil. Then put the transplant into the hole so it is several inches deeper than it was in the pot. Roots will form all along this section of buried stem. Build a watering basin and water thoroughly.

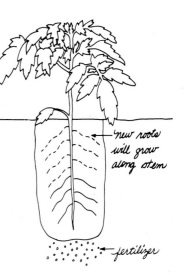

new roots will grow along stem

fertilizer

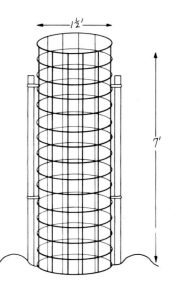

The Fruit Garden

In a nutshell, nothing is as tasty as home-grown fruit, but few plants require so much work, or need so much space in the garden. Be prepared to put some effort into planting, training, pruning, spraying, fertilizing, and thinning. And start practicing patience, because some fruit trees don't begin to bear for several years.

Space is the first concern. A full-sized tree is big indeed, and rambunctious blackberry bushes can consume an entire garden. Even strawberries need a good-sized bed if you're going to harvest more than a bowl full. It isn't a good idea to plant even two fruits that ripen at the same time — you won't know what to do with it all. Make a list of all the fruits you want to grow, then write down at what time of year each ripens. Note that different varieties of the same fruit ripen at different times, sometimes only weeks apart, but enough to help spread out the harvest.

In most cases you shouldn't plant full-sized fruit trees. It's better to plant several dwarf or semi-dwarf trees — they'll produce less fruit, but there will still be more than enough. Dwarf and semi-dwarf trees are grown on special roots that restrict their size. There are also what are called "genetic" dwarfs, which are naturally small.

A few fruits are especially valuable because they don't have to be harvested all at once, or because their harvest is easy to preserve: citrus can stay on the tree for months after they are ripe; apricots are especially easy to dry in the sun, or make into jam; nuts can be squirreled away with almost no preparation.

Also valuable are fruits that ripen at times of the year other than midsummer, when most gardens are overflowing with ripening peaches, plums, berries, and the like. Some nontraditional tasting fruits ripen in late fall and winter, or early spring, as well as several citrus.

If you have now made a list of the fruits you want and when they ripen, make a sketch of your garden and see how many you can squeeze in, making sure that one doesn't shade the other. In California, with a little planning, you can have fruit ripening year round.

The Small Fruits

These are the best bets for small gardens. Though the plants are often large, they can be trained to grow in leftover spaces like side yards, or against the house or fence. Other than the small size of their fruits, they have this in common — all need some sort of special treatment each year or they won't produce fruit.

KIWI FRUIT

This fuzzy little fruit (*Actinidia chinensis*) originated in China (where it is known as *yangtao*), became famous in New Zealand, and now seems quite at home in California. If you've never seen the inside of a kiwi, it is a shocking but delicious chartreuse, with tiny edible black seeds. Kiwis grow in most of California, though they do especially well in the Central Valley and northern San Diego County. They don't like to be too close to the coast or the desert. In New Zealand, kiwis are grown on huge overhead trellises. The fruits hang below at eye level, which makes picking easy. A California version of this trellis, scaled to a backyard, is pictured at right. It must be sturdy because the vines are heavy. Vines can grow to thirty feet or more.

Buy only grafted or cutting-grown varieties, like Hayward, Chico, or Monty. You will need a male and a female plant. The first few years be careful not to overwater, but never let the plant go without. In Southern California, you may need to water every few days. If your soil is heavy clay, plant the vines on a gentle mound to improve drainage.

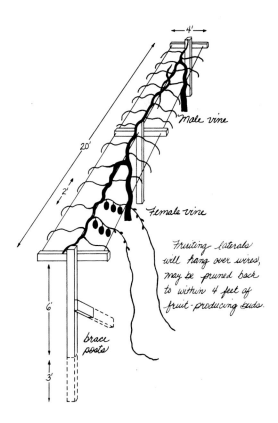

Male vine

Female vine

Fruiting laterals will hang over wires, may be pruned back to within 4 feet of fruit-producing buds.

brace posts

Fertilize in January, again after fruit begins to form. Fruits form on secondary branches, usually called laterals, in late fall or winter when fresh fruit is most appreciated. These side branches will produce for several years but eventually must be replaced with new branches. For how to train and prune, see at right.

GRAPES

Table grapes do best where summers are warm, away from the coast, but a few will grow where summers are cooler. They are pretty plants, shown off atop a gazebo or patio overhead, scrambling along a fence, or planted on a functional trellis with wood posts spaced eight feet apart and wires three and a half feet above the ground. They can be trained on just about anything and at any height. Atop an arbor it might take a little longer to develop a suitably long trunk, but that trunk will be permanent. Only the top needs pruning. Grapes should be planted bare root in winter, then pruned in succeeding winters. Apply two handfuls of an all-purpose fertilizer in late winter. Mildew is a problem on European varieties. Vines are deep-rooted, so water infrequently but thoroughly.

Grapes must be pruned each year because they bear fruit on year-old wood only. The idea is to grow new canes each summer, cut them back in winter, let the remaining part fruit the following summer, then remove them. In the meantime, you bring along another batch of replacement canes. There are two ways to prune, described at right. How you prune is determined by the variety you plant, and grapes

TRAINING AND PRUNING SMALL FRUITS

kiwis. This is about the smallest trellis that will adequately hold one female fruiting vine and a male pollinizer. Use sturdy 4-by-4-inch posts and 2-by-6-inch crossmembers, and heavy gauge wire strung between eye bolts. Plant the female vine in the center and the male at one end. Train vines up their posts, then out along the central wire. It's very important not to let the vines twine around posts or wires. Just tie them on. These major branches, called "cordons," will last the life of the plant. Lateral branches will grow from the cordon and spill over the sides of the trellis. Prune so they are spaced from one to two feet apart.

Fruits are produced from buds near the base of these lateral branches, once the branches are a year old. First to produce are several buds closest to the base, the following year the next buds out along the lateral produce, and the next year a group even farther out. These lateral branches produce for about three years, then they are cut off and new laterals take their place. Lateral branches can grow as long as ten feet, but they may be cut back to about four feet from where the fruit will form. This provides just enough foliage for fruit production.

The male vine is trained

the same way, but it may be kept smaller, with only six or so lateral branches. These can be cut back hard after flowering, again in the fall so it doesn't take much space.

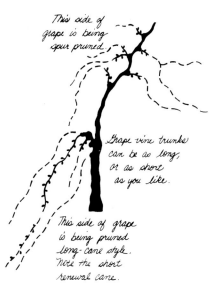

This side of grape is being spur pruned

Grape vine trunks can be as long, or as short as you like.

This side of grape is being pruned long-cane style. Note the short renewal cane.

grapes. The first year after planting, just let the vine grow. The following winter cut off all but one branch, which will become the trunk. In spring several branches will sprout from this; choose the strongest, removing all others, and continue training it up to where you want it to branch, at the top of a trellis or arbor, or patio overhead. Then pinch out the top to force branching. That winter (the third) save only two branches at top and cut them back to several buds each. From here on out, you can prune grapes in one of two ways: long cane pruning and spur pruning. The former method works on most grapes. You simply save several canes each year for fruit, then replace them after they have produced. Each year at *pruning time, keep two to four canes, each with about a dozen buds, plus several short renewal canes that will provide long canes for the following year. All other canes should be cut off at the trunk. Grapes will form on the canes that have been saved, and new canes will grow from the short renewal canes. Several of these will be saved the following winter to provide the next crop.*

Spur pruning works only on certain kinds of grapes and saves only the base of canes. Canes are cut back to short "spurs" of three buds. About a dozen of these are evenly spaced along two permanent branches (cordons). Cordons can be tied to wire trellises and can also be positioned on top of an arbor or fence, as long as they are more or less horizontal. The spurs will produce grapes the next summer, plus new canes. The new canes that sprout from the base of the old spurs become

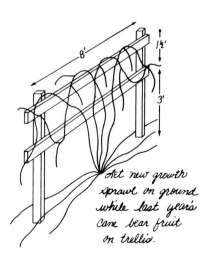

Let new growth sprawl on ground while last year's cane bear fruit on trellis.

the next season's spurs, when they in turn are cut back in winter to just three buds. The

rest of the old spur is then spent and must be cut off.

blackberries. *Blackberries should be spaced about eight feet apart on a trellis similar to the one pictured here. Let new canes that grow in spring and summer sprawl on the ground. When previous year's canes have finished fruiting, usually in August, cut them to the ground and tie new canes to trellis. These will continue growing into fall, so prune tips when they reach the end of the trellis. The following summer they will produce fruit. If any of the canes lying on the ground take root, cut roots off. Blackberries can get away from you, so cut out old canes and trellis new ones promptly.*

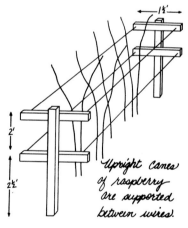

Upright canes of raspberry are supported between wires.

red raspberries. *Raspberries don't sprawl like blackberries and will stand neatly between rows of wire as shown here. Space plants about two feet apart. New canes grow in spring and summer, bear fruit in fall, then fruit again the following spring when they should be cut to the ground to make way for the next crop of canes.*

are roughly divided into two groups: American and European.

American grapes are typified by the Concord variety. They are sometimes called "slipskin" grapes. Most must be pruned to long canes since fruit is produced a few feet from the trunk. American grapes do best where summers aren't too hot, and they are the only grapes that will grow close to the coast. Good varieties include:

Concord. Best near the coast, doesn't like heat.

Golden Muscat. A golden green hybrid between an American and a European grape, excellent in Southern California, elsewhere.

Niabell. Big berries, an early producer, stands heat, good near coast.

Niagara. Greenish fruit, vigorous, good on arbors.

Pierce. Also called "California Concord," it's more vigorous, stands more heat. Perhaps the best for coastal Southern California.

European grapes are typified by Thompson Seedless, the popular market variety. These need much more summer heat and won't succeed anywhere in the fog belt. They are at their best in the hot Central Valley but will do well in any other hot summer areas. If you are in doubt, plant against a south-facing wall to provide some of the extra heat. Several can be pruned to either long canes or short spurs, but a few demand one or the other method. Good varieties include:

Muscat of Alexandria. Large, musky green fruits.

Perlette. An early producer, needs less heat than others. Spur prune.

Red Malaga. Reddish fruit, good on arbors.

Ribier. Huge black fruit. Spur prune.

Ruby Seedless. Dark reddish fruit, very sweet.

Thompson Seedless. The market classic, needs the heat found only in interior valleys, must be pruned to long canes.

BLACKBERRIES AND RED RASPBERRIES

To have berries most of the summer, be sure to plant both

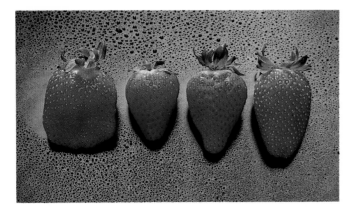

Some super strawberries (left to right): Douglas, Sequoia, Tioga, Tufts

November 1-15: plant from packs; cut off all runners that form while plants are fruiting in winter & spring.

July 1: stop cutting off runners, allow plants to form as many as possible.

October 15: sever runners and carefully dig them up. Gently shake off dirt, cut off all but two good leaves on each plant, put in a plastic bag in refrigerator for 20 days.

November 1-15: take out of refrigerator and carefully replant, after digging out old plants and preparing bed.

blackberries and red raspberries. Raspberries fruit in late spring, then come blackberries around June and July, and in September, raspberries often fruit again, especially in Southern California, where this may be the best crop of the year. Blackberries and raspberries are best planted in the winter, bare root. Both need lots of water while they're growing or setting fruit. Fertilize in late winter, before new growth begins.

Blackberries are the more rambunctious of the two and need a hefty support. New canes grow in the spring and summer, sit semi-dormant through winter, then fruit the following summer, usually on side branches that sprout along the main cane. After the cane has fruited it is cut to the ground. A clever way of dealing with this coming and going of canes is described at left. Here are some good choices in blackberries:

Boysen. The most productive in Southern California, where it was developed. Thornless variety not so good.

Marion. Shiny black berries best in Northern California.

Olallie. Long narrow berries, good anywhere but a little sensitive to heat.

Red raspberries are the kind to grow in California, especially those that fruit again in the fall. Actually, here's what happens: new canes grow in spring while the previous year's canes bear fruit. In fall, new canes bear fruit and the next spring they bear again before being cut to the ground. A good trellis system and pruning advice are described at left. Three good varieties for California that reliably produce fall crops are Heritage, Willamette, and Indian Summer. A new variety that looks promising in Southern California is the locally developed Bababerry.

STRAWBERRIES

Strawberries are extremely easy to grow along coastal California, only a little more difficult farther inland. To get berries as big as the kinds seen at markets, first purchase one of these four varieties: Sequoia, Tufts, Tioga, or Douglas (largest fruit). Next, follow the planting plan outlined at right. It was developed by the University of California's strawberry expert Victor Voth, and it is a backyard version of what commercial growers do.

Basically you plant berries in November from nursery packs (preferred over bare-root plants). By keeping the runners (small plants that grow from parent) cut off during the fruiting season, fruit grows bigger. Runners that grow after July are dug up in October, put in polyethylene bags, and then into the refrigerator where they get some necessary chilling. Last year's plants are now tossed out and the newly chilled runners are planted in their place. This will work for three years in a row, but then it's best to start with fresh plants from a nursery.

Here strawberries are planted in double rows atop raised beds, but they can also be planted in slightly raised single rows that are spaced about eighteen inches apart. The raised rows help drainage, critical to strawberries. In hot interior areas flat plantings irrigated by sprinklers work better. One word of caution: be careful not to plant strawberries too deep or too shallow. Soil should come to the middle of the crown.

PRUNING PRINCIPLES

All deciduous fruit trees (except true genetic dwarfs) require substantial pruning every January or February. Pruning helps keep the size of the tree in bounds so it is easier to reach the fruit but, more important, it encourages the formation of new growth that will produce fruit. It is a process of renewal. On a few trees, fruit may come anywhere along branches but most trees produce fruit on special stubby little branches called spurs. It takes a couple of years for a new tree to produce spurs, and spurs will produce fruit for only a few seasons. So a constant supply of new spurs must be encouraged while the old ones that are no longer productive must slowly be removed.

The first two years. If you buy a small branchless whip bare root, it must be cut back at planting time so it is only two feet tall. In early summer select three of the new branches to become the frame for the future tree. They should be spaced six to nine inches apart and arranged evenly around the tree. Cut off all other branches.

More likely you will purchase a bare-root tree that has branches, so select three of these to become the frame. Again, they should be spaced six to nine inches apart, evenly dispersed around the tree. Cut off all other branches; then cut off the top, just above the highest remaining branch. This may sound radical, but it is absolutely necessary and will actually encourage the

formation of spurs.

The following winter, again prune with a vengeance so there are basically only three strong limbs left and perhaps a few short spurs. More spurs will develop in summer and these will produce fruit the following summer (the third summer after planting).

The third winter and after. From now on, prune to keep the tree in bounds and to encourage new growth. Pruning should also open up the tree so more sunlight can reach the fruiting buds. Trees that become too dense produce little fruit. It is important to prune every year — it should be a yearly chore every January or you will be forced to prune too hard at some time to bring the tree back into production. Even then it will be several years before it is in production.

In general you are thinning the tree — removing small and medium-sized branches without touching the major limbs. Don't just cut off the ends of branches, cut them back to a side branch, usually one that faces out from the center of the tree. Fruiting spurs will sprout along strong branches, even from some major limbs, so it is safe to remove as much as half of the small side branches. Those that remain will go on to produce new spurs. They in turn can be removed after several years, even if they are as thick as two inches in diameter. Other branches will take their place, producing fresh new spurs.

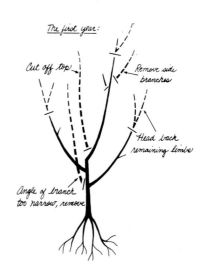

The first year:

Cut off top

Remove side branches

Head back remaining limbs

Angle of branch too narrow, remove

The Deciduous Fruits

All deciduous fruit trees lose their leaves in winter, and most need some chilling each winter. Sometimes different varieties of the same fruit need different amounts of winter chilling (measured in hours that the temperature stays below 45 degrees Fahrenheit). For instance, the common Red Delicious apple needs as much as one thousand hours of chilling, but a variety named Beverly Hills needs only about three hundred hours. In California, where cold is sometimes hard to come by, this is an extremely important bit of information. It can't be overemphasized that if you plant a variety that needs more chilling than your area can provide, you will get little or no fruit. Unfortunately, nurseries cannot always be relied upon to sell only the varieties that do best in your area. It is a good idea to research this in depth, because chilling can vary dramatically within just a few blocks. Ask around your neighborhood, consult several nurseries, find out what does well right where you live. It's a terrible disappointment to plant a fruit tree, waiting the several years required for it to begin producing, only to find the effort fruitless.

Deciduous fruit trees are best planted in January and February, when they are sold bare root. Nurseries have the best selection at this time. Most deciduous fruit trees also need yearly pruning in winter, when they are bare. Pruning renews the specialized branches that produce fruit, and varies from tree to tree.

In winter, deciduous fruit trees should be sprayed with a dormant spray (a mix of insecticidal oil and a fungicide). Fertilize deciduous fruit trees in late winter several weeks before they bloom. A handful of an all-purpose fertilizer is fine for new trees. Simply sprinkle evenly under the tree, cultivate, and let the next rain water it in. Trees in mid-life need about a coffee can full, and mature trees two coffee cans full. In the lists that follow, the best varieties are listed

Almonds

Apricots

along with the month in which the fruit ripens. There are semi-dwarf versions that grow only ten to twelve feet across.

ALMOND

The nuts are almost unnecessary because this peach relative could be grown for looks alone—it has beautiful white spring flowers and a handsome shape. Trees grow to about twenty-five feet and need little pruning. Fruiting spurs last about five years, and branches that no longer produce nuts can be removed. Warm summers are necessary to ripen hulls, which split and release nuts in September and October. Most trees need another variety planted nearby as a pollinizer. These varieties will grow anywhere in California except along the Southern California coast:

All-in-one (no pollinizer needed; October), **Ne Plus Ultra** (use Nonpareil as pollinizer; September), **Nonpareil** (tastiest, use Ne Plus Ultra as pollinizer; August).

APPLE

Here is an example of a deciduous fruit tree that does best in cold climates but can be grown where winters are much milder if you search out the few low-chill varieties. Apples are also available in endless sizes and types. They bear fruit on short stubby spurs that produce for as long as twenty years. Some apples have these spurs spaced close together and these "spur-type" apples produce more fruit in the same amount of space. Spur-type apples also tend to be about two-thirds the normal size, are slower growing, and seldom need pruning. In general apples need little pruning except to control shape and size. The exceptions are "tip bearing" varieties, which produce much of their fruit on the tips of last year's growth and need regular pruning of small branches to encourage new small branches.

Apples are often grafted to dwarfing rootstocks, the most common being East Malling 9 (EM9 or just M 9), which keeps a tree at about six to ten feet tall by about twelve feet wide, and Malling 26 (M 26), which lets trees grow to ten or thirteen feet, spreading to about nineteen

Mission fig

feet. Apples on dwarf rootstocks are easy to train into formal shapes along a trellis (an "apple fence") or against a fence or wall. Spur-type apples on dwarfing rootstock are almost unbelievable — they produce many apples for such a small plant, but because the trees are so small perhaps not enough for real apple fanatics. Spur-type and dwarfed apples also bear earlier, as soon as two years after planting, while standard apples may take four or more years.

These low-chill varieties are the only apples that succeed in Southern California: **Anna** (green, use Dorsett Golden as pollinizer; July), **Beverly Hills** (green, use Winter Banana as pollinizer; August), **Dorsett Golden** (July), **Gordon** (green; September), **Pettingill** (for cooking; September), **Winter Banana** (cooking; September).

These varieties are best in Northern California, though a few have produced in the colder parts of Southern California. These are only the most commonly planted, there are many more worth trying:
Delicious (*the* red apple, not good in hot summer areas, look for spur-type like Red Spur and Crimson Spur, needs pollinizer like Winter Banana or Golden Delicious; September), **Golden Delicious** (*the* yellow apple, spur-types available; September), **Granny Smith** (delicious, tip-bearer; October), **Gravenstein** (green, needs pollinizer; August), **Jonathan** (green; September), **Yellow Newton Pippin** (green, not for Central Valley; October).

APRICOT

Apricots are easy to grow, tough too, and are attractive shade trees in the garden. One variety or another will grow almost anywhere in California, though most are erratic producers near the Southern California coast. They bear on spurs that produce for about four years. Pruning is heavy at first (branches grow too long), less is required later. The object is to encourage new spurs to replace the old. Apricots should be thinned so fruit is at least two inches apart. None of the apricots listed here needs a pollinizer.

These varieties are good anywhere and are the best bets for coastal Southern California:
Blenheim or **Royal** (productive old-timer; June), **Garden Annie** (eight-foot dwarf; May), **Gold Kist** (May), **Newcastle** (June).

These varieties are good anywhere other than coastal Southern California:
Golden Amber (extended harvest; June to July), **Autumn Royal** (September), **Moorpark** (tastiest; June).

FIG

Some people can't start their day without a bowl of figs and cream, so it is fortunate that figs produce two crops a year — one in early summer, one in the fall. Some varieties even ripen as late as December. They thrive near the coast (there is a fig tree ranch in Malibu), but some are just at home inland.

One variety, Mission, does not need pruning, but others do if they are to produce good crops. About one quarter to one third of the branches that grew the previous year should be removed. The lighter the pruning, the heavier the spring crop will be, but heavy pruning encourages a big fall crop. Most can grow to about twenty feet, spreading wider, but are easy to keep about twelve feet tall. Excess figs are easy to dry on a tray in the sun. These are good choices:
Celeste (very sweet), **Conardia** (even sweeter, less fuzzy), **Brown Turkey** (heavy fall crop), **Kadota** (best inland), **Mission** (best all-round, less fuzzy), **Osborn** (best on coast, last crop very late), **White Genoa** (best on coast, almost continuous production).

PEACH AND NECTARINE

Tree-ripened peaches are sweet beyond compare and so juicy that it's a good idea to have a towel nearby to catch those drips that roll down your chin. If you think there are a lot of apples to choose from at planting time, there are twice as many peach varieties, one or another suited to any California climate. Peaches need the most pruning of any fruit tree, up to two thirds of the previous year's growth. They grow fast and will produce too much fruit (which may be inferior) if new growth isn't cut back. Peaches form on branches produced the previous year. You will get plenty of peaches if only a third of this new growth is left on the tree.

Peach-leaf curl, a common disease, is easier to prevent than cure: spray in November and again in January with Bordeaux or lime sulfur. In the following lists note the variety of ripening dates; colors refer to the flesh, not the skin.

These are flavorful peach choices for Northern California and the colder parts of Southern California. None of these requires pollinizers:

Champagne (big, white-fleshed peach; August), **Elberta** and **Early Elberta** (yellow-fleshed favorites; August, July), **Fay Elberta** (tastiest yellow; August), **Nectar** (best white; July), **Rio Grande** (juicy yellow; June), **Rio Oso Gem** (delicious yellow; August), **Saturn** (showy flowers, yellow; July), **Summerset** (yellow; September).

These can be grown anywhere (the earliest peaches are in this group) but they are especially good in Southern California, even near the coast:

Babcock (big, white; June), **Desert Gold** (yellow; May), **Early Amber** (yellow; May), **Four Star Daily News** (pretty flowers, white; June), **Red Baron** (beautiful flowers; July), **Springtime** (juicy white; May), **Shanghai** (extra-sweet white; July), **Tropi-Berta** (juicy yellow; August), **Ventura** (huge crops, yellow; July).

Nectarines are simply fuzzless peaches, though peach-loving people will tell you that nectarines aren't as sweet or juicy. Culture is nearly identical, though there are fewer nectarines for mild-winter areas. These nectarines do well anywhere, even in the milder parts of Southern California, though they are not as reliable as peaches there:

Goldmine (white; August), **Panamint** (best for Southern California coast, yellow; July), **Pioneer** (yellow; July), **Silver Lode** (white; June), **Sunred** (yellow; May).

These nectarines need colder winters. Good in Northern California or inland Southern California:

Armking (big, yellow; June), **Fantasia** (yellow; July), **Snow Queen** (white; June).

Genetic dwarf peaches and nectarines are different. They grow slowly to four or five feet tall and seldom need pruning, though fruit always needs thinning. Though they can be grown in containers, most gardeners have a hard time getting them to produce fruit.

These are genetic dwarf peaches that do fine even in mild-winter areas. All have yellow flesh:

Bonanza II (July), **Empress** (August), **Garden Gold** (August), **Golden Gem** (June), **Southern Rose** (August), **Southern Sweet** (June).

These are genetic dwarf nectarines, worth trying anywhere, though we haven't seen any along the coast. All have yellow flesh:

Garden Beauty (August), **Garden Delight** (July), **Nectarina** (July), **Southern Belle** (August), **Sunbonnet** (July).

EUROPEAN AND ASIAN PEARS

Pears used to be all of one kind — the European type. But in the last few years, Asian or oriental pears, and hybrids between the Asian and European, have appeared in California nurseries. European pears generally need more cold than Southern California can provide. Asian pears seem to grow fine in Southern California, where a test planting at the Irvine Ranch has shown great promise. Asian pears are often

European pear

called "apple-pears" at markets because they have the crunch and approximate shape of an apple, but have their own distinctive taste that is much more pear than apple.

Asian pears need another Asian variety or a Bartlett pear nearby for a pollinizer. European pears don't need a pollinizer, though yields increase if one is nearby. Asian pear trees look very much like European pear trees, but they are a little prettier and need a little more pruning. European pears can often get by with almost no pruning. However, on all pears it's a good idea to keep up with the branches that grow too long. All bear fruit and grow like an apple, with long-lived spurs. They are easily trained and espaliered, seldom getting taller than fifteen feet. Pears are best when picked green and hard and allowed to ripen in a cool place or in the refrigerator.

French prune

These are the favorite European pear varieties that do best in Northern California:

Bartlett (big, yellow; July), **Bosc** (big, dark; September), **Comice** (delicious, green; October), **Seckel** (small, sweet, some success in Southern California; September).

These are hybrid pears. Both reportedly grow in Southern California's colder parts:

Fan Stil (crisp, yellow; August), **Orient** (yellow; September).

These are some of the new Asian varieties: **Chojuro, 20th Century, Shinseiki** (said to be the tastiest), and **Yali** (needs the least chilling). All ripen in August.

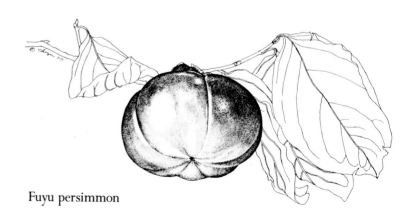

Fuyu persimmon

PERSIMMON

These are handsome trees even without the brilliant orange fruit that decorates the leafless trees in fall and winter. Does well anywhere except along the coast in Southern California. Trees grow to about twenty-five feet, need little pruning There are two types of fruit: astringent fruit must be soft-

Pomegranate

ripe before it is sweet; nonastringent fruit may be eaten while still firm. Here are some good varieties; all ripen in October:

Chocolate (nonastringent), **Fuyu** (nonastringent, better along coast), **Hachiya** (astringent), **Tamopan** (nonastringent).

PLUM AND PRUNE

Plums are probably the easiest fruit trees to grow. What most people call plums are technically Japanese plums, but there are also European plums. The former are usually red; the latter, blue. Prunes are European plums you can dry but they're also delicious fresh, sweeter than other kinds. Both grow into twenty-foot trees. The Japanese kinds need heavy yearly pruning to keep up with rampant growth, while the European kinds need much less. Watch out for long shoots called water spouts; prune these off.

Some plums need a pollinizer nearby, and the variety Santa Rosa is usually the choice. European plums are difficult to grow in Southern California; most Japanese plums grow easily anywhere, except right near the beach in Southern California (even here there are a few that succeed). Here are some good Japanese plums:

Burgundy (red, good along coast; July), **Howard Miracle** (yellow; July), **Inca** (yellow, needs pollinizer, good along coast; August), **Mariposa** (purple red, needs pollinizer; September), **Santa Rosa** (purple red, good along coast, there is an attractive weeping form; June), **Satsuma** (red, needs pollinizer; August), **Sprite** (a cherry-plum cross; July).

Here are some European plums that do best in Northern California but grow in Southern California's inland areas:

French Prune (sweet drying prune; August), **Green Gage** (greenish yellow; July), **Stanley** (large, reliable blue; August).

POMEGRANATE

Most kinds are ornamental plants that don't produce edible fruit. The one that does produce is the variety Wonderful, a handsome fifteen-foot tree that does well anywhere, though fruits are sweeter in hot summer areas. Needs no pruning and gets by with little water or fertilizer. Very easy. Fruit ripens in September.

WALNUT

Walnuts are at their best in Northern California, though they can be grown in Southern California's inland areas. Trees are handsome and big, to forty or more feet, need little pruning, fertilizing, with average irrigation. They usually do not need a pollinizer, but yields increase if one is nearby. These are good varieties:

Chandler, Chico (needs pollinizer, try Serr), **Hartley** (the best), **Placentia** (best in Southern California), **Serr** (use Chico as pollinizer).

Walnut

Avocado

Cherimoya

The Subtropical Fruits

These are quite the opposite of the more common deciduous fruit trees. They detest cold and do best where summers are hot and winters mild. If you can't grow apples, these are your compensation. There are a few exceptions that aren't too picky about how hot or cold it gets, but most do best in the traditional California citrus belts. The conditions in these specialized climatic areas can sometimes be created in gardens by protecting plants from cool ocean winds or frosty inland nights. If you live in a marginal area, a look around the neighborhood should show what you can get away with.

It has been discovered that some very exotic fruits can be grown in California's mild climate, even mangoes and papayas. Subtropical fruits are best planted as weather begins to warm in May or June. Pruning is seldom necessary, but fertilizing is much more important, absolutely essential with most citrus, and pests can be more of a problem.

For more information and possible sources for the more unusual kinds, join the California Rare Fruit Growers, Fullerton Arboretum, California State University, Fullerton, California 92634.

AVOCADO

Growing avocados is a bit of a gamble. All sorts of things may keep them from producing fruit. Trees don't like wind, or soils that are too wet. If they go dry at the wrong time, they won't fruit. Fruit won't form if the weather is chilly at flowering time, and if it gets too hot later, small fruits drop. Avocados tend to bear big crops in alternate years. In addition, trees are big—too big for many gardens, and it is impossible to grow anything under or even near them.

Plant carefully and build a cone-shaped watering basin to make sure water gets to roots. Since roots are close to the surface a thick mulch is important to keep them cool in February and again in early summer. Feed cautiously. Avocados seldom need pruning, and branches may burn if suddenly exposed to sun. Do not plant avocados from pits—the results are unpredictable and trees are often huge and fruitless.

186

These Guatemalan varieties do best in coastal Southern California:

Haas. The most tasty avocado. Fruit has thick rough skin, ripens over a long period, from May through October. Trees aren't too large, growing to twenty feet with a spread of twenty-five.

Fuerte. Excellent fruit with thin skin. Tree is huge, to thirty feet and as wide. Stands more cold (a hybrid between Guatemalan and Mexican kinds).

Reed. Huge fruit, excellent flavor but very sensitive to frost. Trees are narrow and upright, to twenty-five feet or more. Ripens July through September.

Wurtz, Minicado, Littlecado. Probably all the same variety, they get mixed reviews from people who have grown them. They are "dwarfs" growing eight to ten feet tall, but are not always good bearers. Fruit is medium-sized, ripens May through September.

These Mexican varieties stand enough cold to be grown inland in Southern California or in Northern California coastal areas:

Bacon. Good flavor on a medium-sized tree but it bears poor crops where summers are hot. Ripens November through March.

Mexicola. Small black fruit on a smallish tree. Perhaps the most cold hardy. Ripens August through October.

Zutano. Fair taste, medium-sized fruit on a big tree. Takes more summer heat. Ripens October through January.

CHERIMOYA

They look forbidding but that bumpy skin is paper thin and hides a soft, custardy flesh spotted with watermelonlike seeds. Taste is somewhere between a banana and a papaya. Very sensitive to cold, so best grown in coastal Southern California, protected from wind.

Grows into a fifteen-foot tree that sometimes goes briefly deciduous. Grow just like an avocado, but to get lots of good fruit, flowers must be hand pollinated with a small brush. Brush pollen from the anthers of a fully opened flower and put on the pistils of another flower that is only partially opened. Good choices if you can find them are:

Booth. More tolerant of hot or cold weather, fruits to one pound. Ripens December through April.

Pierce. Good crop even without hand pollinization, fruits to two pounds, ripens December through April.

CITRUS

You can grow some kind of citrus almost anywhere in California. There are citrus that require heat (navel oranges, tangerines, grapefruit) doing best where summers get hot, and citrus that need less heat (Valencia oranges, lemons, limes) that do well even where summers are foggy. Most standard citrus grow to twenty feet around, and there are dwarf versions of every kind that grow about half as tall: Eureka and Lisbon lemons, Valencia and navel oranges, and grapefruits grow about eight feet tall as dwarfs. Mandarins and tangelos grow about six feet tall. Dwarf trees also produce proportionately more fruit. Citrus, especially dwarfs, often drop leaves a month or so after planting. To minimize this, plant in May or June, dig a big hole, and thoroughly prepare the soil that goes back into it, then build a small watering basin to make sure the root ball gets watered. Leaves, flowers, or fruit dropping at any other time is usually caused by irregular or inadequate watering, or sometimes poor drainage. Citrus do not need pruning except for the occasional errant and overly long branch. Fertilize lightly in late winter, then in June, again in August.

Grapefruits need the most heat, and do best in the desert but succeed wherever summers are hot. It may take a year or more for fruit to ripen in cooler areas.

The standard yellow grapefruit is Marsh; Ruby is the common red kind. Both ripen November through June. Grapefruitlike pummelos are sometimes grown where it is too cool for true grapefruit. Their rinds are bitter beyond belief but properly peeled they're a reasonable substitute. Reinking and Chandler are two immense varieties.

Oranges do fine in any citrus area of California, though a few are sweeter away from the coast where summers are hot. There are eating kinds that are easy to peel and juice kinds that aren't. Here are some:

Robertson Navel. Eating orange, best with summer heat,

Lemon guavas

Loquats

ripens December through April.

Moro. A blood orange, with soft sweet, berrylike juice, often colored red. Ripens December through April.

Sanguinella. A blood orange that colors well in cooler areas, December through June.

Trovita. An eating orange with no navel, good near coast or where it's hot. Tends to fruit alternate years. Ripens December through March.

Washington Navel. *The* navel orange, prefers warmth found away from coast. Ripens December through February.

Valencia. *The* juice orange, great near coast. Ripens July through November.

Mandarins are even more adaptable than oranges. They include all loose-skinned citrus, and tangerines are simply mandarins more colored than most—the names are really interchangeable. Included here is one tangelo, a mandarin-grapefruit cross, and a tangor, a mandarin-orange cross:

Clementine. Great taste, seedy. Ripens January through March.

Dancy. Sweet, seedy, best in hot areas. Ripens February through March.

Dweet. Tangy, juicy, sweet, seedy, best near coast. Ripens April through May.

Honey. Extra sweet, prolific. Ripens January through March.

Kinnow. Sweet, juicy, seedy; a pretty weeping tree. Ripens February through March. Ripe fruit keeps on tree a long time.

Minneola. The tangelo of markets, with the bump on one end, best with heat. Ripens February to March.

Owari Satsuma. Nearly seedless, good near coast. Ripens November through March.

Lemons and limes stand the most cold, need the least heat—they aren't very picky:

Eureka. The market lemon, best in gardens because it ripens fruit year round, though it makes a straggly bush or tree.

Meyer. Almost doesn't qualify as a lemon, fruit round, thin skinned, not so acid, produces most of the year.

Bearss. The most adaptable lime, some fruit all year but most comes November through June.

Mexican. The bartender's lime, coastal Southern California only. Ripens July through January.

FEIJOA

Also called the pineapple guava (*Feijoa sellowiana*), this native of Brazil has a sweet taste somewhat like a pineapple. The waxy white flower petals are also sweet and edible. The tree is extremely handsome, growing about twenty feet tall. It doesn't require pruning but looks best with a little. Feijoa grows throughout California but fruit is sweetest near the coast. Good varieties are Coolidge and Nazemetz, the latter with fruit almost twice the size. Fruit ripens in fall and winter.

GUAVA

The red-fruited strawberry guava (*Psidium littorale longipes*) and the yellow lemon guava (*P. l. littorale*) are true guavas that can grow anywhere in California but the Central Valley or desert. The names refer to coloration, not taste. Used mostly to make jelly, the small sweet-but-tart fruits can also be eaten fresh. Trees grow to about ten feet tall, are handsome, evergreen. There is also a tropical guava but it is only grown in the mildest parts of Southern California.

LOQUAT

Loquats are handsome trees easily grown in most of California, but the best fruit comes near the coast on grafted varieties. The variety Behlehr is considered the tastiest; Champagne is good near the coast, Gold Nugget is best in warm inland areas. Trees can grow to thirty feet tall, but are usually seen much smaller. They produce more fruit than

Macadamia nuts

even the most loquacious loquat fancier can consume or make into jelly or chutney (branches sometimes break under the weight), so it is a good idea to thin the flowers. Otherwise trees thrive with practically no care. Fruit ripens March through June.

MACADAMIA NUT

If you live in Southern California, reasonably near the coast, you should be growing macadamias. If you live farther inland, or in the San Francisco Bay area, you should consider trying one. Considered by many to be the tastiest of nuts, these Australian natives are also handsome evergreen trees. They are slow growing — to about twenty feet, and it takes a few years before you will get nuts. The shells are as hard as rocks.

When you purchase your tree, it is a good idea to ask the nursery if they also sell one of the special nutcrackers made for macadamias. Even a hammer won't work because it smashes the soft round meat along with the shell.

Macadamias do best protected from the wind, though there are producing trees in Malibu that get severely buffeted. Trees need little pruning. Nuts fall naturally when they're ripe. There are many varieties, but Cate and Beaumont are two of the best, and easiest to locate.

SAPOTE

Though tropical looking and tropical tasting, sapotes will grow anywhere an orange will. The fruit has a thin green skin, custardy white flesh with a few big seeds. The tree is handsome but messy because it produces far more fruit than you can eat, literally thousands of two- to three-inch fruits. It can grow to forty feet, but twenty is more common. Suebelle and Vernon are common varieties. The former ripens almost year round, the latter from November through February.

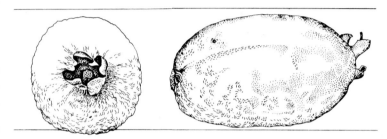

Feijoa

Sapotes

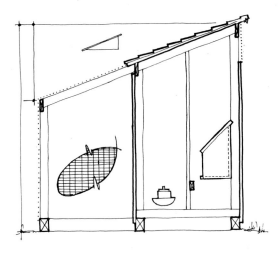

The Backyard Barnyard

The finishing touch to the kitchen garden might be this backyard barnyard. In a sense, it completes the cycle. Leftovers from the garden become food for the animals and they in turn provide a first-rate fertilizer for the plants, and more food for the table. Nothing is wasted.

It's designed to be perfectly legal in the city of Los Angeles, and it was built with the necessary permits. Surprisingly, the keeping of chickens and other small animals is allowed, as it is in most California cities. Inspired by the big barns of old, this two-goat barn and adjoining chicken coop are simple, sleek, functional structures — fun to build and full of rural romance. Like all barns they are also great places for children to play.

While the two-level eight- by twelve-foot barn was specifically designed to house two frolicsome milk goats, it is really an all-purpose building for any number of animals and their supplies, for garden equipment, or whatever — the very definition of the word "barn."

There's room for stalls on the ground floor, and a half-dozen bales of hay can be kept high and dry in the loft above. Our barn even has a working lift to heft the heavy bales up into the loft. The loft is the place children like best. Reached by a built-in ladder, it's a private retreat where bales of alfalfa become tables and chairs and favorite animals are just downstairs.

The chicken coop, designed as a separate eight- by eight-foot building, can house six laying hens in splendid comfort. In fact, it works so well that the chickens can practically take care of themselves. This number of hens will supply a family with at least four eggs a day and possibly some poultry for the table. Goats add milk and cheese to the menu. Combined with a vegetable garden and a few fruit trees, the backyard barnyard can make quite a dent in the food bill and bring a certain sense of self-sufficiency.

BARN RAISING

Building the barn and coop is an easy and satisfying experience — one doesn't often get the chance to build something this substantial from the ground up. The basic frame is 4- by 4-inch lumber, in homage to the mighty posts and beams of yesterday's barns. In between the major posts and beams, we used more conventional 2- by 4-inch lumber. Rafters are also 2-by-4's or 4-by-4's, depending on what size post supports them. There is no separate concrete foundation — pressure-treated 4-by-6's that resist decay are allowed by building codes because these are "outbuildings," subject to less stringent regulation. Metal angle clips are used to fasten all framing members.

Floors are dirt and the roof is a special metal tile system (called "Typhoon Tile") that includes clear plastic inserts, but you can also use ordinary corrugated metal with clear corrugated fiberglass inserts for skylights. The hay lift is a piece of 4- by 6-inch lumber securely fastened with a special 4- by 10-inch purlin hanger, available at lumber yards.

Sheathing everything in exterior sheets of plywood makes it sturdy. Note that the dimensions make it possible to use whole sheets of plywood. It's important to keep overall dimensions a little shorter than the plywood covering, to allow for mistakes in measuring or fitting. Doors are simply cut from the plywood, then braced on the back with 2- by 2-inch lumber.

The coop is a little less complicated, and is as efficient as a machine, with an automatic waterer and feeder that leaves only egg-gathering a daily chore. None of this equipment touches the floor, making cleaning easy. Divided in two halves, the indoor part keeps hens warm and dry, the outdoor area keeps them safe behind 1- by 2-inch welded wire, partially buried underground to keep dogs or the proverbial fox from tunneling under.

Buildings must be located a certain legal distance from houses. In Los Angeles, the coop must be twenty feet from your house, thirty-five feet from the neighbors, five feet from the property line. For goats, the distances increase. Check with building department officials.

Credits

The author thanks editor Joan Fisher and designer Darilyn Lowe for their creative contributions and guidance; his wife, Iris, for her constant help; the staff of Home Magazine, especially Maria La Ganga and Paula Ballo, for their support; Home's former Editor, Carolyn Murray, for help and guidance; Joe Williamson, Garden Editor of Sunset Magazine, who convinced the author that writing about gardening could be almost as satisfying as actually getting out in the garden and growing things; and the dedicated horticulturists who have made the California garden so special, but especially Ed Carman, Francis Ching, Jack Christensen, Paul B. Engler, Mary Ellen Guffey, James Kirk, Fred Lang, John C. MacGregor IV, Dan MacMasters, Chris Rosmini, L. K. Smith, David Verity, and Bill Warriner — all contributed valuable knowledge and know-how to this book.

For their contributions to various parts of this book, especially the section on vegetables and herbs, I wish to thank and acknowledge the Home Magazine writers who produce a regularly appearing column called The Kitchen Garden:

Bill Sidnam

Teddy Colbert

All photographs and illustrations in this book are protected under United States copyright laws and international copyright treaties with copyright ownership belonging to, and all rights reserved by, the following list of photographers and illustrators respectively:

Glen Allison: 1, 2, 8, 12, 26, 27, 28, 29, 38, 39, 40, 43, 52, 53, 55, 80, 81, 98, 99, 100, 101, 111, 114, 116, 117, 129, 131, 135, 139

William Aplin: 111

Jessie Chizu-Baer: 70, 72, 132, 150-155, 158, 160, 163-166, 169-178, 175, 181-189

George de Gennaro: 44, 46, 48, 49

Tom Engler: 118, 119

Steve Fontanini: 79

Jerry Fruchtman: 162

James Goble: 174

Richard Gross: 22, 66, 86, 91, 156, 161

Douglas Kennedy: 156, 168

Kathy Miyamoto: 159, 166, 178

Dawn Navarro: 145

Max Navarro: 144, 190

Jack Nelson: 126, 127, 137

Cathy Pavia: 58, 68, 69, 72, 76, 112, 146, 147, 148, 149

Bobbie Probstein: 33

Susan Ragsdale: 5, 10-20, 25, 27, 28, 30, 32, 36, 38, 41, 42, 47, 49, 52, 54, 57, 62, 63, 77, 84, 93, 103-109, 140, 141, 143, 154, 175, 177, 178, 179, 180

Dick Rosmini: 37

Bill Ross: 24, 28, 31, 33, 35, 41, 42, 43, 53, 54, 60, 64, 65, 68, 69, 73, 79, 80, 81, 88, 89, 90, 91, 92, 108, 110, 111, 112, 114, 115, 121-124, 132, 136, 137, 139

Richard Ruthsatz: 34

Morgan Sinclaire: 38, 82, 83, 88, 89

Robert Smaus: 28, 29, 33, 35, 38, 41, 51, 56, 57, 62, 63, 64, 65, 85, 90, 94-97, 113, 134, 138

Susan Theresa Smith: 74, 75, 171

Richard Sullivan: 157, 159, 168, 179

Sandra Williams: 41